CISI Investment Award Programme

Introduction to Investment

The Foundation Qualification

Edition 9, May 2016
This learning manual relates to syllabus version 16.0 and will cover exams from
1 Aug 2016 to 31 July 2017

APPROVED WORKBOOK

Welcome to the Chartered Institute for Securities & Investment's Introduction to Investment Award study material.

This workbook has been written to prepare you for the Chartered Institute for Securities & Investment's Introduction to Investment Award examination.

Published by:
Chartered Institute for Securities & Investment
© Chartered Institute for Securities & Investment 2016
8 Eastcheap
London
EC3M 1AE
Tel: +44 20 7645 0600
Fax: +44 20 7645 0601

Email: customersupport@cisi.org
www.cisi.org/qualifications

Author:
Kevin Rothwell, Chartered MCSI

Reviewers:
Kevin Petley, Chartered FCSI
Kevin Sloane, Chartered MCSI

This is an educational manual only and the Chartered Institute for Securities & Investment accepts no responsibility for persons undertaking trading or investments in whatever form.

While every effort has been made to ensure its accuracy, no responsibility for loss occasioned to any person acting or refraining from action as a result of any material in this publication can be accepted by the publisher or authors.

All rights reserved. No part of this publication may be reproduced, stored in a retrieval system, or transmitted, in any form or by any means, electronic, mechanical, photocopying, recording or otherwise without the prior permission of the copyright owner.

Warning: any unauthorised act in relation to all or any part of the material in this publication may result in both a civil claim for damages and criminal prosecution.

A learning map, which contains the full syllabus, appears at the end of this manual. The syllabus can also be viewed on cisi.org and is also available by contacting the Customer Support Centre on +44 20 7645 0777. Please note that the examination is based upon the syllabus. Candidates are reminded to check the Candidate Update area details (cisi.org/candidateupdate) on a regular basis for updates as a result of industry change(s) that could affect their examination.

The questions contained in this manual are designed as an aid to revision of different areas of the syllabus and to help you consolidate your learning chapter by chapter. They should not be seen as a 'mock' examination or necessarily indicative of the level of the questions in the corresponding examination.

Learning manual version: 9.1 (May 2016)

Learning and Professional Development with the CISI

The Chartered Institute for Securities & Investment is the leading professional body for those who work in, or aspire to work in, the investment sector, and we are passionately committed to enhancing knowledge, skills and integrity – the three pillars of professionalism at the heart of our Chartered body.

CISI examinations are used extensively by firms to meet the requirements of government regulators. Besides the regulators in the UK, where the CISI head office is based, CISI examinations are recognised by a wide range of governments and their regulators, from Singapore to Dubai and the US. Around 50,000 examinations are taken each year, and it is compulsory for candidates to use CISI learning manuals to prepare for CISI examinations so that they have the best chance of success. Our learning manuals are normally revised every year by experts who themselves work in the industry and also by our Accredited Training Partners, who offer training and elearning to help prepare candidates for the examinations. Information for candidates is also posted on a special area of our website: cisi.org/candidateupdate.

This learning manual not only provides a thorough preparation for the examination it refers to, it is also a valuable desktop reference for practitioners, and studying from it counts towards your Continuing Professional Development (CPD). Mock examination papers, for most of our titles, will be made available on our website, as an additional revision tool.

CISI examination candidates are automatically registered, without additional charge, as student members for one year (should they not be members of the CISI already), and this enables you to use a vast range of online resources, including CISI TV, free of any additional charge. The CISI has more than 40,000 members, and nearly half of them have already completed relevant qualifications and transferred to a core membership grade. You will find more information about the next steps for this at the end of this manual.

With best wishes for your studies.

Lydia Romero, Director of Learning

The Financial Services Industry 1

The workbook commences with an introduction to the financial services industry and examines the role of the industry and the main participants that are seen in financial centres around the globe.

The Economic Environment 15

An appreciation of some key aspects of macro economics is essential to an understanding of the environment in which investment services are delivered. This chapter looks at some key measures of economic data and the role of central banks in management of the economy.

Financial Assets and Markets 35

This chapter starts the review of financial assets and markets by looking at the characteristics of cash deposits, the money markets, property and the foreign exchange markets.

Equities 47

The workbook then moves on to examine some of the main asset classes in detail, starting with equities. It begins with the features, benefits and risks of owning shares or stocks, looks at corporate actions and some of the main world stock markets and indices, and outlines the methods by which shares are traded and settled.

Bonds 77

A review of bonds follows which includes looking at the key characteristics and types of government and corporate bonds and the risks and returns associated with them.

Derivatives 93

Next there is a brief review of derivatives to provide an understanding of the key features of futures, options and swaps and the terminology associated with them.

Investment Funds 109

The workbook then turns to the major area of investment funds or mutual funds/ collective investment schemes. The chapter looks at open-ended and closed-ended funds, exchange-traded funds and hedge funds, and how they are traded.

8 Financial Services Regulation and Professional Integrity 129

An understanding of regulation is essential in today's investment industry. This chapter provides an overview of international regulation and looks at specific areas such as money laundering, insider trading and bribery as well as a section on professional integrity and ethics.

9 Taxation, Investment Wrappers and Trusts 165

Having reviewed the essential regulations covering provision of financial services, the workbook then moves on to look at the main types of investment wrappers seen in the UK, including ISAs and pensions, and also looks at the principles of taxation and the use of trusts.

10 Other Financial Products 179

The workbook concludes with a review of the other types of financial products, including loans, mortgages, and protection products including life assurance.

Glossary and Abbreviations 197

Multiple Choice Questions 213

Syllabus Learning Map 229

It is estimated that this workbook will require approximately 70 hours of study time.

What next?
See the back of this book for details of CISI membership.

Need more support to pass your exam?
See our section on Accredited Training Partners.

Want to leave feedback?
Please email your comments to learningresources@cisi.org

Chapter One
The Financial Services Industry

1.	Introduction	3
2.	Professional and Retail Business	3
3.	Industry Participants	7
4.	Investment Distribution Channels	12

This syllabus area will provide approximately 2 of the 50 examination questions

1. Introduction

The financial services industry in developed countries is a major contributor to the economy. In the UK, for example, the activities of the firms located in and around the City of London provide considerable employment, as well as overseas earnings for the economy.

The financial services industry provides the link between organisations needing capital and those with capital available for investment. For example, an organisation needing capital might be a growing company, and the capital might be provided by individuals saving for their retirement in a pension fund. It is the financial services industry that channels money invested to those organisations that need it, and provides execution, payment, advisory and management services.

Stock markets and investment instruments are not unique to one country, and there is increasing similarity in the instruments that are traded on all world markets and in the way that trading and settlement systems are developing.

With this background, therefore, it is important to understand the core role that the financial services industry undertakes within the economy and some of the key features of the global financial services sector. This will be considered in the following sections.

2. Professional and Retail Business

Learning Objective

1.1.2　Know the function of and differences between retail and professional business and who the main customers are in each case: retail clients and professional clients

Within the financial services industry there are two distinct areas, namely the wholesale and retail sectors. The wholesale sector is also sometimes referred to as the professional sector or institutional sector.

The activities that take place in wholesale financial markets are shown below and are expanded on in Sections 2.1 to 2.5.

The financial activities that make up the **wholesale/professional sector** include:

- **equity markets** – the trading of quoted shares
- **bond markets** – the trading of government, supranational or corporate debt
- **foreign exchange** – the trading of currencies
- **derivatives** – the trading of options, swaps, futures and forwards
- **insurance markets** – major corporate insurance (including professional indemnity), re-insurance, captive insurance and risk-sharing insurance.

Other activities that take place in the wholesale sector include:

- **fund management** – managing the investment portfolios of collective investment schemes, pension funds and insurance funds
- **investment banking** – banking services tailored to organisations, such as undertaking mergers and acquisitions, equity trading, fixed income trading and private equity
- **custodian banking** – provision of services to asset managers involving the safekeeping of assets; the administration of the underlying investments; settlement; corporate actions and other specialised activities.

By contrast, the **retail sector** focuses on services provided to personal customers:

- **retail banking** – the traditional range of current accounts, deposit accounts, lending and credit cards
- **insurance** – the provision of a range of life assurance and protection solutions for areas such as medical insurance, critical illness cover, motor insurance, property insurance, income protection and mortgage protection
- **pensions** – the provision of investment accounts specifically designed to capture savings during a person's working life and provide benefits on retirement
- **investment services** – a range of investment products and vehicles ranging from execution-only stockbroking to full wealth management services and private banking
- **financial planning and financial advice** – helping individuals to understand and plan for their financial future.

2.1 Equity Markets

Equity markets are the best known financial markets and facilitate the trading of shares in quoted companies.

According to the statistics from the World Federation of Exchanges, the total value of shares quoted on the world's stock exchanges was over US$60 trillion at the end of 2015 (note: not all stock exchanges provide data to the World Federation of Exchanges so actual figures may well be higher).

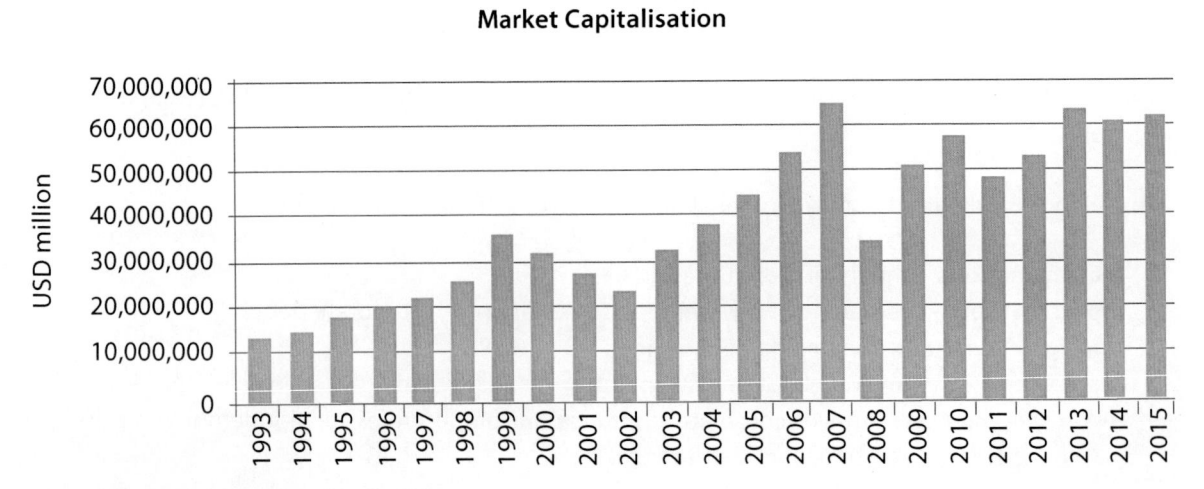

Market Capitalisation

Source: World Federation of Exchanges

- The New York Stock Exchange (NYSE) is the largest exchange in the world and had a domestic market capitalisation of close to US$18 trillion at the end of 2015 (domestic market capitalisation is the value of shares listed on an exchange).
- The other major US market, NASDAQ, was ranked as the second largest with a domestic market capitalisation of over US$7 trillion, meaning that the two New York exchanges account for around one-third of all exchange business.
- Japan Exchange Group, which includes the Tokyo Stock Exchange (TSE), is the world's third largest market and had a domestic market capitalisation of close to US$5 trillion.
- In Europe, the largest exchanges are the London Stock Exchange (LSE), Euronext, Deutsche Börse, SIX Swiss Exchange and the Spanish exchanges.

Rivals to traditional stock exchanges have also arisen with the development of technology and communication networks known as **multilateral trading facilities (MTFs)**. These are systems that bring together multiple parties that are interested in buying and selling financial instruments including shares, bonds and derivatives. These systems are also known as crossing networks or matching engines that are operated by an investment firm or another market operator.

We will look in more detail at equities and equity markets in Chapter 4.

2.2 Bond Markets

Although less well known than equity markets, bond markets are larger both in size and value of trading. However, the volume of bond trading is lower, as most trades tend to be very large indeed when compared to equity market trades. The amounts outstanding on the global bond market now exceed around US$100 trillion. Domestic bond markets accounted for 70% of the total, and international bonds for the remainder.

The instruments traded range from domestic bonds issued by companies and governments, to international bonds issued by companies, by governments and by supranational agencies such as the World Bank. The US has the largest bond market, but trading in international bonds is predominantly undertaken in European markets.

We will look in more detail at bonds in Chapter 5.

2.3 Foreign Exchange Markets

Foreign exchange markets are the largest of all financial markets, with average daily turnover in excess of US$5 trillion.

The rate at which one currency is exchanged for another is set by supply and demand and by the strength of one currency in relation to another. For example, if there is strong demand from Japanese investors for US assets, such as property, bonds or shares, the US dollar will rise in value.

There is an active foreign exchange market that enables governments, companies and individuals to deal with their cash inflows and outflows denominated in overseas currencies. The market is provided by the major banks, who each provide rates of exchange at which they are willing to buy or sell currencies. Historically, most foreign exchange deals were arranged over the telephone; now, however, electronic trading is becoming increasingly prevalent.

As foreign exchange is an OTC (over-the-counter) market, meaning one where brokers/dealers negotiate directly with one another, there is no central exchange or clearing house. Instead, FX trading is distributed among major financial centres.

The Bank for International Settlements (BIS) releases figures on the composition of the foreign exchange market every three years. The latest report for 2013 shows that market activity has become ever more concentrated in a handful of global centres. As you can see in the chart below, FX transactions are concentrated in five countries, with the UK as the main global centre.

Main Countries for FX Trading 2013

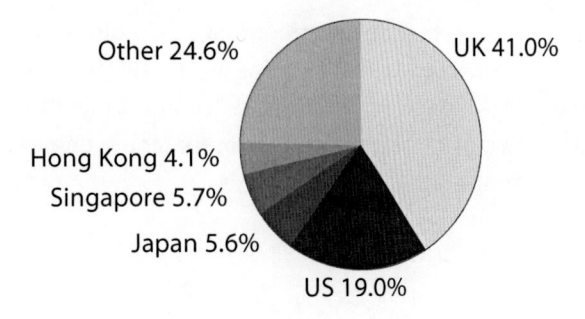

- Other 24.6%
- UK 41.0%
- Hong Kong 4.1%
- Singapore 5.7%
- Japan 5.6%
- US 19.0%

Source: *Bank for International Settlements*

2.4 Derivatives Markets

Derivatives markets trade a range of complex products based on underlying instruments that include currencies, indices, interest rates, equities, commodities and credit risk.

Derivatives based on these underlying elements are available on both the **exchange-traded** market and the **over-the-counter (OTC)** market (see Chapter 6, Section 1.1). The largest of the exchange-traded derivatives markets is the Chicago Mercantile Exchange (CME), while Europe dominates trading in the OTC derivatives markets worldwide. Based on the value of the notional amounts outstanding, the OTC derivatives markets worldwide are about four times the size of stock quoted on stock exchanges.

Interest rate derivatives contracts account for three-quarters of outstanding derivatives contracts, mostly through interest rate swaps. In terms of currencies, the interest rate derivatives market is dominated by the euro and the US dollar, which have accounted for most of the growth in this market since 2001. The growth in the market came about as a reaction to the 2000-02 stock market crash as traders sought to hedge their position against interest rate risk.

We will look in more detail at derivatives in Chapter 6.

2.5 Insurance Markets

Insurance markets specialise in the management of risk.

Globally, the US, Japan and the UK are the largest insurance markets, accounting for around 50% of worldwide premium income.

The market is led by a number of major players who dominate insurance activity in their market or regionally. These include well known household names such as Allianz Worldwide, AXA, AIG, Generali Group and Aviva.

Another well-known organisation is Lloyd's of London, which with its 300-year-plus history is one of the largest insurance organisations in the world. It is not an insurance company but a marketplace that brings together a range of insurers, both individuals and companies, each of whom accepts insurance risks as a member of one or more underwriting syndicates. A small number of individual members (traditionally known as 'names') are liable to the full extent of their private wealth to meet their insurance commitments, while the corporate entities trade with limited liability. Lloyd's names join together in syndicates and each syndicate will 'write insurance', ie, take on all or part of an insurance risk. There are many syndicates, and each name will belong to one or more. Each syndicate hopes that premiums received will exceed claims paid out, in which case each name will receive a share of profits (after deducting administration expenses).

Lloyd's insures specialist and complex risks in casualty, property, energy, motor, aviation, marine and reinsurance. It has a reputation for innovation, for example, developing policies for aviation, burglary and cybercrime, and is known across the world as the place to bring unusual, specialist and complicated risks.

3. Industry Participants

Learning Objective

1.1.1 Know the role of the following within the financial services industry: retail banks; building societies; investment banks; pension funds; insurance companies; fund managers; stockbrokers; custodians; platforms; third party administrators (TPAs); industry trade and professional bodies

The following sections provide descriptions of some of the main participants in the financial services industry.

3.1 Retail Banks

Retail (or high street) banks provide services such as taking deposits from and lending funds to retail customers, as well as providing payment and money transmission services. They may also provide similar services to business customers.

Historically these banks have tended to operate through a network of branches located on the high street. They also provide internet and telephone banking.

As well as providing traditional banking services, larger retail banks also offer other financial products such as investments, pensions and insurance.

3.2 Savings Institutions

As well as retail banks, most countries also have savings institutions which started off by specialising in offering savings products to retail customers, but which now tend to offer a similar range of services to those offered by banks.

In the UK, they are usually known as **building societies**. They were established in the 19th century when small numbers of people would group together and pool their savings, allowing some members to build or buy houses. Building societies are jointly owned by the individuals who have deposited money with or borrowed money from them – the 'members'. It is for this reason that such savings organisations are often described as 'mutual societies'.

Over the years, many smaller building societies have merged or been taken over by larger ones or banks. In the late 1980s, legislation was introduced allowing building societies to become companies – a process known as **demutualisation**. Some large building societies remain as mutuals, such as the Nationwide Building Society. They continue to specialise in services for retail customers, especially the provision of deposit accounts and mortgages.

3.3 Investment Banks

Investment banks provide advice and arrange finance for companies that want to float on the stock market, raise additional finance by issuing further shares or bonds, or carry out mergers and acquisitions. They also provide services for those who might want to invest in shares and bonds, for example, pension funds and asset managers.

Typically, an investment banking group provides some or all of the following services, either in divisions of the bank or in associated companies within the group:

- **corporate finance and advisory work**, normally in connection with new issues of securities for raising finance, takeovers, mergers and acquisitions
- **banking**, for governments, institutions and companies
- **Treasury dealing** for corporate clients in foreign currencies, with financial engineering services to protect them from interest rate and exchange rate fluctuations
- **investment management** for sizeable investors such as corporate pension funds, charities and private clients. This may be either via direct investment for the wealthier, or by way of collective investment schemes (CISs) (or 'investment funds'; see Chapter 7). In larger firms, the value of funds under management runs into many billions of pounds
- **securities trading** in equities, bonds and derivatives, and the provision of broking and distribution facilities.

Only a few investment banks provide services in all these areas. Most others tend to specialise to some degree and concentrate on only a few product lines. A number of banks have diversified their range of activities by developing businesses such as proprietary trading, servicing hedge funds, or making private equity investments.

3.4 Pension Funds

Pension funds are one of the key methods by which individuals can make provision for retirement. There is a variety of pension schemes available, ranging from those provided by employers to self-directed schemes.

Pension funds are large, long-term investors in shares, bonds and cash. Some also invest in physical assets, like property. To meet their aim of providing a pension on retirement, the sums of money invested in pensions are substantial.

3.5 Insurance Companies

One of the key functions of the financial services industry is to ensure risks are managed effectively. The insurance industry provides solutions for much more than the standard areas of life and general insurance cover.

Protection planning is a key area of financial advice, and the insurance industry offers a wide range of products to meet many potential scenarios. These products range from payment protection policies designed to pay out in the event that an individual is unable to meet repayments on loans and mortgages, to fleet insurance against the risk of an airline's planes crashing (see Chapter 10, Section 4).

Insurance companies collect **premiums** in exchange for the cover provided. This premium income is used to buy investments such as shares and bonds and as a result, the insurance industry is a major player in the stock market. Insurance companies will subsequently realise these investments to pay any claims that may arise on the various policies.

The UK insurance industry is the largest in Europe and the third largest in the world after the US and Japan.

3.6 Fund Managers

Fund management is the professional management of investment portfolios for a variety of institutions and private investors.

The UK is the largest centre for fund management in Europe, second in size globally only to the US. The fund management industry in the UK serves a large number of domestic and overseas clients and attracts significant overseas funds. London is the leading international centre for fund management.

Fund managers, also known as investment or asset managers, run portfolios of investments for others. They invest money held by institutions, such as pension funds and insurance companies, as well as for collective investment schemes such as unit trusts and open-ended investment companies (OEICs) and for wealthier individuals. Some are organisations that focus solely on this activity; others are divisions of larger entities, such as insurance companies or banks.

Fund management is also known as **asset management** or **investment management**.

Investment managers who buy and sell shares, bonds and other assets in order to increase the value of their clients' portfolios can conveniently be subdivided into institutional and private client fund managers. **Institutional** fund managers work on behalf of institutions, for example, investing money for a company's pension fund or an insurance company's fund, or managing the investments in a unit trust. **Private client** fund managers invest the money of relatively wealthy individuals. Institutional portfolios are usually larger than those of regular private clients.

Fund managers charge their clients for managing their money; their **charges** are often based on a small percentage of the value of the fund being managed.

Other areas of fund management include the provision of investment management services to institutional entities, such as companies, charities and local government authorities.

3.7 Stockbrokers

Stockbrokers arrange trades in financial instruments on behalf of their clients, which include investment institutions, fund managers and private clients. They may advise investors about which shares, bonds or funds they should buy or, alternatively, they may offer execution-only services (see Section 4.2). Many stockbrokers now offer wealth management services to their clients and so are also referred to as wealth managers.

Like fund managers, firms of stockbrokers can be independent companies, but some are divisions of larger entities, such as investment banks. They earn their profits by charging **fees** for their advice and **commissions** on transactions. Also like fund managers, stockbrokers may look after client assets and charge custody and portfolio management fees.

3.8 Custodian Banks

Custodians are banks that specialise in safe custody services, looking after portfolios of shares and bonds on behalf of others, such as fund managers, pension funds and insurance companies.

The core activities they undertake include:

- holding assets in safekeeping, such as equities and bonds
- arranging settlement of any purchases and sales of securities
- processing corporate actions, including collecting income from assets, namely dividends in the case of equities and interest in the case of bonds
- providing information on the underlying companies and their annual general meetings
- managing cash transactions
- performing foreign exchange transactions when required
- providing regular reporting on all their activities to their clients.

Competition has driven down the charges that a custodian can make for its traditional custody services and has resulted in consolidation within the industry. The custody business is now dominated by a small number of **global custodians**, which are often divisions of investment banks.

3.9 Platforms

Platforms are online services used by intermediaries, such as independent financial advisers, to view and administer their clients' investment portfolios.

They offer a range of tools which allow advisers to see and analyse a client's overall portfolio and to choose products for them. As well as providing facilities for investments to be bought and sold, platforms generally arrange custody for clients' assets. Examples of platforms include those offered by Cofunds and Hargreaves Lansdown.

The term 'platform' refers to both wraps and fund supermarkets. These are similar, but while fund supermarkets tend to offer wide ranges of unit trusts and OEICs, wraps often offer greater access to other products too, such as Individual Savings Accounts (ISAs), pension plans and insurance bonds. Wrap accounts enable advisers to take a holistic view of the various assets that a client has in a variety of accounts. Advisers also benefit from using wrap accounts to simplify and bring some level of automation to their back office using internet technology.

Platform providers also make their services available direct to investors, and platforms earn their income by charging for their services.

The advantage of platforms for fund management groups is the ability of the platform to distribute their products to financial advisers.

3.10 Third Party Administrators (TPAs)

Third party administrators (TPAs) undertake investment administration on behalf of other firms, and specialise in this area of the investment industry.

The number of TPA firms and the scale of their operations has grown with the increasing use of **outsourcing**. The rationale behind outsourcing is that it enables a firm to focus on the core areas of its business (for example, investment management and stock selection, or the provision of appropriate financial planning) and fix its costs, and leaves a specialist firm to carry out the administrative functions, which it can process more efficiently and cost-effectively.

3.11 Trade and Professional Bodies

The investment industry is a dynamic, rapidly changing business, and one that requires co-operation between firms to ensure that the views of various industry sections are represented, especially to government and regulators. The industry also facilitates and enables cross-firm developments to take place to create an efficient market in which the firms can operate.

This is essentially the role of the numerous professional and trade bodies that exist across the world's financial markets. Examples of such bodies include:

- **Bonds** – International Capital Market Association (ICMA).
- **Derivatives** – FIA Europe; International Swaps and Derivatives Association (ISDA).
- **Fund managers** – Investment Association (IA).
- **Insurance companies** – Association of British Insurers (ABI).

- **Private client investment management** – Wealth Management Association (WMA) (formerly Association of Private Client Investment Managers and Stockbrokers (APCIMS)).
- **Banks** – British Bankers' Association (BBA).
- **Investment funds** – the Tax Incentivised Savings Association (TISA) is an industry-funded body working to improve savings and investment schemes available to UK citizens; the Depositary and Trustee Association represents the industry views of depositaries of open-ended investment companies (OEICs) and trustees of unit trusts within the UK.

4. Investment Distribution Channels

Learning Objective

1.1.3 Know the role of the following investment distribution channels: independent financial adviser; restricted advice; platforms; execution-only; robo-advice

4.1 Financial Advisers

Financial advisers are professionals who offer advice on financial matters to their clients. Some recommend suitable financial products from the whole of the market and others from a narrower range of products.

Typically a financial adviser will conduct a detailed survey of a client's financial position, preferences and objectives; this is sometimes known as a **fact-find**. The adviser will then suggest appropriate action to meet the client's objectives and, if necessary, recommend a suitable financial product to match the client's needs.

Investment firms must now clearly describe their services as either **independent advice** or **restricted advice**. Firms that describe their advice as independent will have to ensure that they genuinely do make their recommendations based on comprehensive and fair analysis of all products available in the market, and provide unbiased, unrestricted advice. If a firm chooses to only give advice on its own range of products – restricted advice – this will have to be made clear. Their activities are supervised by the Financial Conduct Authority (FCA).

4.2 Execution-Only

A firm carries out transactions on an execution-only basis if the customer asks it to buy or sell a specific named investment product without having been prompted or advised by the firm. In such instances, customers are responsible for their own decision about a product's suitability.

The practice of execution-only sales is long-established. To ensure that firms operate within regulatory guidelines they need to record and retain evidence in writing that the firm:

- gave no advice
- made it clear, at the time of the sale, that it was not responsible for the product's suitability.

4.3 Robo-Advice

Robo-advice is the application of technology to the process of providing financial advice, but without the involvement of a financial adviser. A prospective investor enters data and financial information about themselves, and the system then uses an algorithm to score the information and decide what investments should be chosen. The system then presents the investment strategy, which is usually passively focused around index funds or exchange-traded funds (ETFs), and allows easy implementation.

Robo-advice can be fully automated or provide guidance and tools to enable investors to choose their own solutions. The approach uses an asset and risk model, as well as the construction of risk-targeted portfolios or funds to achieve a client's objectives, and then the ongoing monitoring and rebalancing against those objectives.

Robo-advice is already established in the US, with some of the industry's largest players involved. It is expected to appear shortly in the UK to fill the gaps in the advice market and, particularly, for pensions planning, as a result of major changes to how pension benefits can be taken (See Chapter 9, Section 4.2).

End of Chapter Questions

Think of an answer for each question and refer to the appropriate section for confirmation.

1. Name four main activities undertaken by the professional financial services sector and five by the retail sector.
   Answer Reference: Section 2

2. What is the main service provided by investment banks?
   Answer Reference: Sections 2 & 3.3

3. How does a mutual savings institution differ from a retail bank?
   Answer Reference: Sections 3.1 & 3.2

4. What are the main types of services provided by investment banks?
   Answer Reference: Section 3.3

5. What is protection planning and what scenarios can protection policies provide cover for?
   Answer Reference: Section 3.5

6. What services does a custodian offer?
   Answer Reference: Section 3.8

7. What is a platform and why are they a useful distribution channel?
   Answer Reference: Section 3.9

8. What is the role of a third party administrator?
   Answer Reference: Section 3.10

9. What are the two types of financial adviser, and how does the range of products they advise on differ?
   Answer Reference: Section 4.1

10. What records should be kept when a transaction is undertaken on an execution-only basis?
    Answer Reference: Section 4.2

Chapter Two
The Economic Environment

1. Introduction	17
2. **Factors Determining Economic Activity**	17
3. Central Banks	19
4. Inflation	23
5. **Key Economic Indicators**	25

This syllabus area will provide approximately 3 of the 50 examination questions

1. Introduction

In this chapter, we turn to the broader economic environment in which the financial services industry operates.

First we will look at how economic activity is determined in various economic and political systems, and then look at the role of the central banks in the management of that economic activity.

The chapter concludes with an explanation of some of the key economic measures that provide an indication of the state of an economy.

2. Factors Determining Economic Activity

Learning Objective

2.1.1 Know the factors which determine the level of economic activity: state-controlled economies; market economies; mixed economies; open economies

2.1 State-Controlled Economies

A state-controlled economy is one in which the state (in the form of the government) decides what is produced and how it is distributed. The best-known example of a state-controlled economy was the Soviet Union throughout most of the 20th century.

Sometimes these economies are referred to as 'planned economies', because the production and allocation of resources is planned in advance rather than being allowed to respond to market forces. However, the need for careful planning and control can bring about excessive layers of bureaucracy, and state control inevitably removes a great deal of individual choice.

These factors have contributed to the reform of the economies of the former Soviet states and the introduction of a more 'mixed' economy (covered in more detail in Section 2.3).

2.2 Market Economies

In a market economy, the forces of supply and demand determine how resources are allocated.

Businesses produce goods and services to meet the demand from consumers. The interaction of demand from consumers and supply from businesses in the market will determine the **market-clearing price**. This is the price that reflects the balance between what consumers will willingly pay for goods and services and what suppliers will willingly accept for them. If there is oversupply, the price will be low and some producers will leave the market. If there is undersupply, the price will be high, which will attract new producers into the market.

There is a market not only for goods and services, but also for productive assets, such as capital goods (eg, machinery), labour and money. For the labour market it is the wage level that is effectively the 'price', and for the money market it is the interest rate.

People compete for jobs and companies compete for customers in a market economy. Scarce resources, including skilled labour, such as a football player, or a financial asset, such as a share in a successful company, will have a high value. In a market economy, competition means that inferior football players and shares in unsuccessful companies will be much cheaper and ultimately competition could bring about the collapse of the unsuccessful company, and result in the inferior football player searching for an alternative career.

2.3 Mixed Economies

A mixed economy combines a market economy with some element of state control. The vast majority of economies are mixed to a greater or lesser extent.

While most of us would agree that unsuccessful companies should be allowed to fail, we generally feel that the less able in society should be cushioned against the full force of the market economy.

In a mixed economy, the government will provide a welfare system to support the unemployed, the infirm and the elderly, in tandem with the market-driven aspects of the economy. Governments will also spend money running key areas such as defence, education, public transport, health and police services.

Governments raise finance for their public expenditure by:

- collecting taxes directly from wage-earners and companies
- collecting indirect taxes (eg, VAT and taxes on petrol, cigarettes and alcohol)
- raising money through borrowing in the capital markets.

Civil servants, primarily working for the government to raise money and spend it, tend to be one of the largest groups in the labour market. In the UK it is the civil servants working for the Treasury who raise money and allocate it to the 'spending departments', such as the National Health Service (NHS).

2.4 Open Economies

The term 'open economy' relates to a country's economic relationship with outside countries. In an open economy there are few barriers to trade or controls over foreign exchange.

Although most western governments create barriers to protect their citizens against illegal drugs and other dangers, they generally have policies to allow or encourage free trade.

From time to time, issues will arise when one country believes another is taking unfair advantage of trade policies and employs some form of retaliatory action, possibly including the imposition of **sanctions**. When a country prevents other countries from trading freely with it in order to preserve its domestic market, it is usually referred to as **protectionism**.

The **World Trade Organisation (WTO)** exists to promote the growth of free trade between economies. It is therefore sometimes called upon to arbitrate when disputes arise.

3. Central Banks

Learning Objective

2.1.2 Know the function of central banks: the Bank of England; the Federal Reserve; the European Central Bank

Traditionally, the role of government has been to manage the economy through taxation and through economic and monetary policy, and to ensure a fair society by the state provision of welfare and benefits to those who meet certain criteria, while leaving business relatively free to address the challenges and opportunities that arise.

Governments can use a variety of policies when attempting to reduce the impact of fluctuations in economic activity. Collectively these measures are known as **stabilisation policies** and are categorised under the broad headings of fiscal policy and monetary policy. **Fiscal policy** involves making adjustments using government spending and taxation, whilst **monetary policy** involves making adjustments to interest rates and the money supply.

Rather than following one or other type of policy, most governments now adopt a pragmatic approach to controlling the level of economic activity through a combination of fiscal and monetary policy. In an increasingly integrated world, however, controlling the level of activity in an open economy in isolation is difficult, as financial markets, rather than individual governments and central banks, tend to dictate economic policy.

Governments implement their economic policies using their central bank, and a consideration of their role in this implementation is explained below.

3.1 The Role of Central Banks

Central banks operate at the very centre of a nation's financial system. They are public bodies but, increasingly, they operate independently of government control or political interference. They usually have some or all of the following responsibilities:

- Acting as banker to the banking system by accepting deposits from, and lending to, commercial banks.
- Acting as banker to the government.
- Managing the national debt.
- Regulating the domestic banking system.
- Acting as lender of last resort in financial crises to prevent the systemic collapse of the banking system.
- Setting the official short-term rate of interest.
- Controlling the money supply.
- Issuing notes and coins.
- Holding the nation's gold and foreign currency reserves.
- Influencing the value of a nation's currency through activities such as intervention in the currency markets.
- Providing a depositors' protection scheme for bank deposits.

3.2 Bank of England (BoE)

The Bank of England is the central bank of the United Kingdom. It was founded in 1694 and its roles and functions have evolved and changed over its 300-year-plus history. Since its foundation it has been the government's banker and, since the late 18th century, it has been banker to the banking system more generally – the bankers' bank. As well as providing banking services to its customers, the Bank of England manages the UK's foreign exchange and gold reserves.

The Bank has two core purposes – monetary stability and financial stability.

- **Monetary stability** means stable prices and confidence in the currency. Stable prices involve meeting the government's inflation target which, since November 2003, has been a rolling two-year target of 2% for the consumer prices index (CPI). This it does by setting the base rate, the UK's administratively set short-term interest rate.
- **Financial stability** refers to detecting and reducing threats to the financial system as a whole. A sound and stable financial system is important in its own right, and vital to the efficient conduct of monetary policy.

3.2.1 Monetary Stability

Learning Objective

2.1.3 Know the functions of the Monetary Policy Committee

The Bank is perhaps most visible to the general public through its banknotes and, since the late 1990s, its **interest rate** decisions. The Bank has had a monopoly on the issue of banknotes in England and Wales since the early 20th century. But it is only since 1997 that the Bank has had statutory responsibility for setting the UK's official interest rate.

Interest rate decisions are taken by the Bank's **Monetary Policy Committee (MPC)**. The MPC's primary focus is to ensure that inflation is kept within a government-set range, set each year by the Chancellor of the Exchequer. The MPC does this by setting the **base rate**. This is the MPC's sole policy instrument.

At its monthly meetings, the MPC must gauge all of those factors that can influence inflation over both the short and medium term. These include the level of the exchange rate, the rate at which the economy is growing, how much consumers are borrowing and spending, wage inflation, and any changes to government spending and taxation plans.

When setting the base rate, however, it must also be mindful of the impact any changes will have on the sustainability of economic growth and employment in the UK and the time lag between a change in rate and the effects it will have on the economy. Depending on the sector of the economy we are looking at, this can be anything from a very short period of time (eg, credit card spending when consumers are already stretched), to a year or more (businesses altering their investment and expansion plans).

Quantitative Easing

The last economic cycle saw governments across the world, including the UK, follow a policy of reducing interest rates to counter the effect of a slowing global economy and the risks of depression.

When a central bank is concerned about the risks of very low inflation, it cuts the base rate to reduce the cost of money and provide a stimulus to the economy.

The key difference in the last recession was that interest rates were reduced massively by central banks in developed countries. When they are close to zero, central banks need an alternative policy instrument. This involves injecting money directly into the economy in a process that has become known as quantitative easing.

Quantitative easing involves the central bank creating money, which it then uses to buy assets such as government bonds and high-quality debt from private companies, resulting in more money in the wider economy.

Creating more money does not involve printing more banknotes. Instead, the central bank buys assets from private sector institutions and credits the seller's bank account, so the seller has more money in their bank account, while the central bank holds assets as part of its reserves. The end result is more money out in the wider economy.

Injecting more money into the economy through the purchase of bonds can have a number of effects:

- The seller of the bonds ends up with more money and so may spend it, which will help boost growth.
- Alternatively, they may buy other assets instead and in doing so boost prices and provide liquidity to other sectors of the economy, resulting in people feeling better off and so spending more.
- Buying assets means higher asset prices and lower yields, which brings down the cost of borrowing for businesses and households, encouraging a further boost to spending.
- Banks find themselves holding more reserves, which might lead them to boost their lending to consumers and business; again, borrowing increases and so does spending.

The theory is that the extra money works its way through the economy, resulting in higher spending and therefore growth, or reducing the impact of recession and preventing the onset of a depression.

3.2.2 Financial Stability

Since the financial crisis of 2007–08, the Bank's role of protecting and enhancing the stability of the financial system has gained greater emphasis and importance.

The purpose of preserving financial stability is to maintain the three vital functions which the financial system performs in the economy:

- providing the main mechanism for paying for goods, services and financial assets
- intermediating between savers and borrowers, and channelling savings into investment via debt and equity instruments
- insuring against and dispersing risk.

In April 2013, the UK government brought in a major reform of the regulatory regime which has significantly increased and broadened the Bank's role and responsibilities for financial stability. These changes are a result of the weaknesses identified as a result of the financial crisis, of which perhaps the most significant failing was that no single institution had the responsibility, authority or powers to oversee the financial system as a whole.

In June 2011, the government announced details of its plans to establish a new committee at the Bank of England — the Financial Policy Committee (FPC). The FPC is tasked with monitoring the stability and resilience of the UK financial system and using its powers to tackle those risks. It also gives direction and recommendations to the newly formed Prudential Regulation Authority (PRA) and Financial Conduct Authority (FCA). The PRA is part of the BoE and has assumed responsibility for the supervision of banks and key market infrastructure firms (such as the London Clearing House and Euroclear UK & Ireland).

3.2.3 Other Bank of England Responsibilities

In addition to these responsibilities, the Bank also assumes responsibility for all other traditional central bank activities listed in Section 3.1 – with the exception of managing the national debt and providing a depositors' protection scheme for bank deposits. Managing the national debt is undertaken by the Debt Management Office (DMO), and operating the depositor protection scheme by the Financial Services Compensation Scheme (FSCS).

3.3 Federal Reserve (Fed)

The Federal Reserve System in the US dates back to 1913. The Fed, as it is known, comprises 12 regional Federal Reserve Banks, each of which monitors the activities of, and provides liquidity to, the banks in its region.

Although free from political interference, the Fed is governed by a seven-strong board appointed by the President of the United States. This governing board, together with the presidents of five of the 12 Federal Reserve Banks, makes up the **Federal Open Market Committee (FOMC)**. The chairman of the FOMC, also appointed by the US President, takes responsibility for the committee's decisions, which are directed towards its statutory duty of promoting price stability and sustainable economic growth. The FOMC meets every six weeks or so to examine the latest economic data in order to gauge the health of the economy and determine whether the economically sensitive Fed funds rate should be altered. In late 2015, it made the decision to raise interest rates for the first time since the 2008 financial crisis.

As lender of last resort to the US banking system, the Fed has, in recent years, rescued a number of US financial institutions and markets from collapse during the financial crisis. In doing so, it has prevented widespread panic and prevented systemic risk from spreading throughout the financial system (known as 'contagion').

3.4 European Central Bank (ECB)

Based in Frankfurt, the ECB assumed its central banking responsibilities upon the creation of the euro, on 1 January 1999. The ECB is principally responsible for setting monetary policy for the entire eurozone, with the objective of maintaining internal price stability. Its objective of keeping inflation, as defined by the harmonised index of consumer prices (HICP), *'close to but below 2% in the medium term'* is achieved by influencing those factors that may affect inflation, such as the external value of the euro and growth in the money supply.

The ECB sets its monetary policy through its president and council; the latter comprises the governors of each of the eurozone's national central banks. Although the ECB acts independently of EU member governments when implementing monetary policy, it has on occasion succumbed to political persuasion. It used to be one of the few central banks that does not act as a lender of last resort to the banking system, but that changed when the eurozone crisis forced it to support banks and economies in struggling European countries.

In 2014, the ECB was given a supervisory role to monitor the financial stability of banks in eurozone states. The Single Supervisory Mechanism (SSM) is a new framework for banking supervision in Europe and comprises the ECB and national supervisory authorities of participating EU countries. Its main aims are to:

- ensure the safety and soundness of the European banking system
- increase financial integration and stability in Europe.

The SSM is an important milestone towards a banking union within the EU.

4. Inflation

In this section we look at the impact of inflation. We will look first at how goods and services are paid for and how credit is created, and then examine the interaction of credit creation with inflation.

4.1 Credit Creation

Learning Objective

2.1.4   Know how goods and services are paid for and how credit is created

Most of what we buy is not paid for using cash. We find it more convenient to pay by card or cheque.

It is fairly easy (subject to the borrower's credit status) to buy something now and pay later, for example by going overdrawn, using a credit card or taking out a loan. Loans will often be for more substantial purchases such as a house or a car. Buying now and paying later is generally referred to as purchasing goods and services 'on credit'.

The banking system provides a mechanism by which credit can be created. This means that banks can increase the total amount of money supply in the economy.

Example

New Bank plc sets up business and is granted a banking licence. It is authorised to take deposits and make loans. Because New Bank knows that only a small proportion of the deposited funds are likely to be demanded at any one time, it will be able to lend the deposited money to others. New Bank will make profits by lending money out at a higher rate than it pays depositors.

These loans provide an increase in the money supply in circulation – New Bank is creating credit.

By this action of lending to borrowers, banks create money and advance this to industry, consumers and governments. This money circulates within the economy, being spent on goods and services by the people who have borrowed it from the banks. The people to whom it is paid (the providers of those goods and services) will then deposit it in their own bank accounts, allowing the banks to use it to create fresh credit all over again.

It is estimated that this 'credit creation' process accounts for 96% of the money in circulation in most industrialised nations, with only 4% being in the form of notes and coins created by the government.

If this process were uncontrolled it would lead to a rapid increase in the money supply and, with too much money chasing too few goods, the result would be an increase in inflation. Understandably therefore, central banks aim to keep the amount of credit creation under control as part of their overall monetary policy. They will aim to ensure that the amount of credit creation is below the level at which it would increase the money supply so much that inflation accelerates.

Nowadays, the UK's central bank (the Bank of England) does this by influencing people's appetite for borrowing through interest rates.

4.2 The Impact of Inflation

Learning Objective

2.1.5 Understand the impact of inflation/deflation on economic behaviour

---

Inflation is a persistent increase in the general level of prices.

There are a number of reasons for prices to increase, such as excess demand in the economy, scarcity of resources and key workers, or rapidly increasing government spending. Most western governments seek to control inflation at a level of about 2–3% per annum without letting it get too high (or too low).

High levels of inflation can cause problems:

- Businesses have to continually update prices to keep pace with inflation.
- Employees find the real value of their salaries eroded.
- Those on fixed levels of income, such as pensioners, will suffer as the price increases are not matched by increases in income.

- Exports may become less competitive.
- The real value of future pensions and investment income becomes difficult to assess, which might act as a disincentive to save.

There are, however, some positive aspects to high levels of inflation:

- Rising house prices contribute to a 'feel good' factor (although this might contribute to further inflation as house-owners become more eager to borrow and spend).
- Borrowers benefit, because the value of borrowers' debt falls in real terms – ie, after adjusting for the effect of inflation.
- Inflation also erodes the real value of a country's national debt and so can benefit an economy in difficult times.

Deflation is defined as a general fall in price levels. Although not experienced as a worldwide phenomenon since the 1930s, it has been seen more recently in many economies.

Deflation typically results from negative demand shocks, such as the recent falls in oil and commodity prices, and from excess capacity and production. It creates a vicious circle of reduced spending and a reluctance to borrow as the real burden of debt in an environment of falling prices increases.

It should be noted that falling prices are not necessarily a destructive force per se and; indeed, they can be beneficial if they are as a result of positive supply shocks, such as rising productivity growth and greater price competition caused by the globalisation of the world economy and increased price transparency.

5. Key Economic Indicators

As well as being essential to the management of the economy, indicators can provide investors with a guide to the health of the economy and aid long-term investment decisions.

5.1 Inflation Measures

Learning Objective

2.1.6 Know the meaning of the following measures of inflation: consumer prices index; retail prices index

Inflation is measured by reference to an 'index', made up of a notional basket of all the things the 'average' person is assumed to spend money on. But different people spend their money on different things – so there are several inflation indices, reflecting different ways of calculating the general rise in price levels and the cost of living. These are known collectively as consumer price indices.

They may be used for several purposes – for example:

- as an indicator of inflationary pressures in the economy
- as a benchmark for wage negotiations
- to determine annual increases in government benefits payments.

Some of the main measures of inflation are:

- **Consumer prices index (CPI)** – this is a measure of inflation that is prepared in a standard way throughout the European Union (EU). It excludes mortgage interest payments, mostly because a large proportion of the population in continental Europe rent their homes, rather than buy them. It also excludes other housing costs aside from mortgage interest costs (for example, it excludes the 'depreciation component', an amount which the RPI uses to allow for the cost of maintaining a home in a constant condition). It was originally known as the **harmonised index of consumer prices (HICP)**.
- **Retail prices index (RPI)** – the RPI (also known as the 'headline' rate) measures the increase in general household spending, including mortgage and rent payments, food, transport and entertainment. Originally launched in 1947, this measures the rate at which the prices of a representative basket of goods and services purchased by the average UK household – that is, excluding pensioners and the top 4% of income-earners – have changed over the course of a month. Needless to say, the composition and weighting of the various goods and services in the basket has altered dramatically since its inception.

In the UK, the government uses the CPI for a range of purposes, principally those when it needs to measure inflation on a like-for-like basis with those other European countries that use the same standard method of calculation.

Consumer Prices Index (2009–15)

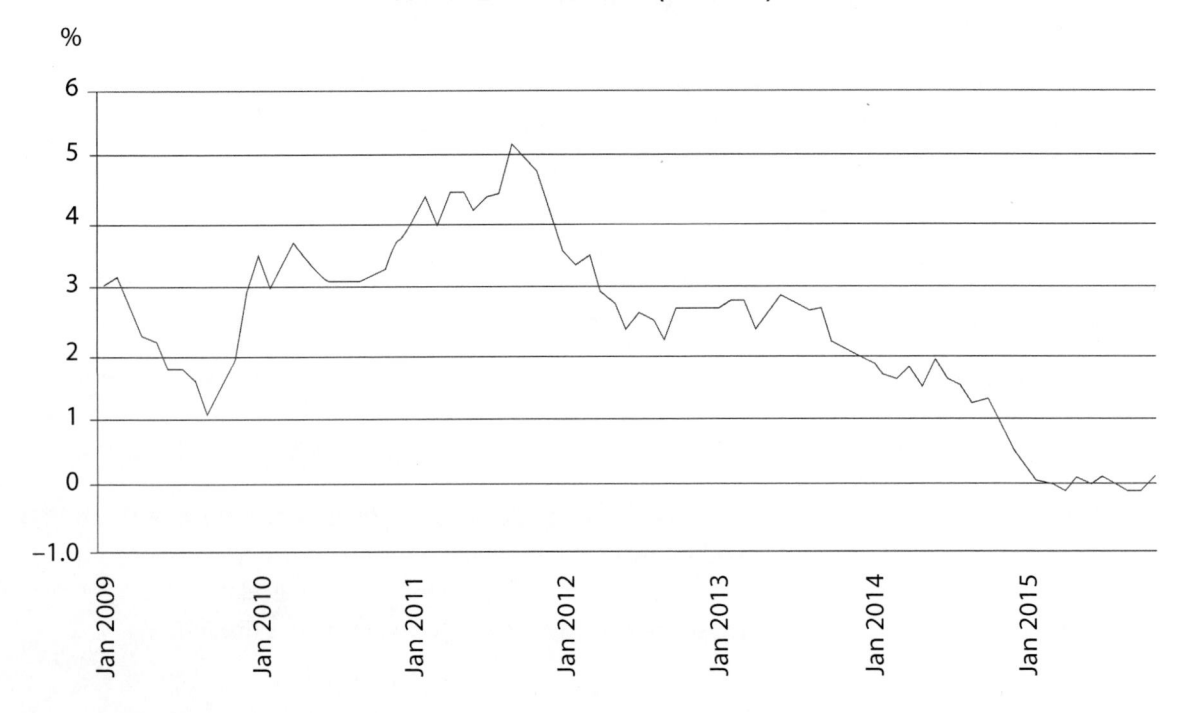

Source: Office for National Statistics

The Economic Environment

5.2 Measures of Economic Data

Learning Objective

2.1.7 Understand the impact of the following economic data: gross domestic product (GDP); balance of payments; budget deficit/surplus; level of unemployment; exchange rates

In addition to inflation measures, there are a number of other economic statistics carefully watched by the government and by other market participants as potentially significant indicators of how the economy is performing.

5.2.1 Gross Domestic Product (GDP)

At the very simplest level, an economy comprises two distinct groups: individuals and firms. Individuals supply firms with the productive resources of the economy in exchange for an income. In turn, these individuals use this income to buy the entire output produced by firms employing these resources. This gives rise to what is known as the **circular flow of income**.

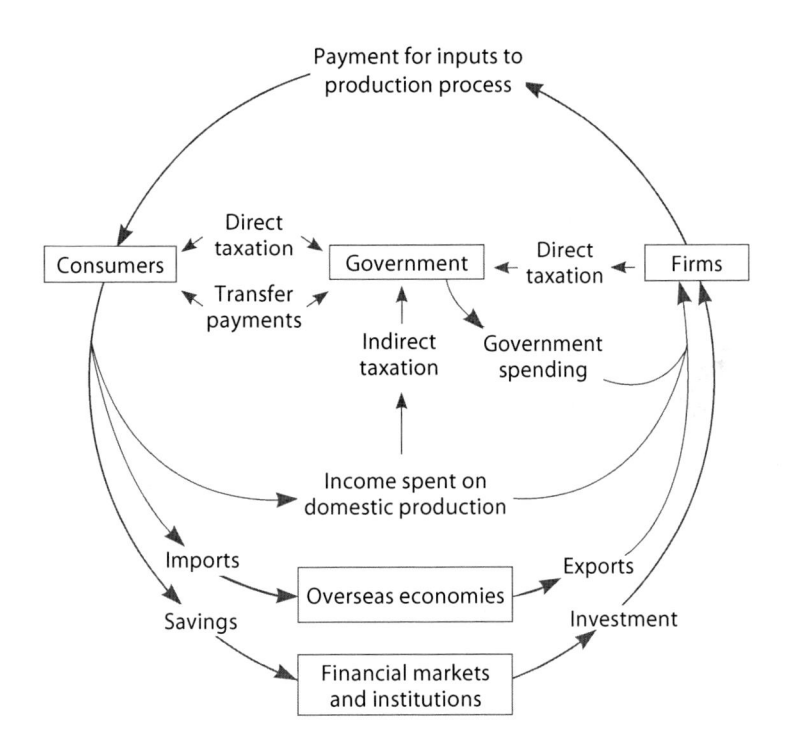

This economic activity can be measured in one of three ways:

- by the total income paid by firms to individuals
- by individuals' total expenditure on firms' output
- by the value of total output generated by firms.

GDP is the most commonly used measure of a country's output. It measures economic activity on an expenditure basis and is typically calculated quarterly as below:

	Gross Domestic Product
	consumer spending
plus	government spending
plus	investment
plus	exports
less	imports
equals	GDP

5.2.2 Economic Growth and the Economic Cycle

There are many sources from which economic growth can emanate, but in the long run the rate of sustainable growth (or **trend rate of growth**) ultimately depends on:

- the growth and productivity of the labour force
- the rate at which an economy efficiently channels its domestic savings and capital attracted from overseas into new and innovative technology and replaces obsolescent capital equipment
- the extent to which an economy's infrastructure is maintained and developed to cope with growing transport, communication and energy needs.

In a mature economy, the labour force typically grows at about 1% per annum, though in countries such as the US, where immigrant labour is increasingly employed, the annual growth rate has been in excess of this. Long-term productivity growth is dependent on factors such as education and training and the utilisation of labour-saving new technology. Moreover, productivity gains are more difficult to extract in a post-industrialised economy than in one with a large manufacturing base.

The fact that actual growth fluctuates and deviates from trend growth in the short term gives rise to the **economic cycle**, or business cycle. When an economy is growing in excess of its trend growth rate, actual output will exceed potential output, often with inflationary consequences. However, when a country's output contracts – that is, when its economic growth rate turns negative for at least two consecutive calendar quarters – the economy is said to be in recession, or entering a deflationary period, resulting in spare capacity and unemployment.

This is demonstrated in the following diagram.

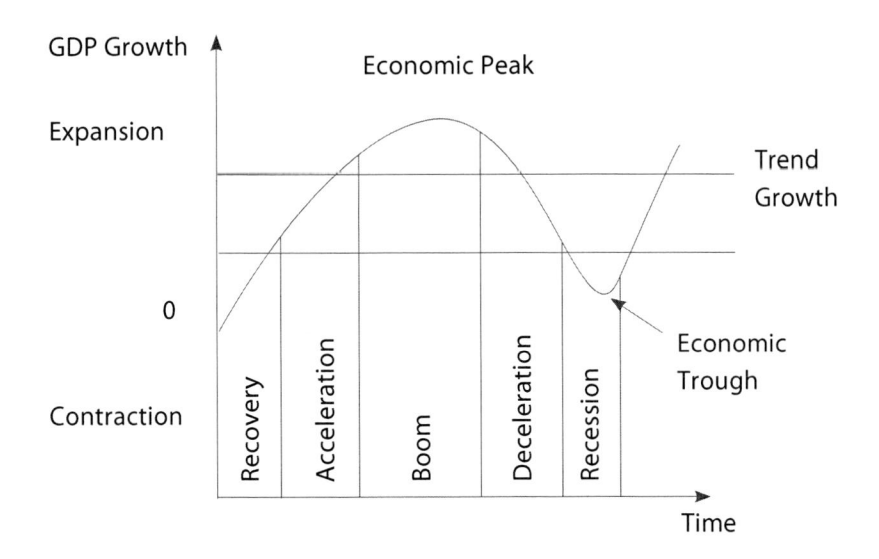

5.2.3 Balance of Payments

The balance of payments is a summary of all the transactions between the UK and the rest of the world. If the UK imports more than it exports, there is a **balance of payments deficit**. If the UK exports more than it imports, there is a **balance of payments surplus**.

The main components of the balance of payments are the trade balance, the current account and the capital account.

The **trade balance** comprises a **visible** trade balance – the difference between the value of imported and exported goods, such as those arising from the trade of raw materials and manufactured goods; and an **invisible** trade balance – the difference between the value of imported and exported services, arising from services such as banking, financial services and tourism. If a country has a **trade deficit** in one of these areas or overall, this means that it imports more than it exports, and, if it has a **trade surplus**, it exports more than it imports.

The **current account** is used to calculate the total value of goods and services that flow into and out of a country. The current account comprises the trade balance figures for the visibles and invisibles. To these figures are added other receipts such as dividends from overseas assets and remittances from nationals working abroad.

The results of the current account calculations provide details of the balance of trade a country has with the rest of the world. Being a post-industrial economy, the UK typically runs a deficit on visible trade but an invisible trade surplus. Also, because it is an open economy, imports and exports combined total over 50% of UK GDP.

The **capital account** records international capital transactions related to investment in business, real estate, bonds and stocks. This includes transactions relating to the ownership of fixed assets and the purchase and sale of domestic and foreign investment assets. These are usually divided into categories such as foreign direct investment, when an overseas firm acquires a new plant or an existing business; portfolio investment, which includes trading in stocks and bonds; and other investments, which include transactions in currency and bank deposits.

For the balance of payments to balance, the current account must equal the capital account plus or minus a balancing item – used to rectify the many errors in compiling the balance of payments – plus or minus any change in central bank foreign currency reserves.

A current account deficit resulting from a country being a net importer of overseas goods and services must be met by a net inflow of capital from overseas, taking account of any measurement errors and any central bank intervention in the foreign currency market.

Having the right **exchange rate** is critical to the level of international trade undertaken, to a country's international competitiveness and therefore to its economic position. This can be understood by looking at what happens if a country's exchange rate alters.

- If the value of its currency **rises**, then exports will be less competitive unless producers reduce their prices, and imports will be cheaper and therefore more competitive. The result will be either to reduce a trade surplus or worsen a trade deficit.
- If its value **falls** against other currencies then the reverse happens: exports will be cheaper in foreign market and thus more competitive, and imports will be more expensive and less competitive. A trade surplus or deficit will therefore see an improving position.

5.2.4 Budget Deficit and National Debt

A key function of government is to manage the public finances, and so a key economic indicator is the level of public sector debt, or the **national debt** as it is more frequently referred to.

In the past a state would incur budget deficits, usually as a result of wars, and finance these through taxation. In the UK, this changed in the late 1600s when the government's need to finance another war with France led to the creation of the Bank of England in 1694 and the first issue of state public debt in England.

Following on from this, the early 1700s saw the emergence of banking and financial markets and the ability to raise money by creating debt through the issue of bills and bonds and the beginning of the national debt. Some key statistics from the Office for National Statistics (ONS) show how the national debt has grown since then:

- The national debt rose from £12 million in 1700 to £850 million by the end of the Napoleonic Wars in 1815.
- The two world wars of the 20th century caused debt levels to rise, from £650 million in 1914 to £7.4 billion by 1919, and from £7.1 billion in 1939 to £24.7 billion in 1946.
- The period of relatively high inflation in the 1970s and 1980s saw debt rise from £33.1 billion in 1970 to £197.4 billion in 1988.
- The national debt has now ballooned to around £1,500 billion.

The national debt continues to rise as the effects of previous overspending and the recession are felt.

There are a wide number of measures used as key economic indicators, which can be quite confusing. Each measures different sets of data, but essentially they fall into two main types:

- **Government debt** – essentially this is what the government owes. The most widely quoted is **public sector net debt**.
- **Government deficit** – essentially the shortfall between what the government receives in tax receipts and what it spends. The most widely quoted is **public sector net cash requirement (PSNCR)**.

Debt measures are also usually presented as a percentage of GDP, since comparisons over time need to allow for effects such as inflation. Dividing by GDP is the conventional way of doing this.

So, PSNCR is the difference between government expenditure and government income, the latter mainly from taxes. In a buoyant economy, government spending tends to be less than income, with substantial tax revenues generated from corporate profits and high levels of employment. This enables the government to reduce public sector (ie, government) borrowing.

In a slowing economy, government spending tends to exceed tax revenues and the government will need to raise borrowing by issuing government bonds. This is currently the case in the UK, where the budget deficit exploded as the recession reduced tax receipts and pushed up spending on unemployment benefit. If left unaddressed, high levels of public borrowing and debt risk undermining growth and economic stability.

As mentioned earlier, excessive government spending, causing a growing PSNCR, has the potential to bring about an increase in the rate of inflation.

5.2.5 Level of Unemployment

The extent to which those seeking employment cannot find work is an important indicator of the health of the economy. There is always likely to be some unemployment in an economy – some people might lack the right skills and/or live in employment black spots. Higher levels of unemployment indicate low demand in the economy for goods and services produced and sold to consumers and therefore low demand for UK people to provide them.

High unemployment levels will have a negative impact on the government's finances. The government will need to increase social security payments, and its income will decrease because of the lack of tax revenues from the unemployed.

The following chart shows how the UK unemployment rate has varied since the 1970s.

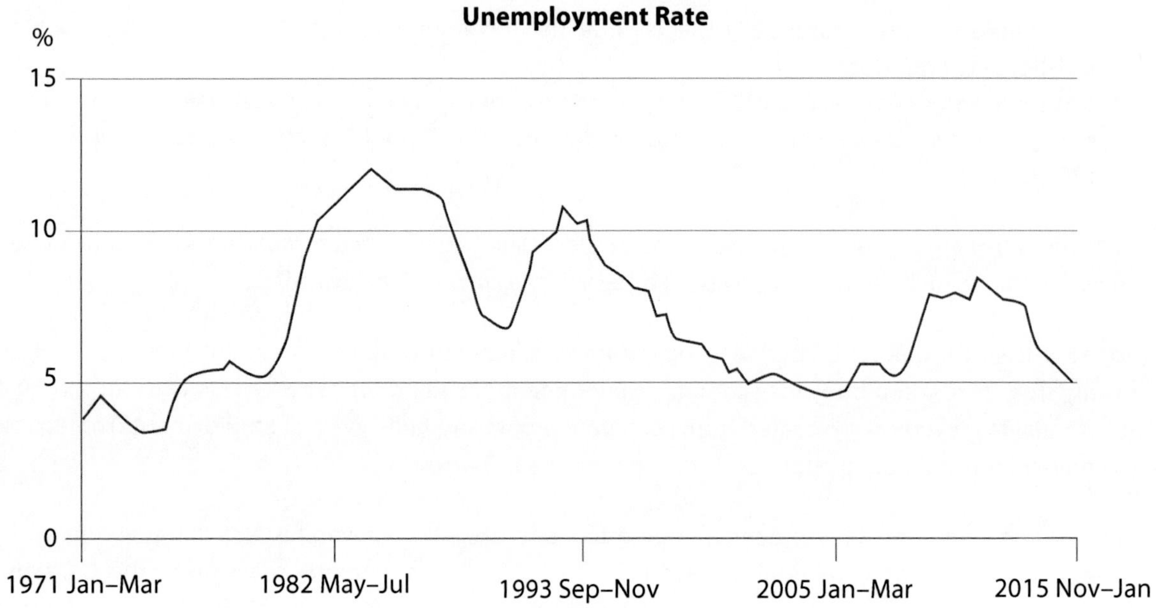
Unemployment Rate
%
15
10
5
0
1971 Jan–Mar
1982 May–Jul
1993 Sep–Nov
2005 Jan–Mar
2015 Nov–Jan

End of Chapter Questions

Think of an answer for each question and refer to the appropriate section for confirmation.

1. What are the key differences between state-controlled and market economies?
   Answer Reference: Sections 2.1 & 2.2

2. Which international organisation has the role of reducing trade barriers?
   Answer Reference: Section 2.4

3. What is the primary role of the Monetary Policy Committee?
   Answer Reference: Section 3.2.1

4. What would be the effect of uncontrolled growth in the money supply?
   Answer Reference: Section 4.1

5. What are the negative effects of inflation?
   Answer Reference: Section 4.2

6. What are the principal differences between the RPI and the CPI?
   Answer Reference: Section 5.1

7. What economic measure is used as an indicator of the health of the economy?
   Answer Reference: Section 5.2.1

8. What does the balance of payments represent?
   Answer Reference: Section 5.2.3

9. What is the potential impact of increasing levels of government spending?
   Answer Reference: Section 5.2.4

10. What is the impact of high unemployment levels on the economy?
    Answer Reference: Section 5.2.5

Chapter Three
Financial Assets and Markets

1. Introduction	37
2. Cash Deposits	37
3. Money Markets	39
4. Property	41
5. Foreign Exchange	42

This syllabus area will provide approximately 5 of the 50 examination questions

Financial Assets and Markets

1. Introduction

This chapter looks at cash, the money market, the property market and foreign exchange. Subsequent chapters will look at the other main asset classes, which are equities, bonds and derivatives.

2. Cash Deposits

Learning Objective

3.1.1 Know the characteristics of fixed term and instant access deposit accounts

3.1.2 Be able to calculate the net interest due given the gross interest rate, the deposited sum, the period and tax rate

Nearly all investors keep at least part of their wealth in the form of cash, which will be deposited with a bank or other savings institution to earn interest.

Cash deposits comprise accounts held with banks or other savings institutions, such as building societies. They are held by a wide variety of depositors, from retail investors, through to companies, governments and financial institutions.

The main characteristics of cash deposits are:

- The return simply comprises interest income with no potential for capital growth.
- The amount invested (the capital) is repaid in full at the end of the investment term or when withdrawn.

Some accounts are known as **instant access** and the money can be withdrawn at any time; other accounts are for a **fixed term** of a year or more, while others require notice to be given before monies can be withdrawn. The interest rate paid on deposits will vary with the amount of money deposited and the time for which the money is tied up. Large deposits are more economical for a bank or building society to process and will earn a better rate. The rate will also vary because of competition, as deposit-taking institutions will compete intensely with one another to attract new deposits.

Any interest received is liable to income tax, but is now paid gross (without deduction of tax) to investors. More detail on how interest is taxed can be found in Chapter 9.

Until April 2016, interest used to be paid net of tax as deposit-takers were required to deduct tax before it was paid to the depositor and then account for the tax to HM Revenue & Customs (HMRC). From April 2016, however, there has been a new personal savings allowance to remove tax on up to £1,000 of savings income for basic rate taxpayers, and up to £500 for higher rate taxpayers. As part of this change, since April 2016, banks and building societies have been required to stop automatically taking 20% in income tax from the interest earned on non-ISA savings.

Non-taxpayers, such as those on very low incomes, were able to submit a form known as an 'R85' to HMRC and, once approved, interest was paid gross with no deduction of tax at source. This was much easier than having tax deducted at source and having to fill out and submit a tax reclaim form. The changes also removed the need for non-taxpayers to complete an R85.

2.1 Advantages and Disadvantages

Learning Objective

3.1.3 Know the advantages and disadvantages of investing in cash

There are a number of **advantages** to investing in cash:

- One of the key reasons for holding money in the form of cash deposits is liquidity. Liquidity is the ease and speed with which an investment can be turned into cash to meet spending needs. Most investors are likely to have a need for cash at short notice and so should plan to hold some cash on deposit to meet possible needs and emergencies before considering other less liquid investments.
- The other main reasons for holding cash investments are as a savings vehicle and for the interest return that can be earned on them.
- A further advantage is the relative safety that cash investments have and that they are not exposed to market volatility, as is the case with other types of assets.

Although cash investments are relatively simple products, it does not follow that they are free of risks, as bank failures in 2008 so clearly demonstrated. Investing in cash does have some serious **drawbacks**, including:

- Deposit-taking institutions are of varying creditworthiness; the risk that they may default needs to be assessed and taken into account.
- Inflation reduces the real return that is being earned on cash deposits and could mean the real return after tax is negative.
- Interest rates vary and so the returns from cash-based deposits will also vary.
- There is a currency risk, and different regulatory regimes to take into account, where funds are invested offshore or in a different currency.

As a result, when comparing available investment options it is important to consider the risks that exist as well as comparing the interest rates available.

Bank and building society deposits are usually protected by a **compensation scheme**. This will repay any deposited money lost, up to a set maximum, as a result of the collapse of a bank or building society. The sum is fixed so as to be of meaningful protection to most retail investors, although it would be of less help to very substantial depositors. Although most cash products are not regulated, the Prudential Regulatory Authority does regulate banks and other deposit-takers, and depositors based in the UK are covered by the Financial Services Compensation Scheme (FSCS). The FSCS provides protection for the first £75,000 of deposits per person with an authorised institution.

The PRA is required by the European Deposit Guarantee Schemes Directive to recalculate the FSCS deposit protection limit every five years and set it at a sterling amount equivalent to €100,000.

Financial Assets and Markets

From 3 July 2015, depositors with temporary high balances will be covered up to £1 million for six months from the date on which the money is transferred into their account, or the date on which the depositor becomes entitled to the amount, whichever is later. This is to ensure that depositors are protected when they deposit funds as a result of specified events until they have had sufficient time to spread the risk between institutions to appropriately protect these funds. The specified events include funds received following a house sale, funds received from a divorce settlement or inheritance.

3. Money Markets

Learning Objective

3.2.1 Know the difference between a capital market instrument and a money market instrument

3.2.2 Know the definition and features of the following: Treasury bill; commercial paper; certificate of deposit; money market funds

3.2.3 Know the advantages and disadvantages of investing in money market instruments

The **money markets** are the wholesale or institutional markets for cash and are characterised by the issue, trading and redemption of short-dated negotiable securities. These usually have a maturity of up to one year, though three months or less is more typical. By contrast, the **capital markets** are the long-term providers of finance for companies, through investment either in bonds or shares.

Owing to the short-term nature of the money markets, most instruments are issued in bearer form and at a discount to their face value to save on the administration associated with registration and the payment of interest (an explanation of 'bearer' can be found in Chapter 4, Section 10).

Although they are accessible to retail investors indirectly through collective investment schemes, direct investment in money market instruments is often subject to a relatively high minimum subscription and therefore tends to be more suitable for institutional investors.

Both cash deposits and money market instruments provide a low-risk way to generate an income or capital return, as appropriate, while preserving the nominal value of the amount invested. They also play a valuable role in times of market uncertainty. However, they are unsuitable for anything other than the short term as, historically, they have underperformed most other asset types over the medium to long term. Moreover, in the long term, returns from cash deposits, once tax and inflation have been taken into account, have barely been positive.

The main types of UK money market instruments are:

- **Treasury bills** – these are issued weekly by the **Debt Management Office (DMO)** on behalf of the Treasury. The money is used for the government's short-term borrowing needs. Treasury bills are non-interest-bearing instruments (sometimes referred to as 'zero coupon' instruments, see Chapter 5, Section 4.2.6). Instead of interest being paid out on them, they are issued at a **discount to par** – ie, a price of less than £100 per £100 nominal (the amount of the Treasury bill that will be repaid on maturity) – and commonly redeem after one, three or six months. For example, a Treasury bill might be issued for £999 and mature at £1,000 three months later. The investor's return is the difference between the £999 they paid, and the £1,000 they receive on the Treasury bill's maturity.

- **Certificates of deposit (CDs)** – these are issued by banks in return for deposited money: you could think of them as tradable deposit accounts, as they can be bought and sold in a similar way to shares. For example, Lloyds Banking Group might issue a CD to represent a deposit of £1 million from a customer, redeemable in six months. The CD might specify that Lloyds TSB will pay the £1 million back plus interest of, say, 0.5% of £1 million. If the customer needs the money back before six months has elapsed, they can sell the CD to another investor in the money market.
- **Commercial paper (CP)** – this is the corporate equivalent of a Treasury bill. Commercial paper is issued by large companies to meet their short-term borrowing needs. A company's ability to issue commercial paper is typically agreed with banks in advance. For example, a company might agree with its bank to a programme of £10 million-worth of commercial paper. This would enable the company to issue various forms of commercial paper with different maturities (eg, one month, three months and six months) and possibly different currencies, to investors. As with Treasury bills, commercial paper is zero coupon and issued at a discount to its par value.

Settlement of money market instruments is typically achieved through CREST (this is the system used in the UK to settle trades in shares and bonds) and they are commonly settled on the day of the trade or the following business day.

As mentioned earlier, the money market is a highly professional market that is used by banks and companies to manage their liquidity needs. It is not accessible by private investors, who instead need to utilise either money market accounts offered by banks, or **money market funds**.

There is a range of money market funds available and they can offer some advantages over pure money market accounts. There is the obvious advantage that the pooling of funds with other investors gives the investor access to assets they would not otherwise be able to invest in. The returns on money market funds should also be greater than a simple money market account offered by a bank.

Placing funds in a money market account means that the investor is exposed to the risk of that bank. By contrast, a money market fund will invest in a range of instruments from many providers, and as long as they are AAA-rated they can offer high security levels. A rating of AAA is the highest rating assigned by a credit rating agency.

Under UK regulatory rules, money market funds may only invest in approved money market instruments and deposits with credit institutions and meet other conditions on the structure of the underlying portfolio.

The Investment Association (IA) introduced two money market sectors with effect from 1 January 2012. These are based on the European definitions of money market funds that have been adopted by the FCA – short-term money market funds and money market funds.

- **Short-term money market funds** can have a constant or a fluctuating net asset value (NAV). A constant NAV face value means they should have an unchanging net asset value when income in the fund is accrued daily and can either be paid out to the unitholder or used to purchase more units in the scheme.
- **Money market funds** by contrast must have a fluctuating net asset value.

It should be noted that money market funds may invest in instruments in which the capital is at risk and so may not be suitable for many investors. In addition, money market funds may invest in assets denominated in other currencies and so introduce exchange rate risk.

4. Property

Learning Objective

3.3.1 Know the characteristics of property investment: commercial/residential property; direct/indirect investment

3.3.2 Know the potential advantages and disadvantages of investing in property

Property as an asset class is unique in its distinguishing features:

- Each individual property is unique in terms of location, structure and design.
- Valuation is subjective, as property is not traded in a centralised marketplace, and continuous and reliable price data is not available.
- It is subject to complex legal considerations and high transaction costs upon transfer.
- It is relatively illiquid as a result of not being instantly tradable.
- It is also illiquid in another sense: the investor generally has to sell all of the property or nothing at all. It is not generally feasible for a commercial property investor to sell one flat out of an entire block (or, at least, to do so would be commercially unattractive) – and a residential property owner cannot sell their spare bedroom to raise a little cash!
- Since property can only be purchased in discrete and sizeable units, diversification is difficult.
- The supply of land is finite and its availability can be further restricted by legislation and local planning regulations. Therefore, price is predominantly determined by changes in demand.

What is also fundamentally different is the price. Only the largest investors, which generally means institutional investors, can purchase sufficient properties to build a diversified portfolio. These tend to avoid residential property (although some have diversified into sizeable residential property portfolios) and instead they concentrate on commercial property, industrial property and farmland.

Some of the key differences between commercial and residential property are shown in the following table.

	Residential Property	Commercial Property
Direct investment	Range of investment opportunities including second homes, holiday homes and buy to let	Size of investment required means direct investment in commercial property is limited to property companies and institutional investors
Tenancies	Typically short renewable leases	Long-term contracts with periods commonly in excess of ten years
Repairs	Landlord is responsible	Tenant is usually responsible
Returns	Largely linked to increase in house prices	Significant component is return from rental income

As an asset class, direct investment in property has at times provided positive real long-term returns allied to low volatility and a reliable stream of income. An exposure to property can provide diversification benefits within a portfolio of investments owing to its low correlation with both traditional and alternative asset classes. Many private investors have chosen to become involved in the property market through the buy-to-let market.

However, property can be subject to prolonged downturns, and its lack of liquidity, significant maintenance costs, high transaction costs on transfer and the risk of having commercial property with no tenant (and, therefore, no rental income) makes commercial property suitable as an investment only for long-term investing institutions such as pension funds.

Other investors wanting to include property within a diversified portfolio generally seek indirect exposure via a mutual fund, property bonds issued by insurance companies, or shares in publicly quoted property companies. The availability of indirect investment media makes property a more accessible asset class to those running smaller, diversified portfolios.

The IA also has a sector covering funds that predominantly invest in property.

It needs to be remembered, however, that investing via a property fund does not always mean that an investment can be readily realised. During 2008, property prices fell across the board and, as investors started to encash holdings, property funds brought in measures to stem outflows and in some cases imposed 12-month moratoria on encashments.

5. Foreign Exchange

Learning Objective

3.4.1　Know the basic structure of the foreign exchange market including: currency quotes; settlement; spot/forward; short-term currency swaps

The foreign exchange market, which is also known as the Forex or FX market, refers to the trading of one currency for another. It is by far the largest market in the world.

Historically, currencies were backed by gold (as money had 'intrinsic value'); this prevented the value of money from being debased and inflation being triggered. This **gold standard** was replaced after the Second World War by the **Bretton Woods Agreement**. This agreement aimed to prevent speculation in currency markets, by fixing all currencies against the dollar and making the dollar convertible to gold at a fixed rate of $35 per ounce. Under this system, countries were prohibited from devaluing their currencies by more than 10%, which they might have been tempted to do in order to improve their trade position.

The growth of international trade and increasing pressure for the movement of capital eventually destabilised this agreement, and it was finally abandoned in the 1970s. Currencies were allowed to **float freely** against one another, leading to the development of new financial instruments and speculation in the currency markets.

Trading in currencies became 24-hour, as it could take place in the various time zones of Asia, Europe and America. London, being placed between the Asian and American time zones, was well placed to take advantage of this, and has grown to become the world's largest Forex market. Other large centres include the US, Japan and Singapore.

Trading of foreign currencies is always done in pairs. These are **currency pairs** when one currency is bought and the other is sold, and the prices at which these take place make up the **exchange rate**. When the exchange rate is being quoted, the name of the currency is abbreviated to a three-digit reference; so, for example, sterling is abbreviated to GBP, which you can think of as an abbreviation for Great British Pounds.

The most commonly quoted currency pairs are:

- US dollar and Japanese yen (USD/JPY)
- Euro and US dollar (EUR/USD)
- US dollar and Swiss franc (USD/CHF)
- British pound and US dollar (GBP/USD)
- Euro and British pound (EUR/GBP).

When currencies are quoted, the first currency is the base currency and the second is the counter or quote currency. The **base currency** is always equal to one unit of that currency, in other words, one pound, one dollar or one euro. For example, if the EUR/USD exchange rate is 1:1.1165, this means that €1 is worth $1.1165.

When the exchange rate is 'going up', it means that the value of the base currency is rising relative to the other currency and is referred to as currency strengthening; if the opposite is the case, the currency is said to be weakening.

When currency pairs are quoted, a market maker or foreign exchange trader will quote a **bid and ask price**. Staying with the example of the EUR/USD, the quote might be 1.1164/66 – notice that the euro is not mentioned, as standard convention is that the base currency is always one unit. So if you want to **buy** €100,000 then you will need to pay the higher of the two prices and deliver $111,660; if you want to **sell** €100,000 then you get the lower of the two prices and receive $111,640.

The Forex market is renowned for being an over-the-counter (OTC) market, ie, one where brokers and dealers negotiate directly with one another. The main participants are large international banks, which continually provide the market with both bid (buy) and ask (sell) prices. Central banks are also major participants in foreign exchange markets, which they use to try to control the money supply, inflation and interest rates.

There are several types of transactions and financial instruments commonly used:

- **Spot transaction** – the spot rate is the rate quoted by a bank for the exchange of one currency for another with immediate effect. However, it is worth noting that, in many cases, spot trades are settled – that is, the currencies actually change hands and arrive in recipients' bank accounts – two business days after the transaction date (T+2).
- **Forward transaction** – in this type of transaction, money does not actually change hands until some agreed future date. A buyer and seller agree on an exchange rate for any date in the future, for a fixed sum of money, and the transaction occurs on that date, regardless of what the market rates are then. The duration of the trade can be a few days, months or years.

- **Future** – foreign currency futures are a standardised version of forward transactions that are traded on derivatives exchanges for standard sizes and maturity dates. The average contract length is roughly three months.
- **Swap** – the most common type of forward FX transaction is the currency swap. In a swap, two parties exchange currencies for a certain length of time and agree to reverse the transaction at a later date. These are not exchange-traded contracts and instead are negotiated individually between the parties to a swap. They are a type of OTC derivative (see Chapter 6).

Settlement is made through the worldwide international banking system. Banks hold accounts with each other and their overseas branches and subsidiaries, through which settlement is made.

End of Chapter Questions

Think of an answer for each question and refer to the appropriate section for confirmation.

1. What is the maximum amount of compensation per person that would be payable by the FSCS in the event of the failure of a bank?
   Answer Reference: Section 2.1

2. How is the return on a Treasury bill achieved?
   Answer Reference: Section 3

3. What are the advantages and disadvantages of investing in property?
   Answer Reference: Section 4

4. When will a spot Forex trade settle?
   Answer Reference: Section 5

Chapter Four
Equities

1. Introduction	49
2. Company Formation and Administration	49
3. Types of Equities	51
4. The Benefits of Owning Shares	53
5. The Risks of Owning Shares	58
6. Corporate Actions	60
7. Stock Exchanges	65
8. Stock Market Indices	67
9. Trading	69
10. Holding Title	71
11. Clearing and Central Counterparties	72
12. Settlement	73

This syllabus area will provide approximately 8 of the 50 examination questions

1. Introduction

In this chapter we will look in detail at many of the features of equities and how they are traded.

The chapter starts by explaining how a company is formed. We will then consider the features of equities, the benefits and risks of owning shares and the effect of corporate actions, before moving on to the requirements for listing on a stock exchange, looking at world stock exchanges and indices, and then outlining how equities are traded and settled.

2. Company Formation and Administration

Learning Objective

4.1.1 Know how a company is formed and the differences between private and public companies

2.1 Forming a Company

Many businesses, large and small, are set up as companies.

To form a simple company is inexpensive and requires the founders of the company to complete a series of documents and lodge these with the appropriate authority. In the UK these documents are required to be lodged with the Registrar of Companies at Companies House.

To form a company, two documents are required:

- Memorandum of Association
- Articles of Association.

The **Memorandum of Association** confirms the subscribers' intention to form a company under the Companies Act 2006 and that they have agreed to become a member of that company and to take at least one share each.

The **Articles of Association** detail the relationship between the company and one of its key sources of finance; in other words, its owners. The articles include details such as shareholder rights, the frequency of company meetings and the company's borrowing powers.

2.2 Private and Public Companies

Companies are established either as:

- **private companies** – such as ABC ltd, where ltd stands for limited. Such companies can have just one shareholder
- **public companies** – such as XYZ plc, where plc stands for public limited company. Plcs must have a minimum of two shareholders.

It is only plcs that are permitted to issue shares to the public. As a result, all listed companies are plcs, but not all plcs are listed. It is perfectly possible for a company to 'just be' a plc, and not be listed on a stock exchange. The global bank HSBC Holdings is a public limited company and is listed on a number of worldwide stock exchanges including the LSE, NYSE, HKex, Paris Stock Exchange (Euronext) and the Bermuda Stock Exchange (BSX). By contrast, Virgin Holdings, the business empire of Richard Branson, is a public limited company but is not listed.

'Limited', whether as in 'ltd' or 'plc', means that the liability of shareholders for the debts of the company is limited to the amount they agreed to pay to the company on initial subscription.

Example

A UK company is created with a share capital of £100 which is made up of 100 ordinary £1 shares.

Assuming that each share is fully paid (see Section 3.1), an initial shareholder who subscribes for 20 shares will pay £20.

In the event that the company goes into liquidation, the liability of that shareholder for the company's debts is limited to the amount they subscribed, that is, £20.

The position would be different if the shares were only partly paid. For example, the shares might be ordinary £1 shares but only require 50p per share to be paid at the outset, the remainder being payable at some future date. In the event of liquidation, the shareholder may be called on to subscribe the balance to meet the company's debts.

2.3 Company Meetings

Learning Objective

4.1.7 Know the purpose and format of annual general meetings

Public companies must hold **annual general meetings (AGMs)** at which the shareholders are given the opportunity to question the directors about the company's strategy and operations. Public companies must hold an AGM within six months of the financial year end.

The Companies Act provides shareholders with the right to attend, speak and vote at the AGM or to appoint a proxy to vote (but not speak) on their behalf at the meeting.

The shareholders are also given the opportunity to vote on matters such as the appointment and removal of directors and the payment of the final dividend recommended by the directors.

Most matters put to the shareholders are **ordinary resolutions**, requiring a simple majority of those shareholders voting to be passed. Matters of major importance, such as a proposed change to the company's constitution, require a **special resolution** and at least 75% to vote in favour.

Shareholders can either vote in person, or have their vote registered at the meeting by completing a **proxy voting form**, enabling someone else to register their vote on their behalf.

Companies may also hold other meetings during the year to deal with important issues, such as a takeover or capital raising. These are known simply as general meetings. Until 2009, they were referred to as extraordinary general meetings (EGMs), and you may come across that term as it is still often used to differentiate between the two types of meeting.

3. Types of Equities

Learning Objective

4.1.2   Know the features and benefits of ordinary and preference shares: dividend; capital gain

The capital of a company is made up of a combination of borrowing and the money invested by its owners. The long-term borrowings, or debt, of a company are usually referred to as bonds, and the money invested by its owners as shares, stocks or equity. Shares are the equity capital of a company, hence the reason they are referred to as equities. They may comprise ordinary shares and preference shares.

3.1 Ordinary Shares

Ordinary shares carry the full **risk and reward** of investing in a company. If a company does well, its ordinary shareholders should do well. As the shareholders of the company, it is the ordinary shareholders who **vote** 'yes' or 'no' to each resolution put forward by the company directors at company meetings. For example, an offer to take over a company may be made and the directors may propose that it is accepted but this will be subject to a vote by shareholders. If the shareholders vote 'no', then the directors will have to think again.

Ordinary shareholders share in the profits of the company by receiving **dividends** declared by the company, which tend to be paid half-yearly or even quarterly. With the final dividend for the financial year, the company directors will propose a dividend which will need to be ratified by the ordinary shareholders before it is formally declared as payable. The amount of dividend paid will depend on how well the company is doing. However, some companies pay large dividends and others none as they plough all profits made back into their future growth.

If the company does badly, it is the ordinary shareholders that will suffer. If the company closes down, often described as the company being 'wound up', the ordinary shareholders are paid last, after everybody else. If there is nothing left, then the ordinary shareholders get nothing. If there is money left after all creditors and preference shareholders have been paid, it all belongs to the ordinary shareholders.

Some ordinary shares may be referred to as **partly paid** or **contributing** shares. This means that only part of their nominal value has been paid up. For example, if a new company is established with an initial capital of £100, this capital may be made up of 100 ordinary £1 shares. If the shareholders to whom these shares are allocated have paid £1 per share in full, then the shares are termed **fully paid**.

Alternatively, the shareholders may contribute only half of the initial capital, say £50 in total, which would require a payment of 50p per share, ie, one-half of the amount due. The shares would then be termed **partly paid**, but the shareholder has an obligation to pay the remaining amount when called upon to do so by the company.

3.2 Preference Shares

Some companies have preference shares as well as ordinary shares. The company's internal rules (its Articles of Association) set out the specific ways in which the preference shares differ from the ordinary shares.

Preference shares are a hybrid security with elements of both debt and equity. Although they are technically a form of equity investment, they also have characteristics of debt, particularly in that they pay a fixed income. Preference shares have legal priority (known as seniority) over ordinary shareholders in respect of earnings and, in the event of bankruptcy, in respect of assets.

Normally, preference shares:

- are **non-voting**, except in certain special circumstances, such as when their dividends have not been paid
- pay a **fixed dividend** each year, the amount being set when they are first issued and which has to be paid before dividends on ordinary shares can be paid
- **rank ahead of ordinary shares** in terms of being paid back if the company is wound up.

Preference shares may be cumulative, non-cumulative, and/or participating.

If dividends cannot be paid in a particular year, perhaps because the company has insufficient profits, preference shares would get no dividend. However, if they were **cumulative** preference shareholders then the dividend entitlement accumulates. Assuming sufficient profits, the cumulative preference shareholders will have the arrears of dividend paid in the subsequent year. If the shares were **non-cumulative**, the dividend from the first year would be lost.

Participating preference shares entitle the holder to a basic dividend of, say, 3p a year, but the directors can award a bigger dividend in a year when the profits exceed a certain level. In other words, the preference shareholder can 'participate' in bumper profits.

Preference shares may also be convertible or redeemable.

Convertible preference shares carry an option to convert into the ordinary shares of the company at set intervals and on pre-set terms.

Redeemable shares, as the name implies, have a date on which they may be redeemed; that is, the nominal value of the shares will be paid back to the preference shareholder and the shares cancelled.

Equities

Example

Banks and other financial institutions are regular issuers of preference shares. So, for example, an investor may have the following holding of a preference share issued by Standard Chartered – £1,000 Standard Chartered $7^3/_8$% non-cumulative irredeemable £1 preference shares.

This means:

- The investor will receive a fixed dividend of $7^3/_8$% each year which is payable in two equal half-yearly instalments on 1 April and 1 November.
- The amount of the dividend is calculated by multiplying the nominal value of shares held (£1,000, ie, 1,000 £1 preference shares) by the interest rate of $7^3/_8$% which gives a total annual dividend of £73.75 gross which will be paid in two instalments.
- The dividend will be paid providing that the company makes sufficient profits, and has to be paid before any dividend can be paid to ordinary shareholders.
- The term 'non-cumulative' means that, if the company does not make sufficient profits to pay the dividend, then it is lost and the arrears are not carried forward.
- The term 'irredeemable' means that there is no fixed date for the shares to be repaid and the capital would only be repaid in the event of the company being wound up. The amount the investor would receive is the nominal value of the shares, in other words £1,000, and they would be paid out before (in preference to) the ordinary shareholders.

4. The Benefits of Owning Shares

Learning Objective

4.1.2 Know the features and benefits of ordinary and preference shares: dividend; capital gain; share benefits; right to subscribe for new shares; right to vote

4.1.3 Be able to calculate share dividend yield

Holding shares in a company is having an ownership stake in that company. Ownership carries certain benefits and rights, and ordinary shareholders expect to be the major beneficiaries of a company's success.

As we will see in Section 5, shares carry risks. As a reward for taking this risk, shareholders hope to benefit from the success of the company. This reward or return can take one of the following forms.

4.1 Dividends

A dividend is the return that an investor gets for providing the risk capital for a business. Companies pay dividends out of their profits, which form part of their **distributable reserves**. Distributable reserves are the post-tax profits made over the life of a company, in excess of dividends paid.

Example

ABC plc was formed some years ago. Over the company's life it has made £20 million in profits and paid dividends of £13 million. Distributable reserves at the beginning of the year are, therefore, £7 million.

This year, ABC plc makes post-tax profits of £3 million and decides to pay a dividend of £1 million.

At the end of the year distributable reserves are:

	Millions
Opening balance	7
Profit after tax for year	3
	10
Dividend	(1)
Closing balance	9

Despite only making £3 million in the current year, it would be perfectly legal for ABC plc to pay dividends of more than £3 million, because it can use the undistributed profits from previous years. This would be described as a **naked** or **uncovered** dividend, because the current year's profits were insufficient to fully cover the dividend. Companies occasionally do this, but it is obviously not possible to maintain this long term.

UK companies seek, if possible, to pay steadily growing dividends. A fall in dividend payments can lead to a negative reaction among shareholders and a general fall in the willingness to hold the company's shares, or to provide additional capital.

4.1.1 Dividend Yield

Potential shareholders will compare the dividend paid on a company's shares with alternative investments. These would include other shares, bonds and bank deposits. This involves calculating the **dividend yield**.

Example

ABC plc has 20 million ordinary shares, each trading at £2.50. It pays out a total of £1 million in dividends.

Its dividend yield is calculated by expressing the dividend as a percentage of the total value of the company's shares (the market capitalisation):

$$\frac{\text{Dividend (£1m)}}{\text{Market capitalisation}} \times 100$$

So the dividend yield is:

[£1m/(20m x £2.50)] x 100 = 2%

Since ABC plc paid £1 million to shareholders of 20 million shares, the dividend yield can also be calculated on a per-share basis.

The dividend per share is £1 million/20 million shares, ie, £0.05. So £0.05/£2.50 (the share price) is again 2%.

Some companies have a higher-than-average dividend yield, which may be for one of the following reasons:

- The company is mature and continues to generate healthy levels of cash, but has limited growth potential, perhaps because the government regulates its selling prices, and so there is no great investor appetite for its shares. Examples are utilities such as water or electricity companies.
- The company has a low share price for some other reason, perhaps because it is, or is expected to be, relatively unsuccessful; its comparatively high current dividend is therefore not expected to be sustained and its share price is not expected to rise.

In contrast, some companies might have dividend yields that are relatively low. This is generally because:

- the share price is high, because the company is viewed by investors as having high growth prospects
- a large proportion of the profit being generated by the company is being ploughed back into the business, rather than being paid out as dividends.

4.2 Capital Gains

Capital gains can be made on shares if their prices increase over time. If an investor purchases a share for £3 and two years later that share price has risen to £5, then the investor has made a £2 capital gain.

However, the shares need to be sold to realise any capital gains. If he does not sell the share, then the gain is described as being **unrealised**; and he runs the risk of the share price falling before he does realise the share and 'bank' his profits.

In the recent past, the long-term total financial return from UK equities has been fairly evenly split between dividends and capital gain. Whereas dividends need to be reinvested in order to accumulate wealth, capital gains simply build up.

4.3 Shareholder Benefits

Some companies provide perks to shareholders, such as a telecoms company offering its shareholders a discounted price on their mobile phones or a shipping company offering cheap ferry tickets. Such benefits can be a pleasant bonus for small investors, but are not normally a big factor in investment decisions.

4.4 Shareholder Rights

4.4.1 Right to Subscribe for New Shares

Rights issues are one method by which a company can raise additional capital, with existing shareholders having the right to subscribe for new shares. See also Section 6.2.

If a company were able to issue new shares to anyone, then existing shareholders could lose control of the company, or at least see their share of ownership diluted. As a result, under UK legislation, existing shareholders in UK companies are given **pre-emptive rights** to subscribe for new shares. What this means is that, unless the shareholders agree to permit the company to issue shares to others, they must be given the option to subscribe for any new share offering before it is offered to the wider public, and in many cases they receive some compensation if they decide not to do so.

Pre-emptive rights are illustrated in the following example.

Example

An investor, Mr B, holds 20,000 ordinary shares of the 100,000 issued ordinary shares in ABC plc. He therefore owns 20% of ABC plc.

If ABC plc planned to increase the number of issued ordinary shares, by allowing investors to subscribe for 50,000 new ordinary shares, Mr B would be offered 20% of the new shares, ie, 10,000. This would enable Mr B to retain his 20% ownership of the enlarged company.

In summary:

Before the issue

Mr B	=	20,000	(20%)
Other shareholders	=	80,000	(80%)
Total	=	100,000	(100%)

New issue

Mr B	=	10,000
Other shareholders	=	40,000
Total	=	50,000

After the issue

Mr B	=	30,000	(20%)
Other shareholders	=	120,000	(80%)
Total	=	150,000	(100%)

If this were not the case, Mr B's stake in ABC plc would be diluted, as shown below:

Before the issue

Mr B	=	20,000	(20%)
Other shareholders	=	80,000	(80%)
Total	=	100,000	(100%)

New issue

Mr B	=	nil	
Other shareholders	=	50,000	
Total	=	50,000	

After the issue

Mr B	=	20,000	(13.3%)
Other shareholders	=	130,000	(86.7%)
Total	=	150,000	(100%)

A rights issue is one method by which a company can raise additional capital, complying with pre-emptive rights, with existing shareholders having the right to subscribe for new shares. The mechanics of a rights issue will be looked at in Section 6.2.

4.4.2 Right to Vote

Ordinary shareholders have the right to vote on matters presented to them at company meetings. This would include the right to vote on proposed dividends and other matters, such as the appointment, or reappointment, of directors.

The votes are normally allocated on the basis of **one share = one vote**. The votes are cast in one of two ways:

- The individual shareholder can attend the company meeting and vote.
- The individual shareholder can appoint someone else to vote on their behalf – this is commonly referred to as **voting by proxy**.

However, some companies issue different share classes, for some of which voting rights are restricted or non-existent. This allows some shareholders to control the company while only holding a small proportion of the shares.

5. The Risks of Owning Shares

Learning Objective

4.1.4 Understand the advantages, disadvantages and risks associated with owning shares: price risk; liquidity risk; issuer risk

Shares are relatively high risk but have the potential for relatively high returns when a company is successful. The main risks associated with holding shares can be classified under the following three headings.

5.1 Price Risk

Price risk is the risk that share prices in general might fall. Even though the company involved might maintain dividend payments, investors could face a loss of capital.

Market-wide falls in equity prices occur, unfortunately, on a fairly frequent basis. For example, worldwide equities fell by nearly 20% on 19 October 1987, with some shares falling by even more than this. That day is generally referred to as Black Monday and the Dow Jones index fell by 22.3%, wiping US$500 billion off share prices.

Markets across the world followed suit and collapsed in the same fashion. Central banks intervened to prevent a depression and a banking crisis and, remarkably, the markets recovered much of their losses quite quickly from this worst-ever one-day crash.

After the 1987 crash, global markets resumed the bull market trend driven by computer technology. The arrival of the internet age sparked suggestions that a new economy was in development and led to a surge in internet stocks. Many of these stocks were quoted on the NASDAQ exchange, whose index went from 600 to 5000 by the year 2000. This led the Chairman of the Federal Reserve to describe investor behaviour as 'irrational exuberance'.

In mid-2000, reality started to settle in and the 'dot.com' bubble was firmly popped, with NASDAQ crashing to below the 2000 mark. Economies went into recession and heralded the decline in world stock markets, which continued in many until 2003.

The markets then had a period of growth, until the sub-prime crisis and credit crunch brought about another fall in stock markets. In 2008, the NASDAQ composite had its worst ever fall, declining by 40.54% over the year, the Dow Jones Industrial Average (DJIA) fell 33.84%, and the FTSE 100 tumbled 31% in the largest annual drop seen since its launch in 1984 (see following graph).

FTSE 100 Since 2000

All of this clearly demonstrates the risks associated with equity investment from general price collapses. In addition to these market-wide movements, any single company can experience dramatic falls in its share price when it discloses bad news, such as the loss of a major contract.

Price risk varies between companies: volatile shares tend to exhibit more price risk than more 'defensive' shares, such as utility companies and general retailers.

5.2 Liquidity Risk

Liquidity risk is the risk that shares may be difficult to sell at a reasonable price or traded quickly enough in the market to prevent a loss. It essentially occurs when there is difficulty in finding a counterparty who is willing to trade in a share.

This typically occurs in respect of shares in 'thinly traded' companies – private companies, or those in which there is not much trading activity.

It can also happen, to a lesser degree, if share prices in general are falling, in which case the spread between the bid price (the price at which dealers will buy shares) and the offer price (the price at which dealers will sell shares) may widen.

Example

Prices for ABC plc shares might be 720–722p on a normal day.

To begin to see a capital gain, an investor who buys shares (at 722p) needs the price to rise so that the bid (the price at which he could sell) has risen by more than 2p (eg, from 720 to 723p).

If there was a general market downturn, the dealer might widen the price spread to, say, 700–720 to deter sellers. An investor wanting to sell would be forced to accept the much lower price.

Shares in smaller companies tend to have a greater liquidity risk than shares in larger companies – smaller companies also tend to have a wider price spread than larger, more actively traded companies.

5.3 Issuer Risk

This is the risk that the issuing company collapses and the ordinary shares become worthless.

In general, it is very unlikely that larger, well-established companies would collapse, and the risk could be seen, therefore, as insignificant. However, events such as the collapse of Northern Rock, HBOS, Bradford & Bingley, Woolworths and Comet show that the risk is a real and present one and cannot be ignored.

Shares in new companies, which have not yet managed to report profits, may have substantial issuer risk.

6. Corporate Actions

Learning Objective

4.1.5 Know the definition of a corporate action and the difference between mandatory, voluntary and mandatory with options

4.1.6 Understand the following terms: bonus/scrip/capitalisation issues; rights issues; dividend payments; takeover/merger (may be tested by the use of a simple calculation)

A corporate action occurs when a company does something that affects its shareholders or bondholders. For example, most companies pay dividends to their shareholders twice a year.

Corporate actions can be classified into three types:

1. A **mandatory corporate action** is one mandated by the company, not requiring any intervention from the shareholders or bondholders. The most obvious example of a mandatory corporate action is the payment of a dividend, since all qualifying shareholders automatically receive the dividend.
2. A **mandatory corporate action with options** is an action that has some sort of default option that will occur if the shareholder does not intervene. However, until the date at which the default option occurs, the individual shareholders are given the choice to select another option. An example of a mandatory with options corporate action is a rights issue (detailed below).
3. A **voluntary corporate action** is an action that requires the shareholder to make a decision. An example is a takeover bid – if the company is being bid for, each individual shareholder will need to choose whether to accept the offer or not.

This classification is the one that is used throughout Europe and by the international central securities depositories Euroclear and Clearstream. It should be noted that, in the US, corporate actions are simply divided into two classifications: voluntary and mandatory. The major difference between the two is therefore the existence of the category of mandatory events with options. In the US these types of events are split into two or more different events that have to be processed.

Equities

6.1 Securities Ratios

Before we look at various types of corporate action, it is necessary to know how the terms of a corporate action such as a rights issue or bonus issue are expressed – a securities ratio.

When a corporate action is announced, the terms of the event will specify what is to happen. This could be as simple as the amount of dividend that is to be paid per share. For other events, the terms will announce how many new shares the holder is entitled to receive for each existing share that they hold.

So, for example, a company may announce a bonus issue whereby it gives new shares to its investors in proportion to the shares they already hold. The terms of the bonus issue may be expressed as 1:4, which means that the investor will receive one new share for each existing four shares held. This is the standard approach used in European and Asian markets and can be simply remembered by always expressing the terms as the investor will receive 'X new shares for each Y existing shares'.

The approach differs in the US. Here, the first number in the securities ratio indicates the final holding after the event; the second number is the original number of shares held. The above example expressed in US terms would be 5:4. So, for example, if a US company announced a 5:4 bonus issue and the investor held 10,000 shares, then the investor would end up with 12,500 shares.

6.2 Rights Issues

A company may wish to raise additional finance by issuing new shares. This might be to provide funds for expansion, or to repay bank loans or bond finance. In such circumstances, a company may approach its existing shareholders with a 'cash call' – they have already bought some shares in the company, so would they like to buy some more?

UK company law gives a series of protections to existing shareholders. As already stated, they have pre-emptive rights – the right to buy shares so that their proportionate holding is not diluted. A rights issue can be defined as an offer of new shares to existing shareholders, pro rata to their initial holding. Since it is an offer and the shareholders have a choice, rights issues are examples of a 'mandatory with options' type of corporate action.

As an example of a rights issue, the company might offer shareholders the right that for every two shares owned, they can buy one more at a specified price that is at a discount to the current market price.

The initial response to the announcement of a planned rights issue will reflect the market's view of the scheme. If it is to finance expansion, and the strategy makes sense to the investors, the share price could well rise. If investors have a very negative view of why a rights issue is being made (eg, to fund activities that investors view negatively) and of what it says for the future of the company, the share price can fall substantially.

The company and their investment banking advisers will therefore have to consider the numbers carefully. If the price at which new shares are offered is too high, the cash call might flop. This would be embarrassing – and potentially costly for any institution that has underwritten the issue. (**Underwriters** of a share issue agree, for a fee, to buy any portion of the issue not taken up by shareholders at the issue price. The underwriters then sell the shares they have bought when market conditions seem opportune to them, and may make a gain or a loss on this sale. The underwriters agree to buy the shares if no one else will, and the company's investment bank will probably underwrite some of the issue itself.)

This situation was seen during the financial crisis with HBOS and RBS, when the price of shares on the open market fell below the discounted rights issue price. The rights issues were flops and the underwriters ended up having to take up the new shares.

Example

ABC plc has 100 million shares in issue, currently trading at £4.00 each.

To raise finance for expansion, it decides to offer its existing shareholders the right to buy one new share for every four previously held. This would be described as a 1 for 4 rights issue (but see Section 6.1).

The price of the rights would be set at a discount to the prevailing market price at, say, £2.00.

Each shareholder is given choices as to how to proceed following a rights issue. For an individual holding four shares in ABC plc, they could:

- **Take up the rights**, by paying the £2.00 and increasing their holding in ABC plc to five shares.
- **Sell the rights on to another investor.** The rights entitlement is transferable (often described as **renounceable**) and will have a value because it enables the purchase of a share at the discounted price of £2.00.
- **Do nothing.** If the investor chooses this option, the company's advisers will sell the rights at the best available price and pass on the proceeds (after charges) to the shareholder.
- Alternatively, the investor could **sell sufficient** of the rights to raise cash and use this to take up the rest. As an example, if an investor had a holding of, say, 4,000 shares then they would have the right to buy 1,000. They could sell sufficient of the rights to raise cash and use this cash to take up the rest.

The share price of the investor's existing shares will also adjust to reflect the additional shares that are being issued. So if the investor originally had four shares priced at £4 each, worth £16, and they can acquire one new share at £2.00, on taking the rights up the investor will have five shares worth £18 or £3.60 each.

The share price will therefore change to reflect the effect of the rights issue once the shares go ex-rights (this is the point at which the shares and the rights are traded as two separate instruments).

The adjusted share price of £3.60 is known as the **theoretical ex-rights price** – theoretical because the actual price will also be determined by demand and supply.

The rights can be sold, and the price is known as the **premium**. In the example above, if the theoretical ex-rights price is £3.60 and a new share can be acquired for £2.00, then the right to acquire one has a value. That value is the premium and would be £1.60, although again the actual price would depend upon demand and supply.

6.3 Bonus Issues

A bonus issue (also known as a **scrip** or **capitalisation** issue) is a corporate action when the company gives existing shareholders extra shares without their having to subscribe any further funds.

The company is simply increasing the number of shares held by each shareholder, and 'capitalises' earnings by transfer to shareholders' funds. It is a mandatory corporate action.

Example

XYZ plc's shares currently trade at £12.00 each.

The company decided to make a 1 for 1 bonus issue, giving each shareholder an additional share for each share they currently hold.

The result is that a single shareholder who held one share worth £12.00 now has two shares worth the same amount in total. As the number of shares has doubled, the share price halves to £6.00.

The reason for making a bonus issue is to increase the liquidity of the company's shares in the market and to bring about a lower share price. The logic is that, if a company's share price becomes too high, it may be unattractive to investors. Traditionally, most large UK companies tried to keep their share prices below £10, but that is less common today.

6.4 Dividends

Dividends are an example of a mandatory corporate action and represent the part of a company's profit that is passed to its shareholders.

Dividends for many large UK companies are paid twice a year, with the first dividend being declared by the directors and paid approximately halfway through the year (commonly referred to as the **interim dividend**). The second dividend is paid after approval by shareholders at the company's AGM, held after the end of the company's financial year, and is referred to as the **final dividend** for the year.

The amount paid per share depends on factors such as the overall profitability of the company and any plans it might have for future expansion.

The individual shareholders will receive the dividends by cheque, or by the money being transferred straight into their bank accounts or be paid through CREST.

A practical difficulty, especially in a large company, where shares change hands frequently, is determining who is the correct person to receive dividends. The London Stock Exchange, therefore, has procedures to minimise the extent that people receive dividends they are not entitled to, or fail to receive the dividend to which they are entitled. The shares are bought and sold with the right to receive the next declared dividend up to a date shortly before the dividend payment is made. Up to that point the shares are described as **cum-dividend**. If the shares are purchased cum-dividend, the purchaser will receive the declared dividend. At a certain point between the declaration date and the dividend payment date, the shares go **ex-dividend**. Buyers of shares when they are ex-dividend are not entitled to the declared dividend.

In October 2014, the standard settlement period across Europe for equity trades changed to T+2; this means that a trade is settled two business days after it is executed so, for example, a trade executed on Monday would settle on Wednesday. As a result, the dividend timetable also changed as the following example illustrates.

Example

The sequence of events for a company listed on the LSE might be as follows:

ABC plc calculates its interim profits (for the six months to 30 June) and decides to pay a dividend of 8p per share. It announces ('declares') the dividend on 1 September and states that it will be due to those shareholders who are entered on the shareholders' register on Friday 7 October. (The actual payment of the dividend will then be made to those shareholders at a later specified date.)

This latter date (always on a Friday) is variously known as the:

- record date
- register date
- books closed date.

Given the record date of Friday 7 October, the LSE sets the ex-dividend date as Thursday 6 October.

On this day the shares will go ex-dividend and should fall in price by 8p. This is because new buyers of ABC plc's shares will not be entitled to the dividend.

Mistakes can happen. If an investor bought shares in ABC plc on 5 October, and for some reason the trade did not settle on Friday 7 October, they would not receive the dividend. A dividend claim would be made, and the buyer's broker would then recover the money via the seller's broker.

6.5 Takeovers and Mergers

Companies seeking to expand can grow either organically or by buying other companies. In a takeover, which may be friendly or hostile, one company (the predator) seeks to acquire another company (the target). When they acquire shares in the other company they are under an obligation to report their share purchases once they reach a certain percentage.

In a successful **takeover** the predator company will buy more than 50% of the shares of the target company. When the predator holds more than half of the shares of the target company, the predator is described as having 'gained control' of the target company. Usually, the predator company will look to buy all of the shares in the target company, perhaps for cash, but usually using its own shares, or a mixture of cash and shares.

A **merger** is a similar transaction when the two companies are of similar size and agree to merge their interests. However, in a merger it is usual for one company to exchange new shares for the shares of the other. As a result, the two companies effectively merge together to form a bigger entity.

Equities

7. Stock Exchanges

7.1 Primary and Secondary Markets

Learning Objective

4.1.8 Know the function of a stock exchange: primary/secondary market; listing

When a company decides to seek a listing for its shares, the process is known by one of a number of terms:

- becoming **listed** or **quoted**
- **floating** on the stock market
- **going public**
- making an **initial public offering (IPO)**.

Typically, a company making an IPO will have been in existence for many years, and will have grown to a point where it wishes to expand further.

Other relevant terminology is 'primary market' and 'secondary market'. The term **primary market** refers to the marketing of new shares in a company to investors for the first time. Once they have acquired shares, an investor will at some point wish to dispose of some or all of their shares and will often do this through a stock exchange. This latter process is referred to as dealing on the **secondary market**.

Primary markets exist to raise capital and enable surplus funds to be matched with investment opportunities, while secondary markets allow the primary market to function efficiently by facilitating two-way trade in issued securities.

7.2 Advantages and Disadvantages of Listing

The advantages and disadvantages to be considered carefully include the following:

Advantages

- **Capital** – an IPO provides the possibility of raising capital and, once listed, further offers of shares are much easier to make. If the shares being offered to the public are those of the company's original founders, then the IPO offers them an exit route and a means to convert their holdings into cash.
- **Takeovers** – a listed company could use its shares as payment to acquire the shares of other companies as part of a takeover or merger.
- **Status** – being a listed company should help the business in marketing itself to customers, suppliers and potential employees.
- **Employees** – stock options to key staff are a way of providing incentives and retaining employees, and options to buy listed company shares that are easily sold in the market are even more attractive.

Disadvantages

- **Regulation** – listed companies must govern themselves in a more open way than private ones and provide detailed and timely information on their financial situation and progress.
- **Takeovers** – listed companies are at risk of being taken over themselves.
- **Short-termism** – shareholders of listed companies tend to exert pressure on the company to reach short-term goals, rather than be more patient and look for longer-term investment and growth.

7.2.1 Requirements for Listing on the LSE

In the UK, the responsibility for allowing a company to be listed on the LSE rests with a division of the UK regulator, the FCA. The division is known as the **United Kingdom Listing Authority (UKLA)**.

A listing on the LSE is often referred to as a 'full listing'. This distinguishes it from cases where companies are dealt in on the **Alternative Investment Market (AIM)**, where the requirements are less onerous (see Section 7.2.2).

The UKLA has a number of requirements for companies seeking a listing for their shares. These are mainly aimed at making sure the company is sufficiently large and that it complies with the rules on issues such as disclosure of important information, so that its shares may be held by members of the public. The main requirements are:

- The company must be a public limited company (plc).
- The company's expected market capitalisation (the share price multiplied by the number of shares in issue) must be at least £700,000.
- The company should have been trading for at least three years and at least 75% of its business must be supported by a historic revenue-earning record for that period.
- At least 25% of the company's shares should be in public hands or available for purchase by the public. The term 'public' excludes directors of the company and their associates, and significant shareholders who hold 5% or more of the company's shares.
- A trading company must demonstrate that it has sufficient working capital for the next 12 months.

Once listed, companies are expected to fulfil rules known as the **continuing obligations**. For example, they are obliged to issue a half-yearly report and to notify the market of any new price-sensitive information.

7.2.2 The Alternative Investment Market (AIM)

Becoming a fully listed company is not open to any company. Listed status is rightly reserved for large, established companies. Smaller businesses have a range of alternative sources of finance for expansion, including the private equity/venture capital industry and the AIM market.

AIM was established by the LSE as a junior market for younger, smaller companies. Such companies apply to the LSE to join AIM, whereas full listing requires application to the UKLA. The requirements for a listing on AIM, in comparison to the requirements for a full listing, are shown in the following table.

AIM	Full Listing
No trading history required; the company could be newly established.	Three years' trading history is needed.
No minimum market capitalisation required.	£700,000 is the minimum market cap.
No requirement for a minimum proportion of the shares to be held by the 'public'.	At least 25% of the shares must be held by outside investors.

A company wanting to gain admission to AIM is required to appoint a **nominated adviser (NOMAD)** and a **nominated broker**. The role of the NOMAD is to advise the directors of their responsibilities in complying with AIM rules and the content of the prospectus that accompanies the company's application for admission to AIM. The role of the nominated broker is to make a market and facilitate trading in the company's shares, as well as to provide ongoing information about the company to interested parties.

Certain rules are common to both AIM and fully listed companies. They must both release price-sensitive information promptly and produce financial information at the half-yearly (interim) and full year (final) stage.

8. Stock Market Indices

Learning Objective

4.1.9 Know the types and uses of the main global stock exchange indices

Markets worldwide compute one or more indices of prices of the shares of their country's large companies. These indices provide a snapshot of how share prices are progressing across the whole group of constituent companies. They also provide a benchmark for investors, allowing them to assess whether their portfolios of shares are outperforming or underperforming the market in general.

Additionally, in recent decades, many indices have provided the basis for derivatives contracts, such as Footsie (FTSE) Futures and Footsie Options. Indices also provide the basis for many tracker products.

Generally, the constituents of these indices are the largest companies, ranked by their market value or market capitalisation (market cap). However, there are also indices which track all constituents of a market, or which focus specifically on a segment, eg, the smaller companies listed on that market.

As well as considering which market they are tracking, it is important to also understand how the index has been calculated. Early indices, such as the DJIA, are **price-weighted** so that it is only the price of each stock within the index that is considered when calculating the index. This means that no account is taken of the relative size of a company contained within an index, and the share price movement of one can therefore have a disproportionate effect on the index.

Following on from these earlier indices, broader-based indices were calculated based on a greater range of shares and which also took into account the relative **market capitalisation** of each stock in the index to give a more accurate indication of how the market was moving. This development process is ongoing, and most market capitalisation-weighted indices have a further refinement in that they now take account of the **free-float capitalisation** of their constituents. This float-adjusted calculation looks to exclude shareholdings held by large investors and governments that are not readily available for trading.

In the UK, the indices are provided by FTSE International, originally a joint venture between the *Financial Times* and the LSE. The relevant indices in the UK are:

- **FTSE 100** – this is an index of the largest 100 UK companies, commonly referred to as the 'Footsie'. The Footsie covers about 70% of the UK market by value.
- **FTSE 250** – an index of the next 250 medium- or middle-sized (mid cap) companies below the 100.
- **FTSE 350** – a combination of the 100 and the 250 indices. The 350 is broken down into industry sectors, for example, retailing and transport.
- **FTSE All Share** – this index covers over 800 companies (including the FTSE 350) and accounts for about 98% of the UK market by value. It is often used as the benchmark against which diversified share portfolios are assessed.

Reviews of the 100, 250 and, therefore, 350 and the All Share Index, are carried out every three months. Companies whose share price has grown strongly, and whose market capitalisation has increased significantly, will replace those whose price and, hence, market capitalisation is static or falling.

Some of the other main indices that are regularly quoted in the financial press are shown in the table below.

Country	Name
US	Dow Jones Industrial Average (DJIA): providing a narrow view of the US stock market
US	S&P 500 (Standard & Poor's): providing a wider view of the US stock market
US	NASDAQ Composite: focusing on the shares traded on NASDAQ, including many technology companies
Japan	Nikkei 225
France	CAC 40
Germany	Xetra DAX
Hong Kong/China	Hang Seng

9. Trading

Learning Objective

4.1.10 Know how shares are traded: on-exchange/over-the-counter; multilateral trading facilities; order-driven/quote-driven

Trading of shares and bonds takes place either on-exchange or off-exchange. As the name suggests, on-exchange trading is when trading is conducted through a recognised stock exchange. Trades can, however, be undertaken directly between market counterparties away from an exchange in which case they are referred to as 'over-the-counter' trades.

Stock market trading is conducted through trading systems broadly categorised as either:

- quote-driven
- order-driven.

Quote-driven trading systems employ market makers to provide continuous two-way, or bid and offer, prices during the trading day in particular securities, regardless of market conditions. Market makers make a profit, or turn, through this price spread. Although outdated in many respects, many practitioners argue that quote-driven systems provide liquidity to the market when trading would otherwise dry up. The NASDAQ and the LSE's SEAQ trading systems are two of the last remaining examples of quote-driven equity trading systems.

An **order-driven** market is one that employs either an electronic order book such as the LSE's SETS or an auction process such as that on the NYSE floor to match buyers with sellers. In both cases, buyers and sellers are matched in strict chronological order by price and the quantity of shares being traded and do not require market makers.

Most stock exchanges operate order-driven systems and how they operate can be seen by looking at the London Stock Exchange's SETS system as an example.

Example – SETS

The London Stock Exchange's main trading platform is SETS, which is used to trade shares that are contained within the FTSE All Share Index. It combines **electronic order-driven** trading with integrated **market maker liquidity provision**, delivering guaranteed two-way prices for the most liquid securities.

In this system, LSE member firms (investment banks and brokers) input orders via computer terminals. These orders may be for the member firms themselves, or for their clients.

Very simply, the way the system operates is that these orders will be added to the 'buy queue' or the 'sell queue', or executed immediately. Investors who add their order to the relevant queue are prepared to hold out for the price they want.

Those seeking immediate execution will trade against the queue of buyers (if they are selling) or against the sellers' queue (if they are buying).

Example of a SETS screen

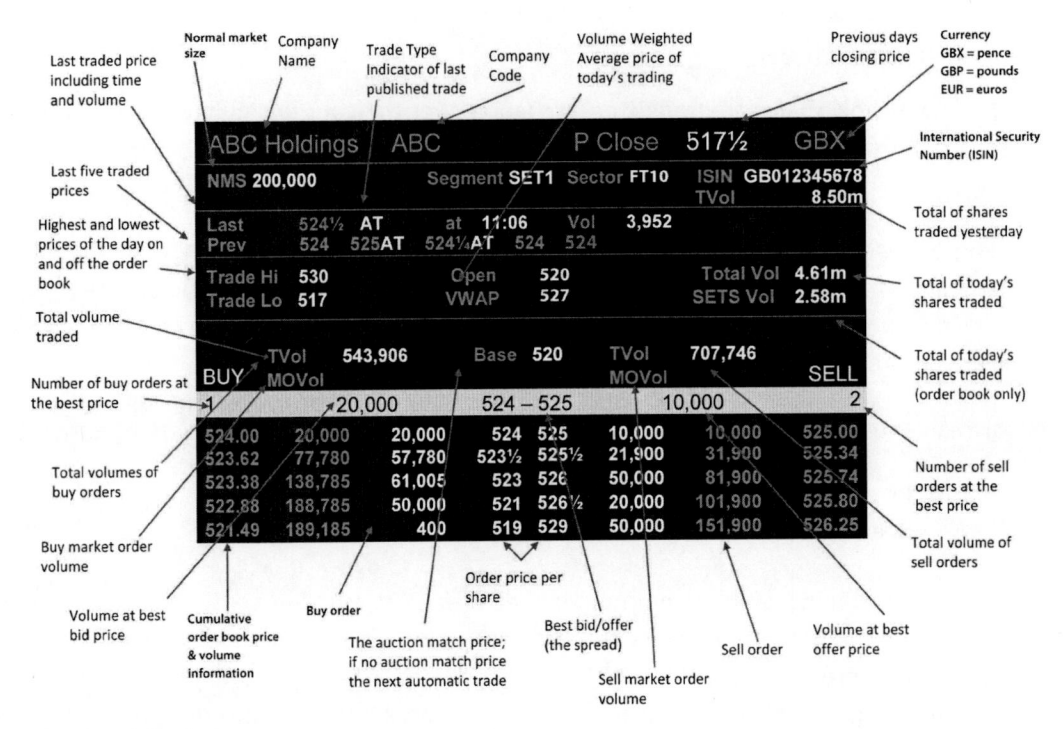

Labels around the SETS screen (clockwise from top-left):
- Last traded price including time and volume
- Normal market size
- Company Name
- Trade Type Indicator of last published trade
- Company Code
- Volume Weighted Average price of today's trading
- Previous days closing price
- Currency: GBX = pence, GBP = pounds, EUR = euros
- International Security Number (ISIN)
- Total of shares traded yesterday
- Total of today's shares traded
- Total of today's shares traded (order book only)
- Number of sell orders at the best price
- Total volume of sell orders
- Volume at best offer price
- Sell order
- Sell market order volume
- Best bid/offer (the spread)
- Order price per share
- The auction match price; if no auction match price the next automatic trade
- Buy order
- Cumulative order book price & volume information
- Volume at best bid price
- Buy market order volume
- Total volumes of buy orders
- Number of buy orders at the best price
- Total volume traded
- Highest and lowest prices of the day on and off the order book
- Last five traded prices

Screen data:

ABC Holdings ABC P Close 517½ GBX
NMS 200,000 Segment SET1 Sector FT10 ISIN GB012345678 TVol 8.50m
Last 524½ AT at 11:06 Vol 3,952
Prev 524 525AT 524¼AT 524 524
Trade Hi 530 Open 520 Total Vol 4.61m
Trade Lo 517 VWAP 527 SETS Vol 2.58m

TVol 543,906 Base 520 TVol 707,746
BUY MOVol MOVol SELL
1 20,000 524 – 525 10,000 2

524.00	20,000	20,000	524	525	10,000	10,000	525.00
523.62	77,780	57,780	523½	525½	21,900	31,900	525.34
523.38	138,785	61,005	523	526	50,000	81,900	525.74
522.88	188,785	50,000	521	526½	20,000	101,900	525.80
521.49	189,185	400	519	529	50,000	151,900	526.25

Source: London Stock Exchange

For a liquid stock, like Vodafone, there will be a 'deep' order book – the term 'deep' implies that there are lots of orders waiting to be dealt on either side. The top of the queues might look like this:

Buy Queue		Sell Queue	
We will buy for at most		We will sell for at least	
7,000 shares	£1.24	3,500 shares	£1.25
5,150 shares	£1.23	1,984 shares [2]	£1.26
19,250 shares [1]	£1.22	75,397 shares [2]	£1.26
44,000 shares [1]	£1.22	17,300 shares	£1.27

Queue priority is given on the basis of price and then time. So, for the equally priced orders noted[1], the order to buy 19,250 shares must have been placed before the 44,000 order – hence its position higher up the queue. Similarly, for the orders noted[2], the order to sell 1,984 shares must have been input before the order to sell 75,397 shares.

The LSE also has other systems including:

- SETSqx for less liquid shares that are not traded on SETS.
- SEAQ for fixed-interest securities and AIM stocks not traded on SETSqx.
- ORB, the electronic order book for retail bonds (ORB), offers continuous two-way pricing for trading in UK gilts and retail-size corporate bonds.

As an alternative to trading on a stock exchange, trades can be conducted through multilateral trading facilities (MTFs). MTFs, sometimes referred to as 'alternative trading systems', are non-exchange trading venues which bring together buyers and sellers of securities. Subscribers can post orders into the system and these will be communicated (typically, electronically via an electronic communication network (ECN)) for other subscribers to view. Matched orders will then proceed to execution. Examples of MTFs include BATS CHI-X Europe and Turquoise.

A further alternative is for a firm to execute client trades against their own account – a role known as a 'systematic internaliser'. Instead of sending orders to a stock exchange, they can match them with other orders on its own book. This means they are able to compete directly with stock exchanges and automated dealing systems, but they have to make such dealings transparent – ie, they have to show a price before a trade is made and have to give information about the transaction, just like conventional trading exchanges, after a trade is made.

10. Holding Title

Learning Objective

4.1.11 Know the method of holding title and related terminology: registered; bearer; immobilised; dematerialised

Shares can be issued in either registered or bearer form.

Holding shares in **registered** form involves the investor's name being recorded on the share register and, often, the investor being issued with a share certificate to reflect their ownership. However, many companies which issue registered shares now do so on a **non-certificated basis**.

The alternative to holding shares in registered form is to hold **bearer** shares. As the name suggests, the person who holds, or is the 'bearer' of, the shares is the owner. Ownership passes by transfer of the share certificate to the new owner. This adds a degree of risk to holding shares in that loss of the certificate might equal loss of the person's investment. As a result, holding bearer shares is relatively rare, especially in the UK. In addition, bearer shares are regarded unfavourably by the regulatory authorities owing to the opportunities they offer for money laundering. Consequently, they are usually immobilised in depositories such as Euroclear, or by their local country registries.

In all but a very few cases, a UK company is required to maintain a **share register**. This is simply a record of all current shareholders in that company, and how many shares they each hold. The share register is kept by the company registrar, who might be an employee of the company itself or a specialist firm of registrars. An electronic register is also kept by CREST so that trades can be settled electronically.

When a shareholder sells some, or all, of their shareholding, there must be a mechanism for updating the register to reflect the buyer and effect the change of ownership and for transferring the money to the seller. This is required in order to settle the transaction – accordingly, it is described as **settlement**.

Historically, each shareholder also held a **share certificate** as evidence of the shares they owned. When shares were sold, the seller sent their share certificate and a stock transfer form, providing details of the new owner, to the company registrar. Acting on these documents, the registrar would delete the seller's name and insert the name of the buyer into the register. The registrar then issued a new certificate to the buyer. This was commonly referred to as **certificated settlement** because the completion of a transaction required the issue of a new share certificate.

Certificated settlement is cumbersome and inefficient, and most markets have moved to having a single central securities depository which hold records of ownership, with transfer of ownership taking place electronically. In the UK, settlement has moved to a paperless, **dematerialised** (or **uncertificated**) form of settlement through a system called **CREST** (see Section 12).

Further developments in settlement took place from October 2014 onwards when rules came in requiring European markets to move to a standardised T+2 settlement period. This reduction in the settlement period is intended to harmonise practices across Europe and help to reduce risk.

Some investors still hold physical share certificates and they have been unable to benefit from shorter settlement periods. Settlement of these trades usually takes place at T+10 or a shorter period to allow all of the paperwork to be completed. As part of the changes to settlement periods, there are separate proposals to phase out the use of paper share certificates.

11. Clearing and Central Counterparties

Learning Objective

4.1.12 Understand the role of the central counterparty in clearing and settlement

Clearing is the process through which the obligations held by buyer and seller to a trade are defined and legally formalised. In simple terms, this procedure establishes what each of the counterparties expects to receive when the trade is settled. It also defines the obligations each must fulfil, in terms of delivering securities or funds, for the trade to settle successfully.

Specifically, the clearing process includes:

- Recording key trade information so that counterparties can agree on the trade's terms.
- Formalising the legal obligation between counterparties.
- Matching and confirming trade details.
- Agreeing procedures for settling the transaction.

Equities

- Calculating settlement obligations and sending out settlement instructions to the brokers, custodians and central securities depository (CSD).
- Managing margin and making margin calls. (Margin relates to collateral paid to the clearing agent by counterparties to guarantee their positions against default up to settlement.)

Trades may be cleared and settled directly between the trading counterparties – known as **bilateral settlement**. When trades are cleared bilaterally, each trading party bears a direct credit risk against each counterparty that it trades with. Hence, it will typically bear direct liability for any losses incurred through counterparty default.

The alternative is to clear trades using a **central counterparty (CCP)**. A CCP interposes itself between the counterparties to a trade, becoming the buyer to every seller and the seller to every buyer. As a result, buyer and seller interact with the CCP and remain anonymous to one another. This process is known as **novation**.

Regulators are increasingly keen to promote the use of CCPs across a wide range of financial products. While this does not eliminate the risk of institutions going into default, it does spread this risk across all participants, and is making these risks progressively easier to monitor and regulate. The risk controls extended by a CCP effectively provide an early warning system to financial regulators of impending risks, and are an important tool in efforts to contain these risks within manageable limits.

Central counterparty (CCP) services have been introduced in a range of markets in order to mitigate this risk. For example, LCH.Clearnet provides CCP services in the UK and Euronext European markets for trading in equity, derivatives and energy products.

12. Settlement

Learning Objective

4.1.13 Understand how settlement takes place: participants; process; settlement cycles

Settlement is the process through which legal title (ie, ownership) of a security is transferred from seller to buyer in exchange for the equivalent value in cash. Ideally, these two transfers should occur simultaneously, known as **delivery versus payment (DvP)**.

CREST is the term that is commonly used to refer to the system operated by Euroclear UK & Ireland, the central securities depository for UK and Irish equities. Some of its key features are:

- Holdings are uncertificated; that is, share certificates are not required to evidence transfer of ownership.
- There is real-time matching of trades.
- Settlement of transactions takes place in sterling, euros or dollars.
- Electronic transfer of title (see below) takes place on settlement.
- Settlement generates guaranteed obligations to pay cash outside CREST.
- Coverage includes shares, corporate and government bonds and other securities held in registered form.

- A range of corporate actions is processed, including dividend distributions and rights issues.
- It also provides a mechanism to facilitate the settlement of trades when the investor holds paper share certificates.

12.1 Settlement in CREST

The diagram below illustrates how a sterling sale of UK-registered shares between two counterparties on a recognised exchange is input, matched and settled in CREST.

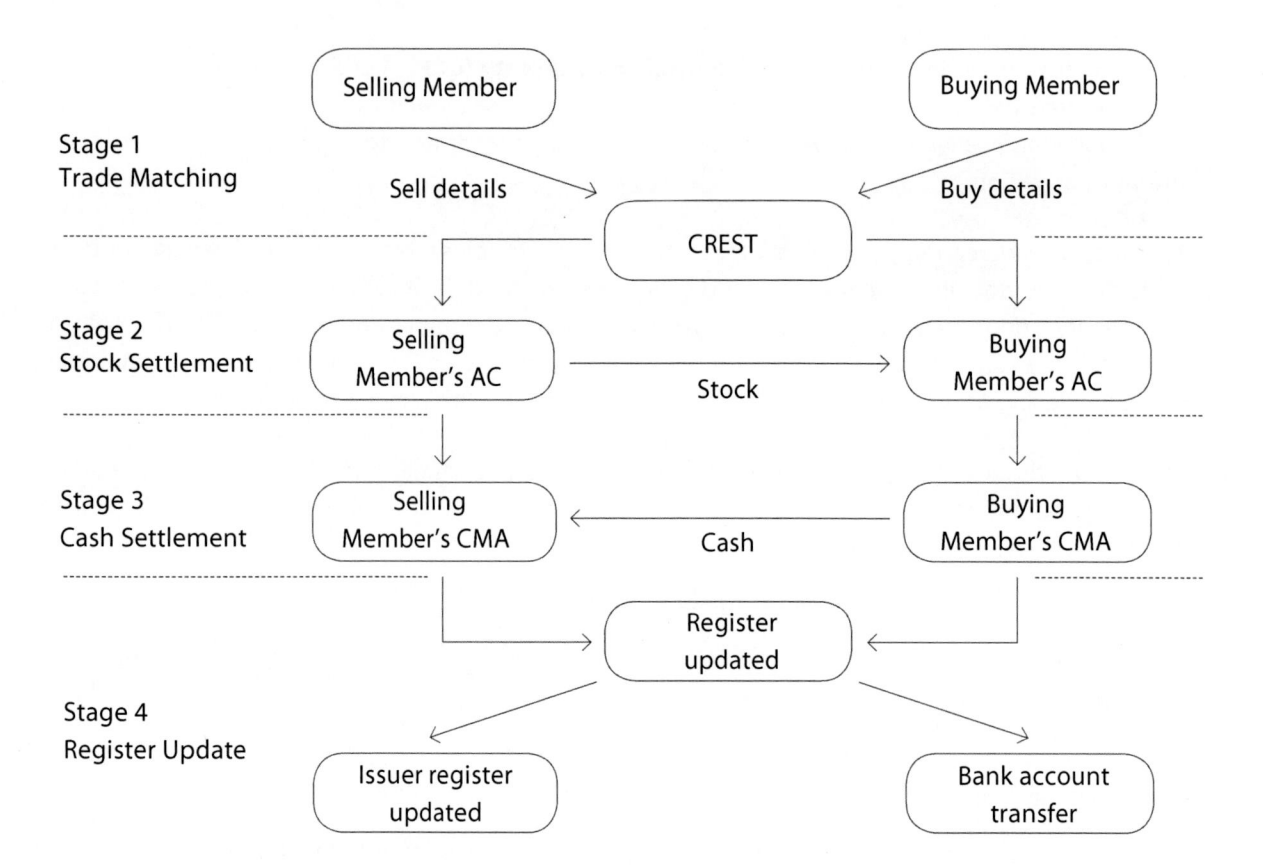

Stage 1 – Trade Matching

- The buying and selling members input instructions in CREST detailing the terms of the agreed trade.
- CREST authenticates these instructions to check that they conform to the authentication procedures stipulated by CREST. If the input data from both members matches, CREST creates a matching transaction.

Stage 2 – Stock Settlement

- On the intended settlement date, CREST checks that the buying member has the funds, the selling member has sufficient stock in its stock account and the buyer's CREST settlement bank has sufficient liquidity at the Bank of England to proceed to settlement of the transaction.
- If so, CREST moves the stock from the selling member's account to the buying member's account.

Stage 3 – Cash Settlement
- CREST also credits the CMA of the selling member and debits the CMA of the buying member, which simultaneously generates a settlement bank payment obligation of the buying member's settlement bank in favour of the Bank of England.
- The selling member's settlement bank receives that payment in Bank of England funds immediately upon the debit of the purchase price from the buying member's CMA.

Stage 4 – Register Update
- CREST then automatically updates its operator register of securities to effect the transfer of shares to the buying member.
- Legal title to the shares passes at this point – ETT, as described earlier.
- This prompts the simultaneous generation by the CREST system of an RUR requiring the issuer to amend its record of uncertificated shares.

In practice, stages 2, 3 and 4 occur simultaneously.

End of Chapter Questions

Think of an answer for each question and refer to the appropriate section for confirmation.

1. What are the constitutional documents of a company more commonly known as?
   Answer Reference: Section 2.1

2. When a shareholder appoints someone to vote on his behalf at a company meeting, what is it referred to as?
   Answer Reference: Sections 2.3 & 4.4.2

3. What are the features of a cumulative preference share?
   Answer Reference: Section 3.2

4. Why might a company have a higher than average dividend yield?
   Answer Reference: Section 4.1.1

5. What options are available to an investor in a rights issue?
   Answer Reference: Section 6.2

6. Under what type of corporate action would an investor receive additional shares without making any payment?
   Answer Reference: Section 6.3

7. Which body is responsible for approving the listing of companies on the London Stock Exchange?
   Answer Reference: Section 7.2.1

8. What is the function of a stock market index?
   Answer Reference: Section 8

9. The CAC 40 index relates to which market?
   Answer Reference: Section 8

10. What is the key characteristic of an order-driven trading system?
    Answer Reference: Section 9

Chapter Five
Bonds

1. Introduction	79
2. Characteristics of Bonds	79
3. Government Bonds	81
4. Corporate Bonds	82
5. Investing in Bonds	88

This syllabus area will provide approximately 5 of the 50 examination questions

1. Introduction

Although bonds do not often generate as much media attention as shares, they are the larger market of the two in terms of global investment value.

Bonds are roughly equally split between government and corporate bonds. Government bonds are issued by national governments, and by supranational agencies such as the European Investment Bank and the World Bank. Corporate bonds are issued by companies, such as the large banks and other large corporate listed companies.

In this chapter, we will first look at the common characteristics of bonds and then consider the key features of both government and corporate bonds.

2. Characteristics of Bonds

Learning Objective

5.1.1 Understand the characteristics and terminology of bonds: coupon; redemption; nominal value

A bond is, very simply, a loan.

A company that needs to raise money to finance an investment could borrow money from their bank, or alternatively they could issue a bond to raise the funds they need.

With a bond, an investor lends in return for the promise to have the loan repaid on a fixed date plus (usually) a series of interest payments. Bonds are commonly referred to as loan stock, debt and (in the case of those that pay fixed income) fixed-interest securities.

The feature that distinguishes a bond from most loans is that a bond is **tradable**. Investors can buy and sell bonds without the need to refer to the original borrower.

Although there are a wide variety of bonds in issue, they all share similar characteristics. These can be described by looking at an example of a UK government bond and explaining what each of the terms means.

To explain the terminology associated with bonds, we will assume that an investor has purchased a holding of £10,000 nominal of 5% Treasury stock 2025.

Nominal[1]	£10,000
Stock[2]	Treasury stock
Coupon	5%[3]
Redemption date	2025[4]
Price[5]	£133.20
Value[6]	£13,320.00

Each of the terms annotated above is explained below:

1. **Nominal** – this is the amount of stock purchased and should not be confused with the amount invested or the cost of purchase. This is the amount on which interest will be paid and the amount that will eventually be repaid. It is also known as the **par** or **face** value of the bond.
2. **Stock** – the name given to identify the stock.
3. **5%** – this is the nominal interest rate payable on the stock, also known as the **coupon**. The rate is quoted gross and will normally be paid in two separate and equal half-yearly interest payments. The annual amount of interest paid is calculated by multiplying the nominal amount of stock held by the coupon; that is, in this case, £10,000 times 5%.
4. **2025** – this is the year in which the stock will be repaid, known as the **redemption date** or **maturity date**. Repayment will take place at the same time as the final interest payment is made. The amount repaid will be the nominal amount of stock held; that is, £10,000.
5. **Price** – the convention in the bond markets is to quote prices per £100 nominal of stock. So, in this example, the price is £133.20 for each £100 nominal of stock and the holding has a market value of £13,320.00 – that is, the nominal value of £10,000 multiplied by the price of £133.20.
6. **Value** – the value of the stock is calculated by multiplying the nominal amount of stock by the current price.

Example

Government bonds are named by their coupon rate and their redemption date, for example, 6% Treasury stock 2028.

The coupon indicates the cash payment per £100 nominal value that the holder will receive each year (unless tax is deducted at source). This interest payment is usually made in two equal semi-annual payments on fixed dates, six months apart.

An investor holding £1,000 nominal of 6% Treasury stock 2028 will receive two coupon payments of £30 each, on 7 June and 7 December each year, until the repayment of £1,000 on 7 December 2028.

3. Government Bonds

Learning Objective

5.2.1 Know the definition and features of government bonds: types; yields

Governments issue bonds to finance their spending and investment plans and to bridge the gap between their actual spending and the tax and other forms of income that they receive. Issuance of bonds is high when tax revenues are significantly lower than government spending.

Western governments are major borrowers of money, so the volume of government bonds in issue is very large and forms a major part of the investment portfolio of many institutional investors (such as pension funds and insurance companies).

UK government bonds are known as **gilts**. When physical certificates were issued, historically they used to have a gold or gilt edge to them, hence they are known as 'gilts' or 'gilt-edged stock'. The bonds are issued on behalf of the government by the Debt Management Office (DMO).

3.1 Types of Government Bonds

There are two main types of UK government bond in issue – conventional bonds and index-linked bonds.

Conventional government bonds are instruments that carry a fixed coupon and a single repayment date, such as in the examples used above of 5% Treasury stock 2025 and 6% Treasury stock 2028. Conventional bonds typically represent around 75% of bonds in issue.

The coupon and redemption amount for index-linked bonds are increased by the amount of inflation over its lifetime. An example is 2½% Treasury index-linked stock 2020. When this stock was issued, it carried a coupon of 2½%, but this is uplifted by the amount of inflation at each interest payment. Similarly, the amount that will be repaid in 2020 is adjusted.

Index-linked bonds are attractive in periods when a government's control of inflation is uncertain because they provide extra protection to the investor. They are also attractive to long-term investors, such as pension funds. These need to invest their funds and know that the returns will maintain their real value after inflation so that they can meet their obligations to pay pensions.

Conventional bonds can be stripped into their individual cash flows – that is, the coupon payments and the bond repayment. 'Stripping' a gilt refers to breaking it down into its individual cash flows which can be traded separately as zero coupon gilts. A three-year gilt will have seven individual cash flows: six (semi-annual) coupon payments and the final maturity repayment. These are known as 'gilt STRIPs'.

In the past, there have also been other types of government bonds, dual-dated and undated. Dual-dated bonds carried a fixed coupon but showed two dates between which they can be repaid. The decision as to when to repay is made by the government and depends on the prevailing rates of interest at that time. The final gilt of this type, 12% Exchequer stock 2013–17, was redeemed on 12 December 2013.

There also used to be a limited number of government stocks which were irredeemable, ie, they had no fixed repayment date. The last remaining 'undated' bonds in the UK gilt portfolio were redeemed in 2015.

4. Corporate Bonds

Learning Objective

5.3.1 Know the definitions and features of the following types of bond: domestic; foreign; eurobond; asset-backed securities including covered bonds; zero coupon; convertible

A corporate bond is a bond that is issued by a company, as the name suggests.

The term is usually applied to longer-term debt instruments, with a maturity date of more than 12 months. The term **commercial paper** (see Chapter 3, Section 3) is used for instruments with a shorter maturity. Only companies with high credit ratings (see Section 5.3) can issue bonds with a maturity greater than ten years at an acceptable cost.

Most corporate bonds are listed on stock exchanges, but the majority of trading in most developed markets takes place in the OTC market – that is directly between market counterparties.

4.1 Features of Corporate Bonds

There is a wide variety of corporate bonds and they can often be differentiated by looking at some of their key features, such as security, and redemption provisions.

4.1.1 Bond Security

When a company is seeking to raise new funds by way of a bond issue, it will often have to offer 'security' to provide the investor with some guarantee for the repayment of the bond. In this context, security usually means some form of charge over the issuer's assets (eg, its property or trade assets) so that, if the issuer defaults, the bondholders have a claim on those assets before other creditors (and so can regard their borrowings as safer than if there were no security).

In some cases, the security takes the form of a **third party guarantee** – for example, a guarantee by a bank that, if the issuer defaults, the bank will repay the bondholders.

The greater the security offered, the lower the cost of borrowing should be.

The security offered may be fixed or floating. **Fixed security** implies that specific assets (eg, a building) of the company are charged as security for the loan. A **floating charge** means that the general assets of the company are offered as security for the loan; this might include cash at the bank, trade debtors, stock, etc.

4.1.2 Redemption Provisions

In some cases, a corporate bond will have a **call provision**, which gives the issuer the option to buy back all or part of the issue before maturity.

This is attractive to the issuer as it gives it the option to refinance the bond (ie, replace it with one at a lower rate of interest) when interest rates are lower than the coupon that is being paid. This is a disadvantage, however, to the investor, who will probably demand a higher yield as compensation.

Call provisions can take various forms. For example, there may be a requirement for the issuer to redeem a specified amount at regular intervals. This is known as a **sinking fund requirement**.

Some bonds are also issued with **put provisions**, known as 'puttable' bonds. These give the bondholder the right to require the issuer to redeem early, on a set date or between specific dates. This makes the bond attractive to investors and may increase the chances of selling a bond issue in the first instance; it does, however, increase the issuer's risk that it will have to refinance the bond at an inconvenient time. An example of a bond with a put provision is shown below in the section on medium-term notes.

4.2 Types of Corporate Bonds

The development of financial engineering techniques in banks around the world has resulted in a large variety of corporate debt being issued and traded. Some of the main types are described below.

4.2.1 Medium-Term Notes (MTNs)

Medium-term notes are standard corporate bonds with maturities up to five years, though the term is also applied to instruments with maturities as long as 30 years. Where they differ from other debt instruments is that they are offered to investors continually over a period of time by an agent of the issuer, instead of in a single tranche of one sizeable underwritten issue.

The market originated in the US to close the funding gap between commercial paper and long-term bonds.

Example

An example of medium-term notes is one issued by Tesco. As part of a larger financing programme, it issued a £200 million tranche of 6% sterling-denominated notes in 1999 which are repayable in 2029.

This bond contains an example of an investor put provision. It provides that, if there is a restructuring event (which for this bond is if anyone becomes entitled to more than 50% of the voting rights in the company) and this results in a rating downgrade, then holders of the bonds can give notice to Tesco requiring it to redeem the bond at par together with any accrued interest.

4.2.2 Fixed-Rate Bonds

The key features of fixed-rate bonds have already been described in Section 2. Essentially, they have fixed coupons which are paid either half-yearly or annually and predetermined redemption dates.

4.2.3 Floating Rate Notes (FRNs)

Floating rate notes are usually referred to as FRNs and are bonds that have variable rates of interest.

The rate of interest will be linked to a benchmark rate, such as the London InterBank Offered Rate (LIBOR). This is the rate of interest at which banks will lend to one another in London, and is often used as a basis for financial instrument cash flows.

An FRN will usually pay interest at LIBOR plus a quoted margin or spread.

4.2.4 Permanent Interest-Bearing Shares (PIBS)

PIBS are a type of instrument that is peculiar to the UK sterling market. The term stands for permanent interest bearing shares and they are issued by building societies. They carry fixed coupons and are irredeemable.

You should note that the name 'shares' is a misnomer. It is in fact a bond, pays interest, and is taxable as such despite its name.

Example

An example of a PIBS is one issued by Coventry Building Society. In 2006, it issued a bond titled 6.092% Permanent Interest Bearing Shares with a redemption date of 31 December 2099 – nearly 90 years away, hence why it qualifies as irredeemable.

We will look separately at some other types of bonds in the following sections.

4.2.5 Convertible Bonds

Convertible bonds are issued by companies. They give the investor holding the bond two possible choices:

- to simply collect the interest payments and then the repayment of the bond on maturity
- to convert the bond into a predefined number of ordinary shares in the issuing company, on a set date or dates, or between a range of set dates, prior to the bond's maturity.

The attractions to the investor are:

- If the company prospers, its share price will rise and, if it does so sufficiently, conversion may lead to capital gains.
- If the company hits problems, the investor can retain the bond – interest will be earned and, as bondholder, the investor would rank ahead of existing shareholders if the company goes bust. (Of course, if the company were seriously insolvent and the bond were unsecured, the bondholder might still not be repaid – but this is a possibility more remote than that of a full loss as a shareholder.)

Bonds

For the company, relatively cheap finance is acquired. Investors will pay a higher price for a bond that is convertible because of the possibility of a capital gain. However, the prospect of dilution of current shareholder interests, as convertible bondholders exercise their options, has to be borne in mind.

4.2.6 Zero Coupon Bonds (ZCBs)

— TAX EVASION ???

A zero coupon bond (ZCB) is a bond that pays no interest. 'Coupon' is an alternative term for the interest payment on a bond.

Example

Imagine that the issuer of a bond (Example plc) offered you the opportunity to purchase a bond with the following features:

- €100 nominal value.
- Issued today.
- Redeems at its par value (that is, €100 nominal value) in five years.
- Pays no interest.

Would you be interested in purchasing the bond? It is tempting to say no – who would want to buy a bond that pays no interest?

However, there is no requirement to pay the par value – a logical investor would presumably happily pay something less than the par value, for example €60. The difference between the price paid of €60 and the par value of €100 recouped after five years would provide the investor with their return of €40 over five years.

The example shows why a zero coupon bond may be attractive. As the example illustrates, these zero coupon bonds are issued at a **discount to their par value** and they repay, or redeem, at par value. All of the return is provided in the form of capital growth rather than income and, as a result, it may be treated differently for tax purposes.

4.3 Domestic and Foreign Bonds

Bonds can be categorised geographically. A **domestic bond** is issued by a domestic issuer into the domestic market, for example, a UK company issuing bonds, denominated in sterling, to UK investors.

In contrast, a **foreign bond** is issued by an overseas entity into a domestic market and is denominated in the domestic currency. Examples of a foreign bond are a German company issuing a sterling bond to UK investors, or a US dollar bond issued in the US by a non-US company.

4.4 Eurobonds

Eurobonds are large international bond issues often made by governments and multinational companies. The eurobond market developed in the early 1970s to accommodate the recycling of substantial OPEC US dollar revenues from Middle East oil sales at a time when US financial institutions were subject to a ceiling on the rate of interest that could be paid on dollar deposits. Since then it has grown exponentially into the world's largest market for longer-term capital, as a result of the corresponding growth in world trade and even more significant growth in international capital flows. Most of the activity is concentrated in London.

Often issued in a number of financial centres simultaneously, the defining characteristic of eurobonds is that they are **denominated in a currency different from that of the financial centre or centres in which they are issued**. An example might be a German company issuing either a euro or a dollar or a sterling bond to Japanese investors.

In this respect, the term 'eurobond' is a bit of a misnomer, as eurobond issues, and the currencies in which they are denominated, are not restricted to those of European financial centres or countries. For example, a dollar-denominated bond sold outside the US (designed to borrow US dollars circulating outside the US) would typically be referred to as a eurodollar bond. The 'euro' prefix simply originates from the depositing of US dollars in the European eurodollar market, and has been applied to the eurobond market since. So, a euro sterling bond issue is one denominated in sterling and issued outside the UK, though not necessarily in a European financial centre.

Eurobonds issued by companies often do not provide any underlying collateral, or security, to the bondholders but are almost always credit-rated by a credit rating agency (see Section 5.3). To prevent the interests of these bondholders being subordinated (made inferior) to those of any subsequent bond issues, the company makes a 'negative pledge' clause. This prevents the company from subsequently making any secured bond issues, or issues which confer greater seniority (ie, priority) or entitlement to the company's assets, in the event of its liquidation, unless an equivalent level of security is provided to existing bondholders.

The eurobond market offers a number of advantages over a domestic bond market that make it an attractive way for companies to raise capital, including:

- a choice of innovative products to more precisely meet issuers' needs
- the ability to reach potential lenders internationally rather than just domestically
- anonymity to investors as issues are made in bearer form
- gross interest payments to investors
- lower funding costs due to the competitive nature and greater liquidity of the market
- the ability to make bond issues at short notice
- less regulation and disclosure.

Most eurobonds are issued as conventional bonds (or 'straights'), with a fixed nominal value, fixed coupon and known redemption date. Other common types include floating rate notes, zero coupon bonds, convertible bonds and dual-currency bonds – but they can also assume a wide range of other innovative features.

4.5 Asset-Backed Securities (ABSs)

There is a large group of bonds that trade under the overall heading of asset-backed securities. These are bundled securities, so-called because they are marketable securities that result from the bundling or packaging together of a set of non-marketable assets.

The assets in this pool, or bundle, range from mortgages and credit card debt to accounts receivable. ('Accounts receivable' is money owed to a company by a customer for goods and services that they have bought and is usually known as this once an invoice has been issued.)

The largest market is for mortgage-backed securities, whose cash flows are backed by the principal and interest payments of a set of mortgages.

Mortgage-backed bonds are created by bundling together a set of mortgages and then issuing bonds that are backed by these assets. These bonds are sold on to investors, who receive interest payments until they are redeemed.

Creating a bond in this way is known as **securitisation**, and it began in the US in 1970 when the government first issued **mortgage certificates**, a security representing ownership of a pool of mortgages.

A significant advantage of asset-backed securities is that they bring together a pool of financial assets that otherwise could not easily be traded in their existing form. The pooling together of a large portfolio of these illiquid assets converts them into instruments that may be offered and sold freely in the capital markets.

4.5.1 Covered Bonds

A variation on asset-backed bonds is covered bonds which are widely used in Europe.

These are issued by financial institutions and are corporate bonds that are backed by cash flows from a pool of mortgages or public sector loans. The pool of assets provides 'cover' for the loan, hence the term 'covered bond'.

They are similar in many ways to asset-backed securities, but the regulatory framework for covered bonds is designed so that bonds that comply with those requirements are considered as particularly safe investments. The main differences are:

- They remain on the issuer's balance sheet.
- The asset pool must provide sufficient collateral to cover bondholder claims throughout the whole term of the covered bond.
- Bondholders must have priority claim on the cover asset pool in case of default of the issuer.

Covered bonds are an important part of the financing of the mortgage and public sector markets in Europe and represent a vital source of term funding for banks. A thriving covered bond market is seen as essential for the future of the European banking sector and the ability of individuals to finance house loans at a reasonable rate.

5. Investing in Bonds

5.1 Advantages, Disadvantages and Risks

Learning Objective

5.4.1 Know the potential advantages and disadvantages of investing in different types of bonds

As one of the main asset classes, bonds clearly have a role to play in most portfolios.

5.1.1 Advantages

Their main advantages are:

- for fixed-interest bonds, a regular and certain flow of income
- for most bonds, a fixed maturity date (but there are bonds which have no redemption date, and others which may be repaid on either of two dates or between two dates – some at the investor's option and some at the issuer's option)
- a range of income yields to suit different investment and tax situations
- relative security of capital for more highly rated bonds.

5.1.2 Disadvantages

Their main disadvantages are:

- the 'real' value of the income flow is eroded by the effects of inflation (except in the case of index-linked bonds)
- bonds carry various elements of risk (see Section 5.1.3).

5.1.3 Risks

As can be seen, there are a number of risks attached to holding bonds.

Corporate bonds generally have **default risk** (the possibility of an issuer defaulting on the payment of interest or capital, eg, the company could go bust) and **price risk**.

Highly rated government bonds are said to have only price risk, as there is little or no risk that the government will fail to pay the interest or repay the capital on the bonds. Recent turmoil in government bond markets, however, such as fears that certain European governments were unable to meet their obligations on these loans, resulted in the prices of their bonds falling significantly.

Price (or market) risk is of particular concern to bondholders, who are open to the effect of **movements in general interest rates**, which can have a significant impact on the value of their holdings.

This is best explained by two simple examples.

Example

Interest rates are approximately 5%, and the government issues a bond with a coupon rate of 5% interest. Three months later, interest rates have doubled to 10%. What will happen to the value of the bond? The value of the bond will fall substantially. Its 5% interest is no longer attractive, so its resale price will fall to compensate and to make the return it offers more competitive.

Example

Interest rates are approximately 5%, and the government issues a bond with a coupon rate of 5% interest. Interest rates generally fall to 2.5%. What will happen to the value of the bond? The value of the bond will rise substantially. Its 5% interest is very attractive, so its resale price will rise to compensate and make the return it offers fall to more realistic levels.

With both of these examples, remember that it is the current value of the bond that is changing. Changes in interest rates do not affect the amount payable at maturity, which will remain as the nominal amount of the stock.

As the above examples illustrate, there is an inverse relationship between interest rates and bond prices:

- If interest rates increase, bond prices will decrease.
- If interest rates decrease, bond prices will increase.

Some of the other main risks associated with holding bonds are:

- **Early redemption** – the risk that the issuer may invoke a call provision (if the bond is callable).
- **Seniority risk** – the seniority with which corporate debt is ranked in the event of the issuer's liquidation. Debt with the highest seniority is repaid first in the event of liquidation; so debt with the highest seniority has a greater chance of being repaid than debt with lower seniority. If the company raises more borrowing and it is entitled to be repaid before the existing bonds, then the bonds have suffered from seniority risk.
- **Inflation risk** – the risk of inflation rising unexpectedly and eroding the real value of the bond's coupon and redemption payment.
- **Liquidity risk** – liquidity is the ease with which a security can be converted into cash. Some bonds are more easily sold at a fair market price than others.
- **Exchange rate risk** – bonds denominated in a currency different from that of the investor's home currency are potentially subject to adverse exchange rate movements.

5.2 Flat Yields

Learning Objective

5.4.2 Be able to calculate the flat yield of a bond

Yields are a measure of the returns to be earned on bonds. The coupon reflects the interest rate payable on the nominal or principal amount. However, an investor will have paid a different amount to purchase the bond, so a method of calculating the true return is needed.

The return, as a percentage of the cost price, which a bond offers is often referred to as the bond's **yield**. The interest paid on a bond as a percentage of its market price is referred to as the **flat** or **running yield**.

The flat yield is calculated by taking the annual coupon and dividing by the bond's price and then multiplying by 100 to obtain a percentage. The bond's price is typically stated as the price payable to purchase £100 nominal value. This is best illustrated by example:

Examples

1. A bond with a coupon of 5%, issued by XYZ plc, redeemable in 2020, is currently trading at £100 per £100 nominal. The flat yield is the coupon divided by the price expressed as a percentage, ie: £5/£100 x 100 = 5%.

2. A bond with a coupon of 4%, issued by ABC plc, redeemable in 2025, is currently trading at £78 per £100 nominal. So an investor could buy £100 nominal value for £78. The flat yield is the coupon divided by the price expressed as a percentage, ie: £4/£78 x 100 = 5.13%.

3. 5% Treasury stock 2028 is priced at £104. So an investor could buy £100 nominal value for £104. The flat yield on this gilt is the coupon divided by the price, ie: £5/£104 x 100 = 4.81%.

The interest earned on a bond is only one part of its total return, however, as the investor may also either make a capital gain or a loss on the bond if it is held until redemption. The **redemption yield** is a measure that incorporates both the income and capital return – assuming the investor holds the bond until its maturity – into one figure.

5.3 Rating Agencies

Learning Objective

5.4.3 Understand the role of credit rating agencies and the differences between investment and non-investment grades

Credit risk, or the probability of an issuer defaulting on their payment obligations, and the extent of the resulting loss, can be assessed by reference to the independent credit ratings given to most bond issues.

There are more than 70 agencies throughout the world, and preferred agencies vary from country to country. The three most prominent credit rating agencies that provide these ratings are Standard & Poor's; Moody's; and Fitch Ratings. The table below shows the credit ratings available from each. Standard & Poor's and Fitch Ratings refine their ratings by adding a plus or minus sign to show relative standing within a category, while Moody's do the same by the addition of a 1, 2 or 3.

As can be seen, bond issues, subject to credit ratings, can be divided into two distinct categories: those accorded an 'investment grade' rating, and those categorised as non-investment grade, or speculative. The latter are also known as 'high-yield' or – for the worst-rated – 'junk' bonds. Investment grade issues offer the greatest liquidity and certainty of repayment.

Bonds will be assessed and given a credit rating when they are first issued and then reassessed if circumstances change, so that their rating can be upgraded or downgraded with a consequent effect on their price.

Bond Credit Ratings				
Credit Risk		Moody's	Standard & Poor's	Fitch Ratings
Investment Grade				
Highest quality		Aaa	AAA	AAA
High quality	Very strong	Aa	AA	AA
Upper medium grade	Strong	A	A	A
Medium grade		Baa	BBB	BBB
Non-Investment Grade				
Lower medium grade	Somewhat speculative	Ba	BB	BB
Low grade	Speculative	B	B	B
Poor quality	May default	Caa	CCC	CCC
Most speculative		C	CC	CC
No interest being paid or bankruptcy petition filed		C	D	C
In default		C	D	D

End of Chapter Questions

Think of an answer for each question and refer to the appropriate section for confirmation.

1. 5% Treasury gilt 2018 is an example of what type of government bond?
   Answer Reference: Section 3.1

2. Which type of government bond would you expect to be most attractive during a period of rising inflation?
   Answer Reference: Section 3.1

3. What is the function of a call provision when attached to a bond?
   Answer Reference: Section 4.1.2

4. What is the typical maturity period for a medium-term note?
   Answer Reference: Section 4.2.1

5. What options does a convertible bond give to an investor?
   Answer Reference: Section 4.2.5

6. What type of bond does not pay interest?
   Answer Reference: Section 4.2.6

7. What types of assets might you see pooled together to provide the backing for an asset-backed security?
   Answer Reference: Section 4.5

8. What will be the impact of a fall in interest rates on bond prices?
   Answer Reference: Section 5.1.3

9. You have a holding of £1,000 Treasury 5% stock 2028 which is priced at 104. What is its flat yield?
   Answer Reference: Section 5.2

10. What credit rating should be looked for in a bond when seeking the greatest liquidity and certainty of repayment?
    Answer Reference: Section 5.3

Chapter Six
Derivatives

1.	**Overview of Derivatives**	**95**
2.	**Futures**	**96**
3.	**Options**	**98**
4.	**Swaps**	**100**
5.	**Derivatives and Commodity Markets**	**102**

This syllabus area will provide approximately 4 of the 50 examination questions

1. Overview of Derivatives

Derivatives are not a new concept – they have been around for hundreds of years. Their origins can be traced back to agricultural markets, where farmers needed a mechanism to guard against price fluctuations caused by gluts of produce and merchants wanted to guard against shortages that might arise from periods of drought.

So, in order to fix the price of agricultural produce in advance of harvest time, farmers and merchants would enter into **forward contracts**. These set the price at which a stated amount of a commodity would be delivered between a farmer and a merchant (termed the 'counterparties' to the trade) at a pre-specified future date.

These early derivative contracts introduced an element of certainty into commerce and gained immense popularity; they led to the opening of the world's first derivatives exchange in 1848, the Chicago Board of Trade (CBOT).

Modern **commodity markets** have their roots in this trading of agricultural products. Commodity markets are where raw or primary products are exchanged or traded on regulated exchanges. They are bought and sold in **standardised contracts** – a standardised contract is one where not only the amount and timing of the contract conforms to the exchange's norm, but also the quality and form of the underlying asset – for example, the dryness of wheat or the purity of metals.

Commodities are sold by producers (eg, farmers, mining companies and oil companies) and purchased by consumers (eg, food manufacturers and industrial goods manufacturers). Much of the buying and selling is undertaken via commodity derivatives, which also offer the ability for producers and consumers to hedge their exposure to price movements. However, there is also substantial trading in commodities (and their derivatives) undertaken by financial firms and speculators seeking to make profits by correctly predicting market movements.

Today, derivatives trading also takes place in financial instruments, indices, metals, energy and a wide range of other assets.

The majority of derivatives take one of four forms: forwards, futures, options and swaps.

1.1 Uses of Derivatives

Learning Objective

6.1.1 Know the uses and application of derivatives

A derivative is a financial instrument whose price is based on the price of another asset, known as the underlying asset or simply 'the underlying'. This underlying asset could be a financial asset or a commodity. Examples of financial assets include bonds, shares, stock market indices and interest rates; for commodities they include oil, silver or wheat.

As we will see later in this chapter, the trading of derivatives can take place either directly between counterparties or on an organised exchange. When trading takes place directly between counterparties it is referred to as **over-the-counter (OTC)** trading, and where it takes place on an exchange, such as LIFFE, the derivatives are referred to as being **exchange-traded**.

Derivatives play a major role in the investment management of many large portfolios and funds, and are used for hedging, anticipating future cash flows, asset allocation change and arbitrage. Each of these uses is expanded on briefly below:

- **Hedging** is a technique employed by portfolio managers to reduce the impact of adverse price movements on a portfolio's value; this could be achieved by selling a sufficient number of futures contracts or buying put options.
- **Anticipating future cash flows.** Closely linked to the idea of hedging, if a portfolio manager expects to receive a large inflow of cash to be invested in a particular asset, then futures can be used to fix the price at which it will be bought and offset the risk that prices will have risen by the time the cash flow is received.
- **Asset allocation changes.** Changes to the asset allocation of a fund, whether to take advantage of anticipated short-term directional market movements or to implement a change in strategy, can be made more swiftly and less expensively using derivatives such as futures than by actually buying and selling securities within the underlying portfolio.
- **Arbitrage** is the process of deriving a risk-free profit from simultaneously buying and selling the same asset in two different markets, when a price difference between the two exists. If the price of a derivative and its underlying asset are mismatched, then the portfolio manager may be able to profit from this pricing anomaly.

2. Futures

2.1 Development of Futures

As mentioned above, the **Chicago Board of Trade (CBOT)** opened the world's first derivatives exchange in 1848. The exchange soon developed a **futures contract** that enabled **standardised** qualities and quantities of grain to be traded for a fixed future price on a stated delivery date. Unlike the **forward contracts** that preceded it, the futures contract could itself be traded.

These futures contracts have subsequently been extended to a wide variety of commodities and are offered by an ever-increasing number of derivatives exchanges.

It was not until 1975 that CBOT introduced the world's first **financial futures contract**. This set the scene for the exponential growth in product innovation and the volume of futures trading that followed.

2.2 Definition and Function of a Future

Learning Objective

6.2.1 Know the definition and function of a future

Derivatives provide a mechanism by which the price of assets or commodities can be traded in the future at a price agreed today without the full value of this transaction being exchanged or settled at the outset.

A future is an agreement between a buyer and a seller. A futures contract is a legally binding obligation between two parties:

- The buyer agrees to pay a prespecified amount for the delivery of a particular prespecified quantity of an asset at a prespecified future date.
- The seller agrees to deliver the asset at the future date, in exchange for the prespecified amount of money.

Example

A buyer might agree with a seller to pay US$30 per barrel for 1,000 barrels of crude oil in three months' time. The buyer might be an electricity-generating company wanting to fix the price it will have to pay for the oil to use in its oil-fired power stations, and the seller might be an oil company wanting to fix the sales price of some of its future oil production.

A futures contract has two distinct features:

- It is **exchange-traded** – for example, on derivatives exchanges such as LIFFE or the IntercontinentalExchange (ICE).
- It is dealt on **standardised terms** – the exchange specifies the quality of the underlying asset, the quantity underlying each contract, the future date and the delivery location – only the price is open to negotiation. In the above example, the oil quality will be based on the oil field from which it originates (eg, Brent crude – from the Brent oil field in the North Sea), the quantity is 1,000 barrels, the date is three months ahead and the location might be the port of Rotterdam.

2.3 Futures Terminology

Learning Objective

6.4.1 Understand the following terms: long; short; open; close; covered; naked

Derivatives markets have specialised terminology that is important to understand.

Staying with the example above, the electricity company is the buyer of the contract, agreeing to purchase 1,000 barrels of crude oil at US$30 per barrel for delivery in three months. The buyer is said to go **long** of the contract, while the seller (the oil company, in the above example) is described as going **short**. Entering into the transaction is known as **opening the trade** and the eventual delivery of the crude oil will **close-out** the trade.

The definitions of these key terms that the futures market uses are as follows:

- **Long** – the term used for the position taken by the buyer of the future. The person who is 'long' of the contract is committed to buying the underlying asset at the pre-agreed price on the specified future date.
- **Short** – the position taken by the seller of the future. The seller is committed to delivering the underlying asset in exchange for the pre-agreed price on the specified future date.
- **Open** – the initial trade. A market participant 'opens' a trade when it first enters into a future. It could be buying a future (opening a long position), or selling a future (opening a short position).
- **Close** – the physical assets underlying most futures that are opened do not end up being delivered: they are 'closed-out' instead. For example, an opening buyer will almost invariably avoid delivery by making a closing sale before the delivery date. If the buyer does not close-out, he will pay the agreed sum and receive the underlying asset. This might be something the buyer is keen to avoid, for example because the buyer is actually a financial institution simply speculating on the price of the underlying asset using futures.
- **Covered** – when the seller of the future has the underlying asset that will be needed if physical delivery takes place.
- **Naked** – when the seller of the future does not have the asset that will be needed if physical delivery of the underlying commodity is required. The risk could be unlimited.

3. Options

Learning Objective

6.3.1 Know the definition and function of an option

6.3.2 Understand the following terms: calls; puts

6.4.1 Understand the following terms: holder; writing; premium; covered; naked

3.1 Development of Options

We now move on to consider options contracts. Options did not really start to flourish until two US academics produced an option pricing model in 1973 that allowed them to be readily priced. This paved the way for the creation of standardised options contracts and the opening of the Chicago Board Options Exchange (CBOE) in the same year. This in turn led to an explosion in product innovation and the creation of other options exchanges, such as LIFFE.

3.2 Definition and Function of an Option

An option gives a buyer the **right**, but not the **obligation**, to buy or sell a specified quantity of an underlying asset at a pre-agreed **exercise price**, on or before a prespecified future date or between two specified dates. The seller, in exchange for the payment of a **premium**, grants the option to the buyer.

When options are traded on an **exchange**, they will be in standardised sizes and terms. From time to time, however, investors may wish to trade an option that is outside these standardised terms and they will do so in the **over-the-counter (OTC)** market. Options can therefore also be traded off-exchange, or OTC, when the contract specification determined by the parties is bespoke.

3.3 Options Terminology

There are two classes of options:

- A **call option** is when the buyer has the right to buy the asset at the exercise price, if they choose to. The seller is obliged to deliver if the buyer exercises the option.
- A **put option** is when the buyer has the right to sell the underlying asset at the exercise price. The seller of the put option is obliged to take delivery and pay the exercise price, if the buyer exercises the option.

The buyers of options are the owners of those options. They are also referred to as **holders**.

The sellers of options are referred to as the **writers** of those options. Their sale is also referred to as 'taking for the call' or 'taking for the put', depending on whether they receive a premium for selling a call option or a put option.

For **exchange-traded contracts**, both buyers and sellers settle the contract with a clearing house that is part of the exchange, rather than with each other. The exchange needs to be able to settle bargains if holders choose to exercise their rights to buy or sell. Since the exchange does not want to be a buyer or seller of the underlying asset, it matches these transactions with deals placed by option writers who have agreed to deliver or receive the matching underlying asset, if called upon to do so.

The **premium** is the money paid by the buyer/holder to the exchange (and then by the exchange to the seller/writer) at the beginning of the option contract; it is not refundable.

The following example of an options contract is intended to assist in understanding the way in which options contracts might be used.

Example

Suppose shares in Jersey plc are trading at 324p and an investor buys a 350p call for three months for a premium of 42p. The investor, Frank, has the right to buy Jersey shares from the writer of the option (another investor – Steve) at 350p if he chooses at the end of the next three months.

If Jersey shares are below 350p three months later, Frank will abandon the option.

If they rise to, say, 600p, Frank will contact Steve and either:

- exercise the option (buy the share at 350p and keep it, or sell it at 600p)
- persuade Steve to give him 600p – 350p = 250p to settle the transaction.

If Frank paid a premium of 42p to Steve, what is Frank's maximum loss and what level does Jersey plc have to reach for Frank to make a profit?

The most Frank can lose is 42p, the premium he has paid.

If the Jersey plc shares rise above 350p + 42p, or 392p, then Frank makes a profit. Frank's potential profit is unlimited.

If the shares rise to 351p then Frank would exercise his right to buy – better to make a penny and cut his losses to 41p than lose the whole 42p.

The most Steve can gain is the premium, ie, 42p. Steve's potential loss, however, is theoretically unlimited, unless he actually holds the underlying shares.

Staying with that example, we can look at the terms 'covered' and 'naked' in relation to options. The writer of the option is hoping that the investor will not exercise his right to buy the underlying shares and then he can simply pocket the premium. This obviously presents a risk because if the price does rise then the writer will need to find the shares to meet his obligation. He may not have the shares to deliver and may have to buy these in the market, in which case his position is referred to as being **naked** (ie, he does not have the underlying asset – the shares). Alternatively, he may hold the shares, and his position would be referred to as **covered**.

4. Swaps

Learning Objective

6.6.1   Know the definition and function of an interest rate swap

6.6.2   Know the definition and function of credit default swaps

4.1 Description of Swaps

A swap is an agreement to exchange one set of cash flows for another. They are most commonly used to switch financing from one currency to another or to replace floating interest with fixed interest.

Swaps are a form of OTC derivative and are negotiated between the parties to meet the different needs of customers, so each tends to be unique.

4.2 Interest Rate Swaps

Interest rate swaps are the most common form of swaps.

They involve an exchange of interest payments and are usually constructed whereby one leg of the swap is a payment of a fixed rate of interest and the other leg is a payment of a floating rate of interest.

They are usually used to hedge exposure to interest rate changes and can be most easily appreciated by looking at an example.

Example

Company A is embarking on a three-year project to build and equip a new manufacturing plant and borrows funds to finance the cost. Because of its size and credit status, it has no choice but to borrow at variable rates.

It can reasonably estimate what additional returns its new plant will generate but, because the interest it is paying will be variable, it is exposed to the risk that the project may turn out to be uneconomic if interest rates rise unexpectedly.

If the company could secure fixed-rate finance, it could remove the risk of interest rate variations and more accurately predict the returns it can make from its investment.

To do this, Company A could enter into an interest rate swap with an investment bank. Under the terms of the swap, Company A pays a fixed rate to the investment bank and in exchange receives an amount of interest calculated on a variable rate. With the amount it receives from the investment bank, it then has the funds to settle its variable-rate lending, even if rates increase. In this way, it has hedged its concerns about interest rates rising.

The two exchanges of cash flow are known as the **legs** of the swap and the amounts to be exchanged are calculated by reference to a **notional amount**. The notional amount in the above example would be the amount that Company A has borrowed to fund its project. It is referred to as the notional amount as it is needed in order to calculate the amounts of interest due, but is never exchanged.

Typically, one party will pay an amount based on a fixed rate to the other party, who will pay back an amount of interest that is variable and usually based on LIBOR (the London Inter-Bank Offered Rate – a rate that is established and published daily) or another benchmark rate. The variable rate will usually be set as LIBOR plus, say, 0.5%, and will be reset quarterly. The variable rate is often described as the floating rate.

4.3 Credit Default Swaps

In recent years there has been significant growth in the use of credit derivatives, of which a credit default swap (CDS) is just one example.

Credit derivatives are instruments whose value depends on agreed credit events relating to a third-party company, for example, changes to the credit rating of that company, or an increase in that company's cost of funds in the market, or credit events relating to it. Credit events are typically defined as including a material default, bankruptcy, a significant fall in an asset's value, or debt restructuring, for a specified reference asset.

The purpose of credit derivatives is to enable an organisation to protect itself against unwanted credit exposure, by passing that exposure on to someone else. Credit derivatives can also be used to increase credit exposure, in return for income.

Although a CDS has the word 'swap' in its name, it is not like other types of swaps, which are based on the exchange of cash flows. A CDS is actually more like an option. In a credit default swap, the party buying credit protection makes a periodic payment (or pays an up-front fee) to a second party, the seller. In return, the buyer receives an agreed compensation if there is a credit event relating to some third party or parties. If such a credit event occurs, the seller makes a predetermined payment to the buyer, and the CDS then terminates.

5. Derivatives and Commodity Markets

Learning Objective

6.5.1 Know the characteristics of the derivatives and commodity markets

As we saw earlier, a derivative is a financial instrument whose price is derived from that of another asset (the other asset being known as the 'underlying asset', or sometimes 'the underlying' for short).

Derivatives are often thought of as dangerous instruments that are impenetrably complex. While derivatives can be complex and present systemic risks, they are chiefly designed to be used to reduce the risk faced by organisations and individuals, a process known as hedging. Equally, many derivatives are not particularly complex.

As an example, imagine that you wanted to purchase a large amount of wheat from a wholesale supplier. You contact the supplier and see that it will cost the sterling equivalent of $5 a bushel. But you discover that the wheat is currently out of stock in the warehouse. However, you can sign a contract to accept delivery of the wheat in one month's time (when the stock will be replenished) and at that stage the store will charge the $5 for each bushel you order now. If you sign, you have agreed to defer delivery for one month – and you have purchased into a derivative.

The physical trading of commodities takes place side by side with the trading of derivatives. The physical market concerns itself with procuring, transporting and consuming real commodities by the shipload on a global basis. This trade is dominated by major international trading houses, governments, and the major producers and consumers. The derivatives markets exist in parallel and serve to provide a price-fixing mechanism whereby all stakeholders in the physical markets can hedge market price risk.

Another aspect of commodity markets, more recent in origin but highly developed, is the use of commodities as an investment asset class in its own right.

5.1 Derivatives Markets

Broadly speaking, there are two distinct groups of derivatives, differentiated by how they are traded. These are OTC derivatives and exchange-traded derivatives (ETDs).

OTC derivatives are negotiated and traded privately between parties without the use of an exchange. Products such as interest rate swaps, forward rate agreements and other exotic derivatives are mainly traded in this way.

The OTC market is the larger of the two in terms of value of contracts traded daily. Trading takes place predominantly in Europe and, particularly, in the UK (note: there is considerable activity taking place at the moment to move OTC trading on-exchange in response to regulatory concerns about the risks posed by OTC derivative trading).

Exchange-traded derivatives are ones that have standardised features and can therefore be traded on an organised exchange, such as single stock or index derivatives. The role of the exchange is to provide a marketplace for trading to take place, but also to stand between each party to a trade to provide a guarantee that the trade will eventually be settled. It does this by acting as an intermediary (central counterparty) for all trades and by requiring participants to post a margin, which is a proportion of the value of the trade, for all transactions that are entered into.

5.2 Physical Markets

There are a number of different commodity markets, which are differentiated by the commodity that is traded. Some of the main ones are:

- agricultural markets
- base and precious metals
- energy markets
- power markets
- plastics markets
- emissions markets
- freight and shipping markets.

As an example, we will consider the features of the base and precious metals markets and energy markets below.

Example

Base and Precious Metals

There are numerous metals produced worldwide and subsequently refined for use in a large variety of products and processes.

As with all other commodity prices, metal prices are influenced by supply and demand.

The factors influencing supply include the availability of raw materials and the costs of extraction and production.

Demand comes from underlying users of the commodity, eg, the demand for metals in rapidly industrialising economies, including China and India. It also originates from investors such as hedge funds which might buy metal futures in anticipation of excess demand, or incorporate commodities into specific funds. Producers use the market for hedging their production. Traditionally, the price of precious metals such as gold will rise in times of crisis – gold is often seen as a safe haven.

Example

Energy Markets

The energy market includes the market for oil (and other oil-based products like petroleum), natural gas and coal.

Oil includes both crude oil and various 'fractions' produced as a result of the refining process, such as naphtha, butanes, kerosene, petrol and heating/gas oil. Crude oil is defined by three primary factors:

Field of origin, for example, Brent, West Texas Intermediate, Dubai.

Density, ie, low density or 'light', high density or 'heavy'.

Sulphur content, ie, low sulphur (known as 'sweet') or high sulphur (known as 'sour').

Demand for oil and gas is ultimately driven by levels of consumption, which in turn is driven by energy needs, eg, from manufacturing industry and transport. Supply of these commodities is finite, and countries with surplus oil and gas reserves are able to export to those countries with insufficient oil and gas to meet their requirements. In the past, oil producing countries that are members of the Organisation of Petroleum Exporting Countries (OPEC) would regularly restrict the supply of oil in order to keep prices high or to drive them up. More recently, prices of oil have dropped significantly due to a combination of oversupply and competition between oil-producing states.

5.3 Derivatives Exchanges

Details of some of the main derivatives exchanges in Europe are shown below.

ICE Futures Europe

In 2001, Euronext purchased a derivatives exchange in London called LIFFE (pronounced 'life') and renamed it Euronext.liffe. LIFFE was originally an acronym for the London International Financial Futures and Options Exchange, originally set up in 1982. It is now part of ICE following the takeover of NYSE Euronext.

ICE Futures Europe is the main exchange for trading financial derivative products in the UK, including futures and options on:

- interest rates and bonds
- equity indices (eg, FTSE)
- individual equities (eg, BP, HSBC).

It also trades derivatives on soft commodities, such as sugar, wheat and cocoa. It also runs futures and options markets in Amsterdam, Brussels, Lisbon and Paris.

Eurex

Eurex is the world's leading international derivatives exchange and is based in Frankfurt. Its principal products are German bond futures and options, the most well-known of which are contracts on the Bund (a German bond). It also trades index products for a range of European markets.

Eurex was created by Deutsche Börse AG and the Swiss Exchange. Trading is on the fully computerised Eurex platform, and its members are linked to the Eurex system via a dedicated wide-area communications network (WAN). This enables members from across Europe and the US to access Eurex outside Switzerland and Germany.

Intercontinental Exchange (ICE)

ICE operates the electronic global futures and OTC marketplace for trading energy commodity contracts. These contracts include crude oil and refined products, natural gas, power and emissions.

The company's regulated futures and options business, formerly known as the International Petroleum Exchange (IPE), now operates under the name ICE Futures. ICE acquired the London-based energy futures and options exchange in 2001 and completed the transition from open outcry to electronic trading in April 2005.

ICE Futures is Europe's leading energy futures and options exchange. ICE's products include derivative contracts based on key energy commodities: crude oil and refined oil products, such as heating oil and jet fuel and other products, like natural gas and electric power. With the acquisition of LIFFE, its range of tradable products expanded to include futures and options on bonds, equities and indices.

ICE's other markets are centred in North America and include trading of agricultural, currency and stock index futures and options. It also took over NYSE Euronext and, as a result, by acquiring LIFFE, became the world's largest derivatives exchange operator.

London Metal Exchange (LME)

The London Metal Exchange is the world's premier non-ferrous metals market and has been operating for over 130 years. Although it is based in London, it is a global market with an international membership and with more than 95% of its business coming from overseas.

Futures and options contracts are traded on a range of metals, including aluminium, copper, nickel, tin, zinc and lead. More recently, it has also launched the world's first futures contracts for plastics.

Trading on the LME takes place in three ways: through open outcry trading in the 'ring', through an inter-office telephone market and through **LME Select**, the exchange's electronic trading platform.

5.4 Investing in Derivatives Markets

Learning Objective

6.5.2 Know the potential advantages and disadvantages of investing in the derivatives and commodity markets

Having looked at various types of derivatives and their main uses, we can summarise some of the main advantages and disadvantages of investing in derivatives.

Advantages

- Enables producers and consumers of goods to agree the price of a commodity today for future delivery, which can remove the uncertainty of what price will be achieved for the producer and the risk of lack of supply for the consumer.
- Enables investment firms to hedge the risk associated with a portfolio or an individual stock.
- Offers the ability to speculate on a wide range of assets and markets to make large bets on price movements using the geared nature of derivatives.

Drawbacks and Risks

- Some types of derivatives investment can involve the investor losing more than their initial outlay and, in some cases, facing potentially unlimited losses.
- Derivatives markets thrive on price volatility, meaning that professional investment skills and experience are required.
- In the OTC markets, there is a risk that a counterparty may default on their obligations, and so it requires great attention to detail in terms of counterparty risk assessment, documentation and the taking of collateral.

End of Chapter Questions

Think of an answer for each question and refer to the appropriate section for confirmation.

1. What are the main investment uses of derivatives?
   Answer Reference: Section 1.1

2. What is the key difference between a future and an option?
   Answer Reference: Sections 2.2 & 3.2

3. What is the seller of a future known as?
   Answer Reference: Section 2.3

4. What is an investor who enters into a contract for the delivery of an asset in three months' time known as?
   Answer Reference: Section 2.3

5. What name is given to the seller of an option?
   Answer Reference: Section 3.3

6. What type of option gives the holder the right to sell an asset?
   Answer Reference: Section 3.3

7. What is the price paid for an option known as and who is it paid to?
   Answer Reference: Section 3.3

8. Which type of derivative is not exchange-traded?
   Answer Reference: Section 4.1

9. What is an interest rate swap?
   Answer Reference: Section 4.2

10. What are the main types of contract traded on the LME and Eurex?
    Answer Reference: Section 5.3

11. What are the main advantages and disadvantages of investing in derivatives?
    Answer Reference: Section 5.4

Chapter Seven
Investment Funds

1. Introduction — 111
2. Unit Trusts — 118
3. Open-Ended Investment Companies (OEICs) — 119
4. Pricing, Dealing and Settlement — 120
5. Investment Trusts — 122
6. Exchange-Traded Funds (ETFs) — 125
7. Summary: Comparison Between Investment Companies — 126
8. Hedge Funds — 127

This syllabus area will provide approximately 7 of the 50 examination questions

Investment Funds

1. Introduction

The asset management industry forms a major part of the UK's financial services industry and is responsible for the investment management of institutional and retail funds totalling over £4 trillion.

The size and scale of the industry can be seen in the regular reports issued by the Investment Association (IA). The IA is the trade body for the UK-based asset management industry. Its members manage a wide variety of investment vehicles including authorised investment funds, pension funds and Stocks & Shares ISAs. Its role is to represent the industry, principally to government and regulators as well as the press and public, and to promote high standards.

How its member firms relate to the rest of the industry can be seen from the diagram below.

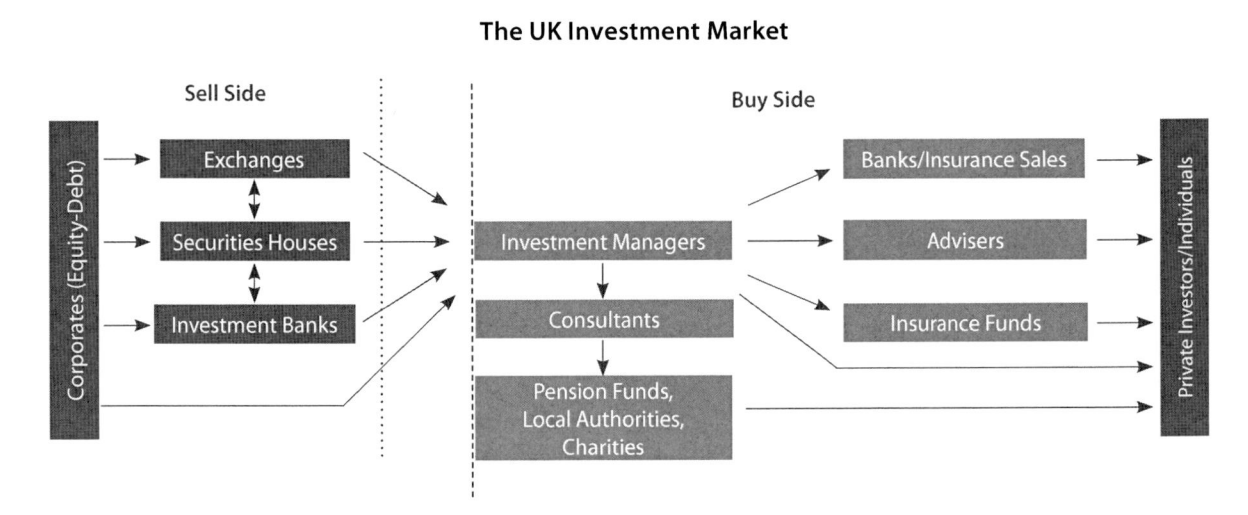

The UK Investment Market

Source: Investment Association (IA)

1.1 Key Considerations

Before we consider the benefits of collective investment and the range of investment styles that are available, we should first look at some of the key considerations that an individual should take into account when determining where to invest and choosing between the types of investment funds that are available.

Before making any investments, the investor should ensure they have sufficient cash resources and then consider some of the following points:

- **What am I investing for?** – the answer, be it retirement, to meet school fees or any other reason, will give some direction to the type of investment that may be suitable.
- **What amount of money will I need?** – an assessment of how much money will eventually be needed determines how much will need to be invested to achieve that goal and whether this is affordable.
- **Over what timescale do I want investment returns?** – this, along with the reason for investing, will give the timescale over which investment needs to be made.

- **What risks am I prepared to take?** – if an individual is going to invest, they will need to be prepared to take some risk in the hope of greater reward. They must be prepared to see at least some fall in the value of their investment without panicking, and be willing to hold on in the hope of future gains. If they are not prepared to take any risk whatsoever, then investing in the stock market is not the right option.
- **What types of assets are right for me?** – each type of asset carries risks and these need to be understood so that the right type of asset can be selected that can meet the individual's long-term objective with an acceptable level of risk.
- **How can I avoid risk?** – risk cannot be totally avoided, but diversifying the range of assets held reduces the risks that are faced.
- **What mix of investments is best suited to my objectives and attitude to risk?** – the right mix of assets – cash, bonds, shares and property – that is best suited will depend on the individual's investment objective, their attitude to risk, and the timescale over which they are investing. The mix will also need to change if the individual's circumstances change and as the time when the investment funds are needed approaches.
- **Do I need income now or later?** – if income is taken to spend, then the investment will grow more slowly, whereas if it is reinvested it will allow interest to be earned on interest, and this compounding of interest will generate further growth.

This is only a brief consideration of some of the many questions that all individuals need to consider both before investing and when reviewing existing investments, so individuals are well advised to seek professional advice from a qualified financial adviser.

1.2 The Benefits of Collective Investment

Learning Objective

7.1.1 Understand the potential advantages and disadvantages of collective investment

When investors decide to invest in a particular asset class, such as equities, there are two ways they can do it – direct investment or indirect investment.

Direct investment is when an individual personally buys shares in a company, such as in BP, the oil giant. Indirect investment is when an individual buys a stake in an investment fund, such as a mutual fund that invests in the shares of a range of different types of companies, perhaps including BP.

Collective investment schemes (funds) pool the resources of a large number of investors, with the aim of pursuing a common investment objective.

This pooling of funds brings a number of benefits, including:

- economies of scale
- diversification
- access to professional investment management
- access to geographical markets, asset classes or investment strategies which might otherwise be inaccessible to the individual investor

- in many cases, the benefit of regulatory oversight
- in some cases, tax deferral.

The value of shares and most other investments can fall as well as rise. Some might fall spectacularly, for example, shares in a company that suddenly collapses, such as Northern Rock and Lehman Brothers. However, if an investor holds a diversified pool of investments in a portfolio, the risk of single constituent investments falling spectacularly can normally be offset by outperformance on the part of other investments. In other words, risk is lessened when the investor holds a diversified portfolio of investments (of course, the opportunity of a startling outperformance is also diversified away – but many investors are happy with this if it reduces their risk of total or significant loss).

However, an investor needs a substantial amount of money before they can create a diversified portfolio of investments directly. If an investor has only £3,000 to invest and wants to buy the shares of 30 different companies, each investment would be £100. This would result in a large amount of the £3,000 being spent on commission, since there will be minimum commission rates of, say, £10 on each purchase. Instead, an investment of £3,000 might go into a fund with, say, 80 different investments, but, because the investment is being pooled with those of lots of other investors, the commission, as a proportion of the fund, is very small.

A fund might be invested in shares from many different sectors; this achieves diversification from an industry perspective (thereby reducing the risk of investing in a number of shares whose performance is closely correlated). Alternatively it may invest in a variety of bonds or a mix of cash, equities, bonds and property. Some collective investments put limited amounts of investment into bank deposits and even into other collective investments.

The other main rationale for investing collectively is to access the investing skills of the fund manager. Fund managers follow their chosen markets closely and will carefully consider what to buy and whether to keep or sell their chosen investments. Few investors have the skill, time or inclination to do this as effectively themselves.

However, fund managers do not manage portfolios for nothing. They might charge investors fees to become involved in their collective investments (entry fees or initial charges) or to leave the collective investment (exit charges) plus annual management fees. These fees are needed to cover the fund managers' salaries, technology, research, their dealing, settlement and risk management systems, and to provide a profit. Equally, there is no guarantee of the investment performance of the fund or of how it will perform in comparison to similar funds or benchmarks.

1.3 Investment Styles

Learning Objective

7.1.2 Know the difference between active and passive management

There is a wide range of funds with many different investment objectives and investment styles. Each of these funds has an investment portfolio managed by a fund manager according to a clearly stated set of objectives. An example of an objective might be to invest in the shares of UK companies with above-average potential for capital growth and to outperform the FTSE All Share index. Other funds' objectives could be to maximise income or to achieve steady growth in capital and income.

In each case it will also be made clear what the fund manager will invest in, ie, shares and/or bonds and/or property and/or cash or money market instruments; and whether derivatives will be used to hedge currency or other market risks.

It is also important to understand the investment style the fund manager adopts. This refers to the fund manager's approach to choosing investments and meeting the fund's objectives. In this section we will look at the differences between active and passive management styles.

1.3.1 Active Management

Active management seeks to outperform a predetermined benchmark over a specified time period. It does so by employing fundamental and technical analysis to assist in the forecasting of future events, which may be economic or specific to a company, so as to determine the portfolio's holdings and the timing of purchases and sales. Actively managed funds usually have higher charges than passive funds.

Two commonly used terms in this context are 'top-down' or 'bottom-up'. **Top-down** means the manager focuses on economic and industry trends rather than the prospects of particular companies. **Bottom-up** means that the analysis of a company's net assets, future profitability and cash flow, and other company-specific indicators, is a priority.

Included in the bottom-up approach is a range of investment styles:

- **growth investing** – which is picking the shares of companies that present opportunities to grow significantly in the long term
- **value investing** – which is picking the shares of companies that are undervalued relative to their present and future profits or cash flows
- **momentum investing** – which is picking the shares whose share price is rising on the basis that this rise will continue
- **contrarian investing** – the flip side of momentum investing, which involves picking shares that are out of favour and may have 'hidden' value.

There is also a significant range of styles used by managers of hedge funds. Hedge funds are considered in Section 8.

1.3.2 Passive Management

Passive management is seen in those types of investment funds that are often described as index tracker funds. **Index-tracking**, or **indexation**, involves constructing a portfolio in such a way that it will track, or mimic, the performance of a recognised index.

Indexation is undertaken on the assumption that securities markets are **efficiently priced** and cannot therefore be consistently outperformed. Consequently, no attempt is made to forecast future events or outperform the broader market.

Investment Funds

The **advantages** of employing indexation are:

- Relatively few active portfolio managers consistently outperform benchmark equity indices.
- The fund's charges will typically be significantly lower than actively managed funds.
- Once set up, passive portfolios are generally less expensive to run than active portfolios, given a lower ratio of staff to funds managed and lower portfolio turnover.

The **disadvantages** of adopting indexation include:

- Performance is affected by the need to manage cash flows, rebalance the portfolio to replicate changes in index-constituent weightings, and adjust the portfolio for stocks coming into, and falling out of, the index. This can lead to tracking error when the performance does not match that of the underlying index.
- Most indices reflect the effect of the value of dividends from constituent equities on the ex-dividend date.
- Indexed portfolios may not meet all of an investor's objectives.
- Indexed portfolios follow the index down in bear markets.

1.3.3 Combining Active and Passive Management

It should be noted that active and passive investment are not necessarily mutually exclusive and there are investment strategies that incorporate both styles, known as **core-satellite management**.

This is achieved by indexing, say, 70–80% of the portfolio's value (the 'core'), so as to minimise the risk of underperformance, and then fine-tuning this by investing the remainder in a number of specialist actively managed funds or individual securities. This is the 'satellite' element of the fund.

1.4 Range of Funds Available

Learning Objective

7.1.4 Know the types of funds and how they are classified

There are almost 2,500 UK-domiciled authorised investment funds available to investors and, unsurprisingly, a method of classifying them is needed in order to allow investors to compare funds with similar objectives.

The **Investment Association (IA)** is the trade body for the UK authorised open-ended funds industry; it maintains a system for classifying funds. The **Association of Investment Companies (AIC)** occupies a similar role for investment trusts (closed-ended companies).

The IA's classification system contains over 30 sectors grouping similar funds together. Most sectors are broadly categorised between those designed to provide 'income' and those designed to provide 'growth'. Those funds that do not fall easily under these headings are in another category entitled 'specialist funds'.

Each of the sectors is made up of funds investing in similar asset categories, in the same stock market sectors or in the same geographical region. So, for example, under the heading of funds principally targeting income you will find sectors that include UK gilts, UK corporate bonds and global bonds. See the table below for an example.

Example

A useful example of how the IA sectors work can be seen by looking at bond funds and how the content of each differs.

UK Gilts	Funds which invest at least 95% of their assets in sterling-denominated (or hedged back to sterling) government-backed securities, with a rating the same as or higher than that of the UK, with at least 80% invested in UK government securities (gilts).
UK Index-Linked Gilts	Funds which invest at least 95% of their assets in sterling-denominated (or hedged back to sterling) government-backed index-linked securities, with a rating the same as or higher than that of the UK, with at least 80% invested in UK index-linked gilts.
£ Corporate Bonds	Funds which invest at least 80% of their assets in sterling-denominated (or hedged back to sterling), triple BBB-minus or above corporate bond securities (as measured by Standard & Poor's or an equivalent external rating agency). This excludes convertibles, preference shares and permanent interest-bearing shares (PIBS).
£ Strategic Bonds	Funds which invest at least 80% of their assets in sterling-denominated (or hedged back to sterling) fixed-interest securities. This includes convertibles, preference shares and permanent interest-bearing shares (PIBS). At any point in time, the asset allocation of these funds could theoretically place the fund in one of the other fixed interest sectors. The funds will remain in this sector on these occasions since it is the manager's stated intention to retain the right to invest across the sterling fixed-interest credit risk spectrum.
£ High Yield	Funds which invest at least 80% of their assets in sterling-denominated (or hedged back to sterling) fixed-interest securities and at least 50% of their assets in below BBB-minus fixed-interest securities (as measured by Standard & Poor's or an equivalent external rating agency), including convertibles, preference shares and permanent interest-bearing shares (PIBs).
Global Bonds	Funds which invest at least 80% of their assets in fixed-interest securities. All funds which contain more than 80% fixed-interest investments are to be classified under this heading regardless of the fact that they may have more than 80% in a particular geographic sector, unless that geographic area is the UK, when the fund should be classified under the relevant UK (sterling) heading.

The sectors are aimed at the needs of the investor who has a desire to compare funds on a like-for-like basis. Sector classification provides groups of similar funds whose performance can be fairly compared by an investor and their adviser.

Investment Funds

1.5 UCITS and NURS

Learning Objective

7.1.3 Know the purpose and principal features of UCITS/NURS

As you would expect, the investment industry has many regulations designed to protect investors. Some of these regulations govern permissible investments and the documentation an investor can expect to receive.

EU directives have been issued in order to promote a single market in investment funds and these heavily influence UK regulation. In the UK, the FCA, through its Collective Investment Schemes Sourcebook (COLL) and Investment Funds Sourcebook (FUND), implements these.

UCITS stands for 'Undertakings for Collective Investment in Transferable Securities' and refers to a series of EU regulations that were originally designed to facilitate the promotion of funds to retail investors across Europe. A UCITS fund, therefore, complies with the requirements of these directives, no matter which EU country it is established in.

The directives have been issued with the intention of creating a framework for cross-border sales of investment funds throughout the EU. They allow an investment fund to be sold throughout the EU, subject to regulation by its home country regulator.

The key point to note, therefore, is that when an investment fund first seeks authorisation from its regulator it will seek authorisation as a UCITS fund. Instead of it just being authorised by the FCA for marketing to the general public in the UK, approval as a UCITS fund means that it can be marketed across Europe.

The original directive was issued in 1985 and established a set of EU-wide rules governing collective investment schemes. Funds set up in accordance with these rules could then be sold across the EU, subject to local tax and marketing laws.

Since then, further directives have been issued which broadened the range of assets a fund can invest in – in particular, allowing managers to use derivatives more freely.

While UCITS regulations are not directly applicable outside the EU, other jurisdictions, such as Switzerland and Hong Kong, recognise UCITS when funds are applying for registration to sell into those countries. In many countries, UCITS is seen as a brand signifying the quality of how a fund is managed, administered and supervised by regulators.

Funds can also be set up under NURS regulations. NURS stands for Non-UCITS Retail Scheme and these are funds that are deemed by the UK regulator to be suitable for retail investors, but do not meet the more prescriptive rules of the European UCITS Directive. These allow a greater range of investment opportunities including direct investment in property. Many fund of funds have adopted NURS as this allows the use of a much wider range of underlying investments.

Both of these approaches allow an investment fund to adopt more flexible approaches to risk and asset allocation.

117

2. Unit Trusts

Learning Objective

7.2.1 Know the definition and legal structure of a unit trust

7.2.2 Know the roles of the manager and the trustee

A unit trust is a collective investment scheme in the form of a **trust** in which the trustee is the legal owner of the underlying assets and the unitholders are the beneficial owners. It may be authorised or unauthorised.

Investors pay money into the trust in exchange for units. The money is invested in a diversified portfolio of assets, usually consisting of shares or bonds or a mix of the two. If the diversified portfolio increases in value, the value of the units will increase. Of course, there is a possibility that the portfolio might fall in value, in which case the units will also decrease in value.

The unit trust is often described as an **open-ended** collective investment scheme because the trust can grow as more investors buy into the fund, or shrink as investors sell units back to the fund and they are either cancelled or reissued to new investors.

The role of the **unit trust manager** is to decide, within the rules of the trust and the various regulations, which investments are included within the unit trust to meet its investment objectives. This will include deciding what to buy and when to buy it, as well as what to sell and when to sell it. The unit trust manager may (and commonly does) outsource this decision-making to a separate investment manager.

The manager also provides a market for the units, by dealing with investors who want to buy or sell units. The manager also carries out the **daily pricing** of units, which is based on the **net asset value (NAV)** of the underlying constituents.

Every unit trust must also appoint a **trustee**. The trustee is the legal owner of the assets in the trust, holding the assets for the benefit of the underlying unit holders.

The trustee also protects the interests of the investors by, among other things, monitoring the actions of the unit trust manager. Whenever new units are created for the trust, they are created by the trustee. The trustees are organisations that the unit holders can 'trust' with their assets.

For authorised unit trusts (AUTs), the trustees are companies subject to special regulation – all part of global banking groups.

3. Open-Ended Investment Companies (OEICs)

Learning Objective

7.3.1 Know the definition and legal structure of an OEIC/ICVC/SICAV

7.3.2 Know the roles of the authorised corporate director and the depository

An open-ended investment company (OEIC) is another form of authorised collective investment scheme. OEICs are referred to as **investment companies with variable capital (ICVCs)** by the FCA.

An ICVC commonly found in Western Europe is the **Société d'Investissement à Capital Variable (SICAV).** Like a UK OEIC, it is an investment company with variable capital. SICAVs are typically set up in Luxembourg by asset management firms so that they can be distributed to investors across Europe or further afield.

An OEIC is a collective investment scheme structured as a **company**, with the investors holding **shares**.

The OEIC invests shareholders' money in a diversified pool of investments. As their name suggests, OEICs are companies, but they differ from conventional companies because they are established under special legislation and not the Companies Acts. They must create new shares and redeem existing ones according to investor demand, unlike ordinary companies. This means they are open-ended in nature, just like unit trusts.

When an OEIC is set up, it is a requirement that an **authorised corporate director (ACD)** and a depository are appointed. The ACD is responsible for the day-to-day management of the fund, including managing the investments, valuing and pricing the fund and dealing with investors. It may undertake these activities itself or delegate them to specialist third parties. It is subject to the same requirements as the manager of an authorised unit trust (AUT).

The OEIC's investments are held by an independent **depository**, responsible for looking after the investments on behalf of the OEIC shareholders and overseeing the activities of the ACD. The depository occupies a similar role to that of the trustee of an authorised unit trust and is subject to the same regulatory requirements.

The register of shareholders is maintained by the ACD.

4. Pricing, Dealing and Settlement

4.1 Pricing and Charges

Learning Objective

7.4.1 Know how unit trusts and OEIC shares are priced

The prices at which authorised unit trusts or OEICs are bought and sold are based on the value of the fund's underlying investments – the **net asset value**. The authorised fund manager is, however, given the flexibility to quote prices, which can be either single-priced or dual-priced (although this decision must be taken at the outset and the manager cannot switch between the two as and when it suits).

Single pricing refers to the use of the mid-market prices of the underlying assets to produce a single price, while **dual pricing** involves using the market's bid and offer prices of the underlying assets to produce separate prices for buying and selling of shares/units in the fund. Traditionally, authorised unit trusts have used dual pricing and OEICs have used single pricing. All funds now have a choice of which pricing methodology they use; whichever is chosen must be disclosed in the prospectus.

When a fund is single-priced, with its underlying investments valued based on their mid-market value, this method of pricing does not provide the ability to recoup dealing expenses and commissions within the spread. Where necessary, such costs are recouped either by applying a separate charge, known as a **dilution levy**, on purchases or redemptions, or by **swinging** the daily price to a dual-priced basis depending on the ratio of buyers and sellers on any day. It is important to note that the initial charge will be charged separately, whichever pricing method is used.

The maximum price at which the fund manager is able to sell new units is prescribed by the FCA. It is known as the **maximum buying price** and, under dual pricing, comprises the creation price (ie, the price the manager must pay to the trustee to create new units, which broadly consists of the value of the underlying investments and an allowance for dealing costs) plus the fund manager's initial charge.

Example

Value of the portfolio (at offer prices) divided by the number of units	100.00p
Add, allowance for dealing costs: brokerage at, say, ¼%	0.25p
Stamp duty at ½%	0.50p
Subtotal (= creation price)	100.75p
Add, fund manager's initial charge at, say, 6.55%	6.55p
Maximum buying price	107.30p

The actual buying price does not have to be 107.30p and, because of the sensitivity of investors to charges, the fund manager may feel that a lower price of, say, 103p per unit is more appropriate.

The price at which the fund manager will repurchase units is calculated in a similar manner. From the investor's viewpoint it is referred to as the selling price, and the **minimum selling price** is also the cancellation price, ie, the price received from the fund by the manager when he cancels the units, using as its starting point the value of the portfolio at bid prices. Again, the manager has flexibility about the price that is set, subject to its being no less than the minimum selling price.

The prices of most individual funds are provided in broadsheet newspapers each day. The telephone numbers and addresses of the fund managers are normally provided alongside the prices.

4.2 Dealing and Settlement

Learning Objective

7.4.2 Know how shares and units are bought and sold

7.4.3 Know how collectives are settled

Investors can buy or sell units in a number of ways:

- direct with the fund manager (either by telephone, via the internet or by post)
- via their broker or financial adviser
- through a fund supermarket or platform.

Whether an investor wishes to buy or sell his units, they will be either bought from, or sold back to, the authorised fund manager. There is no active secondary market in units or shares, except between the investors (or their advisers/intermediaries) and the fund manager. The key point to note, therefore, is that units in AUTs and shares in OEICs are bought from the managers themselves and not via a stock market.

A **fund supermarket** or **platform** is an organisation that specialises in offering investors easy access to a range of unit trusts and OEICs from different providers. They are usually based around an internet platform which takes the investor's order and processes it on their behalf, usually at reduced, or nil, commission rates. They offer online dealing, valuations, portfolio planning tools and access to key features documents and illustrations. Investors can look at their various holdings in different funds in one place, analyse their performance and easily make switches from one fund to another.

Settlement currently takes place directly with each fund group. For **purchases**, once the investment has been made and the amount invested has been received, the fund group will record ownership of the relevant number of units or shares in the fund's share register. When the investor decides to **sell**, they need to instruct the fund manager (or ask their adviser or the supermarket to instruct the fund manager), who then has four days from receipt of the instruction and necessary paperwork in which to settle the sale and remit the proceeds to the investor. Traditionally, this instruction had to be in writing but, since 2009, managers have been able to accept instruction via the internet or over the telephone, using appropriate security checks.

When an order to buy or sell units is undertaken by an organisation that provides dealing services, such as a fund supermarket, it is likely to use a **systems platform** to place those orders with the fund management group.

One widely used system is **EMX**, which can be used by firms to enter customer orders, aggregate these and then send them electronically to the fund group. The firm then receives an electronic confirmation of receipt and, once the deal is traded at the next valuation point, EMX will send an electronic dealing confirmation showing the price at which the deal was done.

EMX was taken over by Euroclear UK & Ireland, the parent company that owns CREST, in late 2006 and it now has an automated **straight-through processing (STP)** platform for fund dealing and settlement.

5. Investment Trusts

Learning Objective

7.5.1   Know the characteristics of an investment trust: share classes; gearing; real estate investment trusts (REITs)

7.5.2   Understand the factors that affect the price of an investment trust

7.5.3   Know the meaning of the discounts and premiums in relation to investment trusts

7.5.4   Know how investment trust shares are traded

Despite its name, an investment trust is actually a company, not a trust. It is a **listed company** and has directors and shareholders. However, like a unit trust, an investment trust will invest in a diversified range of investments, allowing its shareholders to diversify and lessen their risk.

When a new investment company is established and launched, it issues **shares** to new investors. Unlike an authorised unit trust or OEIC, the number of shares is likely to remain fixed for many years. As a result, these investment companies are **closed-ended**, in contrast with AUTs and OEICs which are open-ended.

The cash from the primary issue of shares will be invested in a number of other investments, mainly the shares of other companies. If the value of the investments grows, then the value of the investment trust company's shares should rise too.

5.1   Share Classes

Some investment companies have more than one type of share and, if this is the case, they are known as **split-capital investment trusts**. For example, an investment trust might issue both ordinary shares and preference shares.

Preference shares may be issued on different terms and may, for example, be issued as **convertible preference shares** that are convertible into the ordinary shares or as **zero dividend preference (ZDP)**

shares. As the name suggests, ZDPs receive no dividends and the investor instead receives their return via the difference in the price they paid and the amount they receive when the ZDP is repaid at a fixed future date.

5.2 Real Estate Investment Trusts (REITs)

REITs are investment companies that pool investors' funds to invest in commercial and, possibly, residential property. They became available to UK investors from January 2007 and the main quoted property companies, such as Land Securities and British Land, have converted to REIT status.

One of the main features of REITs is that they provide access to property returns without the previous disadvantage of double taxation. Prior to the introduction of REITs, when an investor held property company shares, not only would the company pay corporation tax, but the investor would be liable to income tax on any dividends and capital gains tax on any growth. Under the rules, a REIT pays no tax on property income or capital gains on property disposals, providing that at least 90% of that income (after expenses) is distributed to shareholders. These property income distributions are then taxed in the hands of the investor as if they had received that income directly themselves (ie, it is not taxed as a dividend).

REITs may also be held in both individual savings accounts (ISAs) and self-invested personal pension schemes (SIPPs).

REITs give investors access to professional property investment and provide new opportunities, such as the ability to invest in commercial property. This allows investors to diversify the risk of holding direct property investments. This type of investment trust company also removes a further risk from holding direct property, namely liquidity risk or the risk that the investment will not be able to be readily realised.

REITs are **closed-ended**; like other investment trusts, they are quoted on the LSE and other trading venues and dealt in the same way.

5.3 Gearing

In contrast with OEICs and authorised unit trusts, investment companies are allowed to borrow more money on a long-term basis by taking out bank loans and/or issuing bonds. This can enable them to invest the borrowed money in more stocks and shares – a process known as **gearing**. This approach can improve returns when markets are rising, but when markets are falling it can exacerbate losses. As a result, the greater the level of gearing used by an investment trust, the greater will be the risk.

5.4 Pricing, Discounts and Premiums

The price of a share (except in the case of an OEIC share, as we have seen) is what someone is prepared to pay for it. The price of an investment trust share is no different.

The share price of an investment trust is thus arrived at in a very different way from the unit price of an authorised unit trust or the share price of an OEIC.

Remember that units in an authorised unit trust are bought and sold by its fund manager at a price that is based on the underlying value of the constituent investments. Similarly, shares in an OEIC are bought and sold by the authorised corporate director (ACD), again at the value of the underlying investments.

The share price of an investment trust, however, is *not* necessarily the same as the value of the underlying investments. The value of the underlying investments determined on a per share basis is referred to as the **net asset value** but, because the share price is driven by supply and demand factors, it may be above or below the net asset value.

- When the investment trust share price is **above the net asset value**, it is said to be trading at a **premium**.
- When the investment trust share price is **below the net asset value**, it is said to be trading at a **discount**.

Example

ABC Investment Trust shares are trading at £2.30. The net asset value per share is £2.00. ABC Investment Trust shares are trading at a premium. The premium is 15% of the underlying net asset value.

Example

XYZ Investment Trust shares are trading at 95p. The net asset value per share is £1.00. XYZ Investment Trust shares are trading at a discount. The discount is 5% of the underlying net asset value.

Investment trust company shares generally trade at a discount to their net asset value, and the extent of the discount is calculated daily and shown in the business pages of newspapers.

A number of factors contribute to the extent of the discount and it will vary across different investment companies. Most importantly, the discount is a function of the market's view of the quality of the management of the investment portfolio, and its choice of underlying investments. A smaller discount (or even a premium) will be displayed when investment trusts are nearing their winding-up, or about to undergo some corporate activity such as a merger/takeover. (You should note that some, but not all, investment trusts have a predetermined date at which the trust will be wound up and the assets returned to the shareholders.)

5.5 Trading in Investment Trust Shares

In the same way as other listed company shares, shares in investment trust companies are bought and sold on the LSE using the SETS trading system.

6. Exchange-Traded Funds (ETFs)

Learning Objective

7.6.1 Know the main characteristics of exchange-traded funds: trading; replication methods

An exchange-traded fund is an investment fund usually designed to track a particular index. This is typically a stock market index, such as the FTSE 100. The investor buys shares in the ETF which are quoted on the stock exchange, as with investment trusts. However, unlike investment trusts, ETFs are **open-ended funds**. This means that, like OEICs, the fund gets bigger as more people invest and smaller as people withdraw their money.

ETF shares may trade at a premium or discount to the underlying investments, but the difference is minimal and the ETF share price essentially reflects the value of the investments in the fund. The investor's return is in the form of dividends paid by the ETF and the possibility of a capital gain (or loss) on sale.

In London, ETFs are traded on the LSE, which has established a special subset of the Exchange for ETFs, called **extraMARK**. Shares in ETFs are bought and sold via stockbrokers and exhibit the following charges:

- There is a spread between the price at which investors buy the shares and the price at which they can sell them. This is usually very small, for example, just 0.1 or 0.2% for, say, an ETF tracking the FTSE 100.
- An annual management charge is deducted from the fund. Typically, this is 0.5% or less.
- The investors pay stockbroker's commission when they buy and sell. However, unlike other shares, there is no stamp duty to pay on purchases.

7. Summary: Comparison Between Investment Companies

The following table summarises the main points about each type of collective investment scheme.

	Authorised Unit Trusts	OEICs	Investment Trusts/REITs	Exchange-Traded Funds	Key Points
Legal Structure	Trust	Company	Company	Company	Despite the name 'investment trust', only unit trusts are truly structured as a trust.
Management	Authorised Manager (company)	Authorised Corporate Director (company)	Board of Directors	Management Company	The companies that act as manager tend to be investment management companies.
Supervision	Trustee	Depository	Board of Directors	Depository	Supervision for open-ended companies (OEICs and ETFs) is provided by a depository.
Regulation	FCA	FCA	UK Listing Authority	FCA and UK Listing Authority	In order to be listed on the exchange, companies have to satisfy the UK Listing Authority.
Open- or closed-ended	Open	Open	Closed	Open	Only investment trust companies are closed-ended.
Pricing	Single- or dual-priced	Single- or dual-priced	Dependent on demand and supply	Largely based on net asset value	It is only investment trust companies where the price can exhibit a substantial discount or premium to NAV.
Trading	Authorised Manager	Authorised Corporate Director	Stock Market	Stock Market	Trading for unit trust and OEICs is with the investment manager, not on the stock market.
Settlement	Authorised Manager	Authorised Corporate Director	CREST	CREST	Stock market-traded funds are settled via CREST.

8. Hedge Funds

Learning Objective

7.7.1 Know the basic characteristics of hedge funds: risks; cost and liquidity; investment strategies

Hedge funds are reputed to be high-risk. However, in some cases this perception stands at odds with reality. In their original incarnation, hedge funds sought to eliminate or reduce market risk. That said, there are now many different styles of hedge fund – some risk-averse, and some employing highly risky strategies. It is, therefore, not wise to generalise about them.

The most obvious market risk is the risk that is faced by an investor in shares – as the broad market moves down, the investor's shares also fall in value.

Traditional **absolute return** hedge funds attempt to profit regardless of the general movements of the market, by carefully selecting a combination of asset classes, including derivatives, and by holding both long and short positions (a short position may be 'naked', ie, involve the selling of shares which the fund does not at that time own in the hope of buying them back more cheaply if the market falls).

However, innovation has resulted in a wide range of complex hedge fund strategies, some of which place a greater emphasis on producing highly geared returns than on controlling market risk.

Many hedge funds have high initial investment levels, meaning that access is effectively restricted to wealthy investors and institutions. However, investors can also gain access to hedge funds through **funds of hedge funds**.

The common aspects of hedge funds are the following:

- **Structure** – most hedge funds are established as unauthorised, and therefore unregulated, collective investment schemes, meaning that they cannot be generally marketed to private individuals because they are considered too risky for the less financially sophisticated investor.
- **High investment entry levels** – most hedge funds require minimum investments in excess of £50,000; some exceed £1 million.
- **Investment flexibility** – because of the lack of regulation, hedge funds are able to invest in whatever assets they wish (subject to compliance with the restrictions in their constitutional documents and prospectus). In addition to being able to take long and short positions in securities such as shares and bonds, some take positions in commodities and currencies. Their investment style is generally aimed at producing 'absolute returns' – positive returns regardless of the general direction of market movements.
- **Gearing** – many hedge funds can borrow funds and use derivatives to potentially enhance their returns.
- **Prime broker** – hedge funds buy and sell investments from, borrow from and, often, entrust the safekeeping of their assets to one main wholesale broker, called their prime broker.
- **Liquidity** – to maximise the hedge fund manager's investment freedom, hedge funds usually impose an initial 'lock-in' period of between one and three months before investors can sell on their investments.
- **Cost** – hedge funds typically levy performance-related fees which the investor pays if certain performance levels are achieved, otherwise paying a fee comparable to that charged by other growth funds. Performance fees can be substantial, with 20% or more of the '**net new highs**' (also called the 'high water mark') being common.

End of Chapter Questions

Think of an answer for each question and refer to the appropriate section for confirmation.

1. How might the pooling of investment aid a retail investor?
   Answer Reference: Section 1.2

2. What is an investment management approach that seeks to produce returns in line with an index known as?
   Answer Reference: Section 1.3.2

3. Why would an investment fund seek UCITS status?
   Answer Reference: Section 1.5

4. Who is the legal owner of the investments held in an OEIC?
   Answer Reference: Section 3

5. In which type of collective investment vehicle would you be most likely to expect to see a fund manager quote bid and offer prices?
   Answer Reference: Section 4.1

6. How does the trading and settlement of an authorised unit trust differ from that of an ETF?
   Answer Reference: Sections 2, 6 & 7

7. What are some of the principal ways in which investment trusts differ from authorised unit trusts and OEICs?
   Answer Reference: Sections 5 & 7

8. Which is an open-ended type of investment vehicle that is traded on a stock exchange?
   Answer Reference: Sections 6 & 7

9. What type of investment vehicle makes extensive use of short positions?
   Answer Reference: Section 8

Chapter Eight
Financial Services Regulation and Professional Integrity

1.	Financial Services Regulation	131
2.	Financial Crime	139
3.	Insider Dealing	147
4.	Market Abuse	148
5.	Data Protection	149
6.	Complaints and Compensation	150
7.	Integrity and Ethics in Professional Practice	152

This syllabus area will provide approximately 6 of the 50 examination questions

Financial Services Regulation and Professional Integrity

1. Financial Services Regulation

An understanding of regulation is essential in today's investment world, and in this chapter we will consider some of the key aspects of regulation.

As this section considers UK regulation, much of the material has been sourced from publications issued by the UK's regulators.

1.1 The Need for Regulation

Learning Objective

8.1.1 Understand the need for regulation

The risk of monetary loss that can arise from dealing in all types of financial transactions has meant that financial markets have always been subject to the need for rules and codes of conduct to protect investors and the public.

As markets developed, there grew a need for market participants to be able to set rules so that there were agreed standards of behaviour, and to provide a mechanism so that disputes could be settled readily. This need developed into what is known as **self-regulation**, when, for example, a stock exchange, as well as providing a secondary market for shares, would also set rules for its members and police their implementation.

As markets, financial institutions and financial services developed, and the potential impact that they could have on both the economy and society grew, self-regulation became increasingly untenable, and most countries moved to a statutory approach and established their own **regulatory bodies**.

A comment by the head of the then UK regulator (the Financial Services Authority (FSA)) in 2005 spelled this out quite succinctly: 'Regulation exists because of the potential economic and social effects of major financial instability, the desirability of maintaining markets which are efficient, orderly and fair and the need to protect retail consumers in their dealings with the financial services industry'.

The development of global markets and a series of crises ranging from Barings Bank to Enron and WorldCom emphasised not only the need for improved regulation and standards, but for **international co-operation** to develop a common approach in a whole range of areas.

This was hugely exacerbated in 2008 as the global community battled against the effects of the financial crisis. With the increasing globalisation of financial markets there is a demand from governments and investment firms for a common approach to regulation in different countries. As a result, there is a significant level of co-operation between financial services regulators worldwide and, increasingly, common standards – money laundering rules being probably the best example.

The main purposes and aims of regulation, in all markets globally, are to:

- maintain and promote the fairness, efficiency, competitiveness, transparency and orderliness of markets
- promote understanding by the public of the operation and functioning of the financial services industry
- provide protection for members of the public investing in or holding financial products
- minimise crime and misconduct in the industry
- reduce systemic risks
- assist in maintaining the market's financial stability by taking appropriate steps.

1.2 The Impact of Regulation

Learning Objective

8.1.2 Know the function and impact of UK, European and US regulators in the financial services industry

As well as aiming to ensure that the EU has world-class regulatory standards, the EU is also particularly concerned with the development of a **single market** in financial services across Europe. This has been a major feature of European financial services legislation for some time, and is the cornerstone of the **Financial Services Action Plan (FSAP).**

Here we will look at how the EU introduces new regulation and how this gets translated into new rules in each EU country.

EU regulation comes about by way of a tiered approach to its creation and implementation. The approach used is known as the **Lamfalussy Process**, named after the chairman of the advisory committee who devised it. It comprises four levels:

- The first level involves the European Council and the European Parliament adopting in a co-decision procedure a piece of legislation – a framework directive – which establishes the core elements of regulation and sets guidelines for its implementation.
- The laws then progress to the second level, where sector-specific committees and regulators advise on the technical detail. The European Commission, based on this advice, then issues rules at a detailed level which do not have to go through the often lengthy co-decision process. The rules are only binding if they are a regulation – instead, directives have to be implemented nationally.
- At the third level, national regulators work on co-ordinating new regulations with other nations.
- The fourth level involves compliance and enforcement of the new rules and laws at national level by the European Commission.

This process was used to introduce the **Markets in Financial Instruments Directive (MiFID)**, which introduced European-wide rules and regulations regarding the conduct of business and organisation of firms within the financial industry. MiFID replaced the Investment Services Directive (ISD), issued in 1993, which had removed a major hurdle to cross-border business by specifying that, if a firm had been authorised in one member state to provide investment services, this single authorisation enabled

Financial Services Regulation and Professional Integrity

the firm to provide those investment services in other member states without requiring any further authorisation. This principle was, and still is, known as the **passport**.

On legislation related to securities markets, the European Commission is guided in its implementation by the **European Securities and Markets Authority (ESMA)**. This is an EU authority which is responsible both for drafting the legislation and for guiding it through EU implementation, overseeing national implementation and enforcement.

1.2.1 UK Regulation

In the UK, the financial services sector underwent a radical change on 1 December 2001 when the **Financial Services and Markets Act 2000 (FSMA)** came into force. Before FSMA, the various sectors of the industry were covered by a series of laws and the requirements of a mix of statutory and self-regulating organisations, regarded by some as unnecessarily complex and confusing.

Under FSMA, the government delegated overall responsibility for the regulation of the financial services industry to the **Financial Services Authority (FSA)**. In July 2009, HM Treasury proposed a series of sweeping policy initiatives around a number of core issues, one of which was the need to strengthen the UK's regulatory framework so that it was better equipped to deal with all firms and, in particular, globally interconnected markets and firms.

Thus, on 1 April 2013, the government transferred operational responsibility for prudential regulation from the FSA to a new subsidiary of the Bank of England, the Prudential Regulation Authority, and responsibility for market conduct to a new organisation called the Financial Conduct Authority.

Financial Policy Committee (FPC)

A new committee has been established in the Bank of England, with responsibility for 'macro-prudential' regulation, or regulation of the stability and resilience of the financial system as a whole. Its role is:

Contributing to the Bank's objective to protect and enhance financial stability, through identifying and taking action to remove or reduce systemic risks, with a view to protecting and enhancing the resilience of the UK financial system.

The FPC has the power to make recommendations on a comply-or-explain basis to the PRA and the FCA; that is, to comply with the recommendation as soon as practicable, or explain to the FPC, in writing and in public, why they have not done so.

Prudential Regulation Authority (PRA)

The Prudential Regulation Authority (PRA) is responsible for prudential regulation of financial firms that manage significant risks on their balance sheets – in other words, it is responsible for the regulation and supervision of 'significant' individual firms including all deposit-taking institutions, insurers and other prudentially significant investment firms. The latter include the supervision of central counterparties and securities settlement systems, and this responsibility sits alongside the BoE's existing responsibilities for overseeing recognised payment systems.

The PRA has a primary objective of enhancing financial stability by promoting the safety and soundness of PRA-authorised firms in a way which minimises the disruption caused by any firms which do fail. In fulfilling its objective, it will take an 'intrusive' approach to regulation and supervision.

Financial Conduct Authority (FCA)

The Financial Conduct Authority focuses on regulation of all firms in retail and wholesale financial markets, as well as the infrastructure that supports these markets. In effect it has responsibility for firms that do not fall under the PRA's scope (approximately 26,000 firms). The FCA's role includes:

- supervision of investment exchanges and monitoring firms' compliance with the Market Abuse Directive (MAD)
- powers to investigate and prosecute insider dealing
- responsibility for overseeing the Financial Ombudsman Service (FOS), the Money Advice Service (MAS) and the Financial Services Compensation Scheme (FSCS), working closely with the FPC and PRA.

Under FSMA, as amended by the **Financial Services Act 2012**, the FCA is responsible for:

- regulating standards of conduct in retail and wholesale markets
- supervising trading infrastructures that support those markets
- the prudential supervision of firms that are not PRA-regulated
- the functions of the UK Listing Authority (UKLA).

Its three **statutory objectives** are to:

- protect consumers
- enhance the integrity of the UK financial system
- help maintain competitive markets and promote effective competition in the interests of consumers.

These are supported by a set of principles of good regulation which the FCA must have regard to when discharging its functions.

HM Treasury is responsible for oversight of how the FCA conducts its operations, and so the FCA is accountable to Treasury ministers, and through them to Parliament.

1.2.2 US Regulation

At first sight, it may seem strange that the UK might be affected by US regulation until you consider the global nature of the firms that operate in the UK. These global operations mean that firms that operate both in the UK and the US are impacted by US regulation, and this has led to increasing co-operation between regulators on both sides of the Atlantic in order to agree and implement similar rules.

Financial Services Regulation and Professional Integrity

1.3 Authorisation

Learning Objective

8.1.3 Understand the reasons for authorisation of firms and approved persons

FSMA makes it an offence for a firm to provide financial services in the UK without being **authorised** to do so. There are certain exemptions from this requirement, for example for the Bank of England.

Authorisation is granted by the relevant regulator. Solo-regulated firms will need to be authorised by the FCA, but, following the establishment of the FCA and the PRA on 1 April 2013, some firms, known as dual-regulated firms, will be regulated by the FCA for the way they conduct their business and by the PRA for prudential requirements.

The regulator looks at each applicant to assess whether the firm is **fit and proper** and meets certain **threshold conditions**. Before granting authorisation, the regulator considers the company's management, its financial strength and the calibre of its staff. The latter is particularly important in certain key roles, which the regulator refers to as **controlled functions**.

By only allowing 'fit and proper' firms to be involved in the financial services industry, the regulator begins to satisfy the statutory objectives of enhancing the integrity of the financial system and of protecting consumers.

Authorised persons are firms but, as firms, they are ultimately operated by individuals – the directors and employees. When a firm applies for authorisation (and when there are changes to key staffing roles) the regulator will assess the calibre of these individuals. Particular individuals, fulfilling key roles within the firm known as 'controlled functions' (see 1.4 below), have to be approved. An individual may be permitted to perform a controlled function only after they have been granted **approved person** status by the regulator. It may grant an application only if it is satisfied that the candidate is a fit and proper person to perform the controlled function stated in the application form.

In assessing the fitness and propriety of a person, the regulator will look at a number of factors against three main criteria:

- **Honesty, integrity and reputation** – here it will consider such issues as any criminal record or history of regulatory misconduct.
- **Competence and capability** to fulfil the role – including achieving success in certain regulatory examinations.
- **Financial soundness** – here it will consider the capital adequacy of the applicant and their financial history; for instance, an undischarged bankrupt would be unlikely to be approved for many roles.

Once authorised, each financial services firm is governed by 11 key **Principles for Businesses** that it must adhere to at all times; if it fails to do so, it will be liable to disciplinary sanctions. The 11 principles are:

1. **Integrity** – a firm must conduct its business with integrity.
2. **Skill, care and diligence** – a firm must conduct its business with due skill, care and diligence.
3. **Management and control** – a firm must take reasonable care to organise and control its affairs responsibly and effectively, with adequate risk management systems.
4. **Financial prudence** – a firm must maintain adequate financial resources.

5. **Market conduct** – a firm must observe proper standards of market conduct.
6. **Customers' interests** – a firm must pay due regard to the interests of its customers and treat them fairly.
7. **Communications with clients** – a firm must pay due regard to the information needs of its clients, and communicate information to them in a way which is clear, fair and not misleading.
8. **Conflicts of interest** – a firm must manage conflicts of interest fairly, both between itself and its customers and between a customer and another client.
9. **Customers: relationships of trust** – a firm must take reasonable care to ensure the suitability of its advice and discretionary decisions for any customer who is entitled to rely upon its judgment.
10. **Clients' assets** – a firm must arrange adequate protection for clients' assets when it is responsible for them.
11. **Relations with regulators** – a firm must deal with its regulators in an open and co-operative way, and must appropriately disclose to the FCA or PRA anything relating to the firm of which the regulator would reasonably expect notice.

1.4 Controlled Functions

Learning Objective

8.1.4 Know the groups of activity (controlled functions) requiring approved person status

Controlled functions are those involved in dealing with customers or their investments, key managers in a firm including finance, compliance and risk, and those exercising a measure of control over the firm as a whole.

The FCA classifies controlled functions into groups, the first of which are **significant influence functions**:

- **Governing function** – for example, the directors of the firm.
- **Significant management function** – senior managers in the larger firms, such as the head of equity dealing.
- **Systems and control function** – mainly those responsible for risk management and internal audit.
- **Required functions** – specific roles, such as the director or senior manager responsible for compliance oversight.

The next group comprises:

- **Customer function** – for example, those individuals managing investments or providing advice to customers. Customer functions are not significant influence functions.

The final group relates to functions involved with setting benchmarks, such as the London Interbank Offered Rate (LIBOR).

The regulator details seven **Statements of Principle for Approved Persons** that controlled functions must observe as they carry out their duties:

1. Act with integrity.
2. Act with due skill, care and diligence.

3. Observe proper standards of market conduct.
4. Deal with regulators in an open and co-operative way.
5. Take reasonable steps to ensure that the business of the firm is organised so that it can be effectively controlled.
6. Exercise due skill, care and diligence in managing the business of the firm.
7. Take reasonable care to ensure the firm complies with the relevant requirements and standards of the regulatory regime.

By targeting these key individuals, the regulator aims to ensure that the culture and operation of a firm meets the spirit, as well as the letter, of the regulations. Breach of the regulations can lead to disciplinary action against the individual, with penalties ranging from public censure to fines, and ultimately being barred from working in the financial services industry.

Regulating the firm, and its key individuals, is essential to ensuring that firms act in an appropriate manner; equally, ensuring that each firm has well-trained and competent staff is a vital component in the quality of the investment and financial advice given to customers.

As a result, the FCA sets the following standards:

- It is the responsibility of the firm to ensure that staff members are appropriately qualified for their role.
- There is an obligation on firms to ensure that their employees continue to be competent.
- It is the firm's responsibility to have a sound training programme in place to ensure that its employees remain up to date with developments in the marketplace.

1.5 Conduct Risk

Learning Objective

8.1.5 Know the outcomes arising from the FCA's approach to managing good conduct within firms including Treating Customers Fairly

Since the financial crisis, conduct risk has become a major area of attention by the FCA and the boards of financial services firms. There is no agreed definition for conduct risk but in simple terms it can be thought of as how to place integrity and trust at the heart of how firms behave and how customers and investors are treated. In essence, therefore, it refers to risks attached to the way in which a firm, and its staff, conduct themselves.

A good starting point is to consider conduct risk as the latest in a series of regulatory thinking that began with treating customers fairly (TCF), which then progressed through principles-based regulation, and then on to outcomes-focused regulation, before becoming conduct risk. All of these expressions have at their heart the same basic idea, namely that regulation through the creation of rules alone is not enough to protect consumers or markets.

1.5.1 Treating Customers Fairly (TCF)

The requirement for firms to treat their customers fairly is firmly rooted in the Principles for Businesses. Principle 6 states that *'a firm must pay due regard to the interests of its customers and treat them fairly'*. The approach adopted to TCF has been not to define precisely what constitutes 'treating customers fairly', but rather to challenge the senior management of firms to work this out for themselves, taking into account the particular types of business they undertake. The objective is for this to be embedded into the culture of a firm at all levels, so that over time it becomes 'business as usual'.

TCF, with its focus on consumer outcomes, still underpins the delivery of the FCA's statutory consumer protection objective. It states:

We expect customers' interests to be at the heart of how firms do business. Customers can expect to get financial services and products that meet their needs from firms that they can trust. Meeting customers' fair and reasonable expectations should be the responsibility of firms, not that of the regulator.

There are six TCF outcomes:

- **Outcome 1** – consumers can be confident that they are dealing with firms where the fair treatment of customers is central to the corporate culture.
- **Outcome 2** – products and services marketed and sold in the retail market are designed to meet the needs of identified consumer groups and are targeted accordingly.
- **Outcome 3** – consumers are provided with clear information and are kept appropriately informed before, during and after the point of sale.
- **Outcome 4** – where consumers receive advice, the advice is suitable and takes account of their circumstances.
- **Outcome 5** – consumers are provided with products that perform as firms have led them to expect, and the associated service is of an acceptable standard and as they have been led to expect.
- **Outcome 6** – consumers do not face unreasonable post-sale barriers imposed by firms to change product, switch provider, submit a claim or make a complaint.

The regulator will look for evidence that firms really have incorporated TCF throughout their operations and processes. It expects to see this incorporated into a firm's systems and controls and all aspects of the business culture, including people issues, such as training and competence, remuneration, and performance management.

It also expects senior management to ensure that they have the right management information and other data to enable them to satisfy themselves that they are treating their customers fairly in practice.

2. Financial Crime

2.1 Money Laundering

Learning Objective

8.2.1 Know what money laundering is, the stages involved and the related criminal offences

2.1.1 Definition and Stages of Money Laundering

Money laundering is the process of turning money that is derived from criminal activities – **dirty money** – into money which appears to have been legitimately acquired and which can therefore be more easily invested and spent.

Money laundering can take many forms, including:

- turning money acquired through criminal activity into **clean money**
- handling the proceeds of crimes such as theft, fraud and tax evasion
- handling stolen goods
- being directly involved with or facilitating the laundering of any criminal or terrorist property
- criminals investing the proceeds of their crimes in the whole range of financial products.

There are three stages to a successful money laundering operation:

- **Placement** – is the first stage and typically involves placing the criminally derived cash into some form of bank or building society account.
- **Layering** – is the second stage and involves moving the money around in order to make it difficult for the authorities to link the placed funds with the ultimate beneficiary of the money. Disguising the original source of the funds might involve buying and selling foreign currencies, shares or bonds.
- **Integration** – is the third and final stage. At this stage, the layering has been successful and the ultimate beneficiary appears to be holding legitimate funds ('clean' money rather than 'dirty' money). The money is integrated back into the financial system and dealt with as if it were legitimate.

Terrorist Financing

There can be considerable similarities between the movement of **terrorist funds** and the laundering of criminal property. Because terrorist groups can have links with other criminal activities, there is inevitably some overlap between anti-money laundering provisions and the rules designed to prevent the financing of terrorist acts. However, these are two major differences to note between terrorist financing and other money laundering activities:

- Often, only quite small sums of money are required to commit terrorist acts, making identification and tracking more difficult.
- If legitimate funds are used to fund terrorist activities, it is difficult to identify when the funds become terrorist funds.

Terrorist organisations can, however, require significant funding, and will employ modern techniques to manage the funds and transfer them between jurisdictions, hence the similarities with money laundering.

2.1.2 Legal and Regulatory Framework

Learning Objective

8.2.2 Know the purpose and the main provisions of the Proceeds of Crime Act and the Money Laundering Regulations

The cross-border nature of money laundering and terrorist financing has led to international co-ordination to ensure that countries have legislation and regulatory processes in place to enable the identification and prosecution of those involved.

Examples include:

- The **Financial Action Task Force (FATF)**, which has issued recommendations aimed at setting minimum standards for action in different countries to ensure that anti-money laundering efforts are consistent internationally; it has also issued special recommendations on terrorist financing.
- **EU directives** targeted at money laundering prevention.
- **Standards issued by international bodies** to encourage due diligence procedures to be followed for customer identification.
- Sanctions by the **United Nations (UN)** and the **EU** to deny access to the financial services sector to individuals and organisations from certain countries.
- Guidance issued by the private sector **Wolfsberg Group** of banks in relation to private banking, correspondent banking and other activities.

In the UK, the approach has been to specify the key elements of the anti-money laundering and countering terrorist financing regime (AML/CTF) as objectives, giving UK financial firms discretion as to how these should be implemented, using a risk-based approach.

The main laws and regulations relating to money laundering and terrorist financing are:

- Proceeds of Crime Act
- Terrorism Act 2000, as amended by the Anti-Terrorism, Crime and Security Act 2001
- Money Laundering Regulations
- HM Treasury Sanctions Notices and news releases
- FCA Handbook
- JMLSG guidance (see Section 2.1.3).

The **Proceeds of Crime Act (as amended) (POCA)** consolidated and extended existing UK legislation regarding money laundering and, as well as making money laundering a criminal offence, established three broad groups of offences related to money laundering that firms and the staff working for them need to avoid committing:

- knowingly assisting in concealing, or arranging for the acquisition, use or possession of criminal property
- failing to report knowledge or suspicions of possible money laundering
- tipping off another person that a money laundering report has been made, which might prejudice the investigation or that a money laundering investigation is being contemplated or carried out.

It also made it an offence to impede any investigation, including:

- destroying or disposing of any documents that are relevant to an investigation
- failure by a firm to comply with a customer information order.

The **Terrorism Act** establishes a series of offences related to involvement in arrangements for facilitating, raising or using funds for terrorism purposes. As with money laundering, there is a duty to report suspicions and it is an offence to fail to report when there are reasonable grounds to have a suspicion or to be involved in an arrangement that facilitates the retention or control of terrorist property by concealment, removal from the jurisdiction, transfer to nominees or in any other way.

The maximum prison terms that can be imposed under both Acts are 14 years for the offence of money laundering, five years for failing to make a report or destroying relevant documents and two years for tipping off. In each case, the penalties can be imprisonment and/or an unlimited fine.

The **Money Laundering Regulations** implemented the EU directive on money laundering and specified the arrangements firms must have in place covering:

- customer due diligence
- reporting
- record-keeping
- internal control
- risk assessment and management
- compliance management
- communication.

HM Treasury maintains a list of individuals and organisations that are subject to financial sanctions, and it is a criminal offence to make payments, or allow payments to be made, to any of these.

The **FCA Handbook** explains the requirements for firms to have effective systems and controls for countering the risk that a firm might be used to further financial crime, and the specific provisions regarding money laundering risks.

2.1.3 Action Required by Firms and Individuals

Learning Objective

8.2.3 Know the action to be taken by those employed in financial services if money laundering activity is suspected and what constitutes satisfactory evidence of identity

As mentioned above, it is up to firms how they implement the requirements of the legislation and the regulations.

The Proceeds of Crime Act, the Terrorism Act and the Money Laundering Regulations require a court to take account of industry guidance when considering whether a person or firm has committed an offence or has complied with the money laundering regulations. This guidance is provided by the **Joint Money Laundering Steering Group (JMLSG)**, an industry body made up of 17 financial sector trade bodies.

Its guidance sets out what is expected of firms and their staff. It emphasises the responsibility of senior management to manage the firm's money laundering and terrorist financing risks, and advises how this should be carried out using a risk-based approach. It sets out a standard approach to the identification and verification of customers, separating out basic identity from other aspects of customer due diligence measures, as well as giving guidance on the obligation to monitor customer activity.

The following sections highlight some of the principal features of the anti-money laundering procedures a firm is expected to put in place.

Internal Controls

There is a requirement for firms to establish and maintain appropriate and risk-based policies and procedures in order to prevent operations related to money laundering or terrorist financing. These controls are expected to be appropriate to the risks faced by the firm.

Money Laundering Reporting Officer (MLRO)

Firms are expected to appoint a director or senior manager to be the Money Laundering Reporting Officer (MLRO), who is responsible for oversight of the firm's compliance with the regulator's rules on systems and controls against money laundering.

The MLRO must receive and review internal disclosure reports and make external reports to the **National Crime Agency (NCA)** when required. The MLRO is also required to carry out regular assessments of the adequacy of the firm's systems and controls and to produce a report at least annually to senior management on its effectiveness.

The MLRO must have authority to act independently, and senior management must ensure that the MLRO has sufficient resources available to effectively carry out his or her responsibilities.

Risk-Based Approach

Senior management are expected to ensure that they have appropriate systems and controls in place to manage the risks associated with the business and its customers. This requires them to assess their money laundering/terrorist financing risk and decide how they will manage it.

It also requires them to determine appropriate customer due diligence measures to be undertaken to ensure that customer identification and acceptance procedures reflect the risk characteristics of customers, based on the type of customer and the business relationship, product or transaction.

Customer Due Diligence (CDD)

The Money Laundering Regulations set out a firm's obligations to conduct customer due diligence, and describe those customers and products when no, or limited, CDD measures are required, and those customers and circumstances when enhanced due diligence is required.

The CDD measures that must be carried out involve:

- identifying the customer and verifying their identity
- identifying the beneficial owner, when relevant, and verifying their identity
- obtaining information on the purpose and intended nature of the business relationship.

Firms must also conduct ongoing monitoring of the business relationship with their customers to identify any unusual activity.

For some particular customers, products or transactions, **simplified due diligence (SDD)** may be applied. Firms must have reasonable grounds for believing that the customer, product or transaction falls within one of the allowed categories, and be able to demonstrate this to their supervisory authority. SDD may be applied to:

- certain other regulated firms in the financial sector
- companies listed on a regulated market
- beneficial owners of pooled accounts held by notaries or independent legal professionals
- UK public authorities
- community institutions
- certain life assurance and e-money products
- certain pension funds
- certain low risk products
- Junior ISAs.

In cases of higher risk and if the customer is not physically present when their identities are verified then **enhanced due diligence (EDD)** measures must be applied on a risk-sensitive basis.

The JMLSG Guidance Notes provide extensive guidance on the customer due diligence to be applied, and the above should be regarded as a very brief summary only; however, the core obligations on firms can be summarised as follows:

- They must carry out prescribed CDD measures for all customers not covered by exemptions.
- They must have systems to deal with identification issues in relation to those who cannot produce the standard evidence.
- They must apply enhanced due diligence to take account of the greater potential for money laundering in higher-risk cases, specifically when the customer is not physically present when being identified, and in respect of **politically exposed persons (PEPs)** and correspondent banking (PEPs are individuals who hold, or have held, a senior political role and when there may be a greater risk of monies arising from corruption).
- Dealing must not take place with some persons/entities, such as those that are on the HM Treasury sanctions list.
- They must have specific policies in relation to the financially (and socially) excluded.
- If satisfactory evidence of identity is not obtained, the business relationship must not proceed further.
- They must have some system for keeping customer information up to date.

Suspicious Activities and Reporting

The regulations require reports to be made of potential money-laundering or terrorist-financing activities. Staff working in the financial sector are required to make reports if they know, or if they suspect, or if they have reasonable grounds for knowing or suspecting, that a person is engaged in money laundering or terrorist financing.

Each firm is expected to provide a framework within which such suspicion reports may be raised and considered by a nominated officer, who may also be the MLRO. The nominated officer must consider each report and determine whether there are sufficient grounds for knowledge or suspicion for a report to be made to the NCA.

Staff Awareness and Training

The best-designed control systems cannot operate effectively without staff who are alert to the risk of money laundering and who are trained in the identification of unusual activities or transactions which may prove to be suspicious.

Firms are therefore required to:

- provide appropriate training to make staff aware of money-laundering and terrorist-financing issues and how these crimes might take place through the firm
- ensure staff are aware of the law, regulations and relevant criminal offences
- consider providing case studies and examples related to the firm's business
- train employees in how to operate a risk-based approach.

Record-Keeping

Record-keeping is an essential component of the audit trail that the money-laundering regulations and FCA rules require to assist in any financial investigations.

Firms are therefore required to maintain appropriate systems for maintaining records and making these available when required and, in particular, should retain:

- copies of the evidence obtained of a customer's identity for five years after the end of the customer relationship
- details of customer transactions for five years from the date of the transaction or five years from when the relationship with the customer ended, whichever is the later
- details of actions taken in respect of internal and external suspicion reports
- details of information considered by the nominated officer in respect of an internal report when no external report is made.

2.2 Bribery

Learning Objective

8.2.4 Know the purpose of the Bribery Act

The Bribery Act 2010 came into force in July 2011 as part of a complete reform of corruption law to provide a modern and comprehensive scheme of bribery offences that will enable courts and prosecutors to respond more effectively to bribery at home or abroad.

The Bribery Act replaces offences at common law and under legislation dating back to the early 1900s. Its key provisions are:

- Two general offences are created covering the offering, promising or giving of an advantage, and the requesting, agreeing to receive or accepting of an advantage.
- There is a discrete offence of bribery of a foreign public official to obtain or retain business or an advantage in the conduct of business.
- A new offence is created, of failure by a commercial organisation to prevent a bribe being paid for or on its behalf.

Penalties include a maximum of ten years' imprisonment, unlimited fines, confiscation of proceeds, debarment from public sector contracts and director disqualification.

For companies, the most important point to note is that there is a new offence of failing to prevent bribery, which does not require any corrupt intent. This offence will make it easier for the Serious Fraud Office (SFO) to prosecute companies when bribery has occurred. The only defence available to a commercial organisation charged with the corporate offence will be for the organisation to show that it had adequate procedures in place to prevent an act of bribery being committed in connection with its business. This requires firms to have an effective compliance programme that has to meet six principles:

- The organisation should develop well-designed policies, procedures and controls to ensure compliance.
- Top-level commitment is required, with the board and senior management making a commitment to conduct business in a fair, honest and ethical manner.
- Risk assessments should be undertaken on an ongoing basis to identify the external and internal risks faced by the company.
- Due diligence should be undertaken on suppliers who undertake services for the company.
- Policies and procedures should be communicated internally along with training of employees, and policy statements or a code of conduct published externally.
- Bribery risks should be monitored, evaluated and reassessed regularly and staff surveys undertaken. Results should be reported regularly to top management and the process independently audited.

2.3 Identity Fraud

Learning Objective

8.2.5 Know how firms can be exploited as a vehicle for financial crime: theft of customer data to facilitate identity fraud

All firms may unwittingly find themselves targeted by criminals and have to be aware of this possibility, and one area that staff working in financial services need to be aware of is the theft of customer data to facilitate identity fraud.

Identity fraud or identity theft is one of the fastest-growing types of fraud in the UK.

- **Identity fraud** is the use of a misappropriated identity in criminal activity, to obtain goods or services by deception. This usually involves the use of stolen or forged identity documents such as a passport or driving licence.
- **Identity theft** (also known as impersonation fraud) is the misappropriation of the identity (such as the name, date of birth, current address or previous addresses) of another person, without their knowledge or consent. These identity details are then used to obtain goods and services in that person's name.

A person's identity (and their ability to prove it) is central to almost all commercial activity. Organisations need to verify that the person applying for credit or investment services is who they say they are and lives where they claim to live.

The procedures used by organisations to check the information supplied by customers help to detect and prevent most identity fraud. However, some fraudulent applications are accepted due to the sophisticated techniques used by the fraudsters.

When opening accounts in banks and other financial organisations, criminals will use data from legitimate persons to provide information for applications and other purposes which, when checked against normal credit reference, postal and other databases, will seem to confirm the genuine nature of the application.

Key to this is accessing what are known as 'breeder' documents – those documents that allow those who possess them to apply for or obtain other documentation and thus build up a profile or 'history' that can satisfy basic CDD processes. The information may either be used quickly before the source of the data is alerted or used, for example, as a facilitator for other identities so as not to alert the source.

Financial Services Regulation and Professional Integrity

3. Insider Dealing

Learning Objective

8.3.1 Know the offences that constitute insider dealing and the instruments covered

When directors or employees of a listed company buy or sell shares in that company, there is a possibility that they may be committing a criminal act – that of insider dealing.

For example, a director may be buying shares in the knowledge that the company's last six months of trade was better than the market expected. The director has the benefit of this information because he is 'inside' the company. Under the Criminal Justice Act 1993 this would be a criminal offence, punishable by a fine and/or a jail term.

The **instruments** covered by the insider dealing legislation in the Criminal Justice Act are described as '**securities**'. For the purposes of this piece of law, securities are:

- shares
- bonds (includes government bonds and others issued by a company or a public sector body)
- warrants
- depositary receipts
- options (to acquire or dispose of securities)
- futures (to acquire or dispose of securities)
- contracts for difference (based on securities, interest rates or share indices).

Note that the definition of 'securities' does not embrace commodities or derivatives on commodities (such as options and futures on agricultural products, metals or energy products), or units/shares in open-ended collective investment schemes (such as OEICs, unit trusts and SICAVs).

To be found guilty of insider dealing, the Criminal Justice Act 1993 defines who is deemed to be an insider, what is deemed to be inside information and the situations that give rise to the offence.

Inside information is information that relates to particular securities or a particular issuer of securities (and not to securities or securities issuers generally) and which:

- is specific or precise
- has not been made public
- if it were made public, would be likely to have a significant effect on the price of the securities.

This is generally referred to as **unpublished price-sensitive information** and the securities are referred to as **price-affected securities**.

Information becomes public when it is published, for example, a UK-listed company publishing price-sensitive news through the LSE's Regulatory News Service. Information can be treated as public even though it may be acquired only by persons exercising diligence or expertise (for example, by careful analysis of published accounts, or by scouring a library).

A person has this price-sensitive information as an **insider** if they know that it is inside information from an inside source. The person may have:

1. gained the information through being a director, employee or shareholder of an issuer of securities
2. gained access to the information by virtue of their employment, office or profession (for example, the auditors to the company)
3. sourced the information from (1) or (2), either directly or indirectly.

The **offence of insider dealing** is committed when an insider acquires or disposes of price-affected securities while in possession of unpublished price-sensitive information. It is also an offence to encourage another person to deal in price-affected securities, or to disclose the information to another person (other than in the proper performance of employment). The acquisition or disposal must occur on a regulated market or through a professional intermediary.

4. Market Abuse

Learning Objective

8.3.2 Know the offences that constitute market abuse and the instruments covered

Market abuse is an offence introduced by the Financial Services and Markets Act 2000 (subsequently amended in the Market Abuse Directive 2005 (MAD)). It relates to behaviour by a person or a group of people working together, which occurs in relation to qualifying investments, on a prescribed market, and which satisfies one or more of the following three conditions:

1. The behaviour is based on information that is not generally available to those using the market and which, if it were available, would have an impact on the price.
2. The behaviour is likely to give a false or misleading impression of the supply, demand or value of the investments concerned.
3. The behaviour is likely to distort the market in the investments.

In all three cases the behaviour is judged on the basis of what a **regular user** of the market would view as a failure to observe the standards of behaviour normally expected in the market.

The Treasury has determined the 'qualifying investments' and 'prescribed markets' – broadly, they are the investments traded on any of the UK's recognised investment exchanges (RIEs), such as the London Stock Exchange (LSE) main market and any investments traded on AIM.

An example of prohibited **market abuse** was the spreading of false rumours in March 2008 about certain companies listed on the LSE. It was suspected that those spreading the rumours were holding short positions in the companies – in other words, they had sold shares which they did not own, in the hope of buying them back at a lower price in the future. The spreading of false rumours was designed to push down the price. Insider dealing is also a type of market abuse.

Financial Services Regulation and Professional Integrity

5. Data Protection

Learning Objective

8.4.1 Understand the impact of the Data Protection Act on firms' activities

The Data Protection Act 1998 details how personal data should be dealt with to protect its integrity and to protect the rights of the persons concerned.

In order to comply with the Act, firms have a number of legal responsibilities, including:

- notifying the Information Commissioner that they are processing information
- processing personal information in accordance with the eight principles of the Data Protection Act
- answering subject access requests received from individuals.

Any firm that is holding and processing personal data is described as a **data controller**, and is required to comply with the Data Protection Act. The firm must be registered with the Information Commissioner.

The Data Protection Act lays down eight data protection principles:

1. Personal data shall be processed fairly and lawfully.
2. Personal data shall be obtained for one or more specified and lawful purposes, and shall not be further processed in any manner that is incompatible with those purposes.
3. Personal data shall be adequate, relevant and not excessive in relation to the purpose or purposes for which it is processed.
4. Personal data shall be accurate and, where necessary, kept up-to-date.
5. Personal data shall not be kept for longer than is necessary for its purpose or purposes.
6. Personal data shall be processed in accordance with the rights of the subject under the Act.
7. Appropriate technical and organisational measures shall be taken against unauthorised or unlawful processing of personal data, and against accidental loss or destruction of, or damage to, the personal data.
8. Personal data shall not be transferred to a country or territory outside the European Economic Area (EEA) unless that country or territory ensures an adequate level of protection in relation to the processing of personal data.

Under these principles, firms are therefore required to take particular care if financial or medical information is held on a laptop or other portable device. Data should be encrypted and organisations must have policies on the appropriate use and security of portable devices and ensuring their staff are properly trained in these.

Other steps that can be taken to keep data safe include the following regulatory recommendations:

- Employees should not have access to data beyond that which is necessary for them to perform their job. When possible, data should be segregated and information such as passport numbers, bank details and social security numbers should be blanked out.
- The firm should look to monitor and control all flows of information in and out of the company.

- All forms of removable media should be disabled, except when there is a genuine business need. There should be no physical means available for unauthorised staff to remove information undetected.
- When laptops or other portable devices are in use, these should be encrypted and wiped afterwards. Usage of such devices should be logged and monitored under the authority of an appropriate individual. Watertight policies on using such devices should be in place.
- Software that tracks all activities, as well as web surfing and email traffic, should be installed on every single terminal on the firm's network, and staff should be aware of this.
- The firm should completely block access to all internet content that allows web-based communication. This includes all web-based email, messaging facilities on social networking sites, external instant messaging and 'peer-to-peer' file-sharing software.
- The firm should conduct due diligence of data security standards of its third party suppliers before contracts are agreed, and review this periodically. If the firm chooses to outsource its IT, conduct checks should be made on their staff also, since they have access to absolutely everything on the firm's network.
- All visitors to the firm's premises should be logged in and out, and be supervised while on site. Logs should be kept for a minimum of 12 months.

If a firm outsources, there are data protection implications. Firms must assess that the organisation can carry out the work in a secure way, check that they are doing so and take proper security measures.

The firm must also have a written contract with the organisation, which lays down how it can use and disclose the information entrusted to it.

6. Complaints and Compensation

Learning Objective

8.5.1 Know the requirements for handling customer complaints, including the role of the Financial Ombudsman Service

6.1 Complaints

It is almost inevitable that customers will raise complaints against a firm providing financial services. Sometimes these complaints will be valid and sometimes not. The FCA requires authorised firms to deal with complaints from **eligible complainants** promptly and fairly. Eligible complainants are, broadly, individuals and small businesses.

The FCA requires firms to have appropriate **written procedures** for handling expressions of dissatisfaction from eligible complainants. However, the firm is able to apply these procedures to other complainants as well, if it so chooses. These procedures should be followed regardless of whether the complaint is oral or written and whether the complaint is justified or not, as long as it relates to the firm's provision of or failure to provide a financial service.

These internal complaints-handling procedures should provide for the receiving of complaints, acknowledgement of complaints in a timely manner, responding to those complaints, appropriately investigating the complaints and notifying the complainants of their right to go to the **Financial Ombudsman Service (FOS)** when relevant. Among other requirements, the complaints-handling procedures require the firm to issue its **final response** to the complainant within **eight weeks** of the date of the original complaint and the complainant must be notified of their right to refer their complaint to the FOS if they are dissatisfied with the firm's response.

The internal complaints-handling procedures must make provision for the complaints to be investigated by an employee of sufficient competence who was not directly involved in the matter that is the subject of the complaint. The person charged with responding to the complaints must have the authority to settle the complaint, including offering redress if appropriate, or should have access to someone with the necessary authority.

The responses should adequately address the subject matter of the complaint and, when a complaint is upheld, offer appropriate redress. If the firm decides that redress is appropriate, the firm must provide the complainant with fair compensation for any acts or omissions for which it was responsible and comply with any offer of redress the complainant accepts. Any redress for financial loss should include consequential or prospective loss, in addition to actual loss.

The firm must take reasonable steps to ensure that all relevant employees (including any of the firm's appointed representatives) are aware of the firm's complaints-handling procedures and endeavour to act in accordance with these.

6.2 The Financial Ombudsman Service (FOS)

Under the provisions of FSMA, the FSA (now the FCA) was given the power to make rules relating to the handling of complaints (see Section 6.1), and an independent body was established to administer and operate a dispute resolution scheme. It is funded by compulsory industry contributions.

The dispute resolution scheme is known as the Financial Ombudsman Service (FOS), and it is designed to resolve complaints about financial services firms quickly and with minimum formality. Eligible complainants are able to refer complaints to the FOS if they are not satisfied with the response of a financial services firm.

The decision of the FOS is binding on firms, although not binding on the person making the complaint.

The Financial Ombudsman can require the firm to pay over money as a result of a complaint. This money award against the firm will be of such amount that the Ombudsman considers to be fair compensation; however, the sum cannot exceed £150,000. Where the decision is made to make a money award, the Ombudsman can award compensation for financial loss, pain and suffering, damage to reputation and distress or inconvenience.

6.3 The Financial Services Compensation Scheme (FSCS)

Learning Objective

8.5.2 Know the circumstances under which the Financial Services Compensation Scheme pays compensation and the compensation payable for investment claims

The Financial Services Compensation Scheme (FSCS) has been established to pay compensation or arrange continuing cover to eligible claimants in the event of a default by an authorised person or firm. Default is, typically, the firm suffering insolvency. It is funded by compulsory financial services industry contributions.

Eligible claimants are, broadly speaking, the less knowledgeable clients of the firm, such as individuals and small organisations. These less knowledgeable clients are generally the firm's 'private customers' and exclude the more knowledgeable 'professional customers'. The scheme is similar to an insurance policy that is paid for by all authorised firms and provides protection to some clients in the event of a firm collapsing. The claims could come from money on deposit with a bank, or claims in connection with investment business, such as the collapse of a fund manager or stockbroker.

The maximum level of compensation for claims against firms declared in default is 100% of the first £50,000 per person per firm for investments, and £75,000 for bank deposits.

7. Integrity and Ethics in Professional Practice

Learning Objective

8.1.7 Understand the key principles of professional integrity and ethical behaviour in financial services

We are all faced with ethical choices on a regular basis, and doing the right thing is usually obvious. Yet there have been many situations in the news recently in which seemingly rational people have behaved unethically.

Is this because they consider that there are some situations when ethics apply and others when they do not? Is it because they did not think that their behaviour was unethical? Or maybe it was just that they thought they could get away with it. Or could it be that, in actual fact, it is a bit more complicated and involves all of these thoughts and actions and some more besides?

Despite the strong relationship between the two, ethics should not be seen as a subset of regulation, but as an important topic in its own right.

7.1 Historical Background

The Greek philosophers Socrates, Plato and Aristotle are widely held to be the fathers of modern ethical philosophy, with Aristotle (384BC–322BC) being the foremost of these. Aristotle's thinking is generally described as 'virtue ethics', with a central philosophy that requires that individuals actively do good, rather than just being a good person. Aristotle has also been linked to the idea of the 'natural law', which suggests that there exists an innate law or coded behaviour which everyone is born with; although this was not a central tenet of his philosophy, the later work of the 12th-century Christian philosopher Thomas Aquinas led to the idea of natural law becoming fundamentally embedded into Christian thinking.

In the 16th, 17th and 18th centuries a number of philosophers developed ethical philosophies; in particular, the work of the German philosopher Immanuel Kant has continued to have a great impact up to the present day. The idea most commonly associated with Kant is the Categorical Imperative, which has been translated as: *'Act only according to that maxim whereby you can, at the same time, will that it should become a universal law.'* This is sometimes known as the universalisation test, and you may notice that this bears considerable similarity to what is frequently referred to as the Golden Rule: *'Do unto others as you would have them do unto you.'* A tenet such as this appears in most forms of belief, and it is therefore so widespread that it may be regarded as a societal rather than a religious norm. Kant also elaborates on his argument of the Categorical Imperative by saying that what really counts is one's intent when doing something, not just doing it out of a sense of duty. *'When moral worth is at issue, what counts is not actions, which one sees, but those inner principles of actions which one does not see.'*

Significant 19th-century figures in the development of ethical thinking include Jeremy Bentham and John Stuart Mill, both of whom were advocates of the 'utilitarianism' school, whose overriding principle was that the most ethical decision is the one which will result in the greatest good for the greatest number of people, within reason.

It should not be assumed that philosophy has not carried on into the 20th and 21st centuries. As society has developed, so has moral and ethical thinking, but, until the advent of mass or universal education within the last 100 years, the majority of teaching or leading of the population in these matters was carried out by religious organisations.

Most developed and many undeveloped societies therefore have similar basic tenets in their mores, and these have formed the roots of the norms of society and have been the foundation for much fundamental legislation.

7.2 Ethical or Unethical Practice?

One of the observations sometimes made about ethics is that the benefit of ignoring ethical standards and behaviour far outweighs the benefit of adhering to them, both from an individual and also a corporate perspective.

What this argument ignores is that, while such a policy may make sense and be sustainable for a short period, in our society the inevitable outcome is likely to be at least social and at worst criminal sanctions.

An obvious example is the selling of products that carry a high level of commission for the salesman. Although there may be benefits to all three parties to the transaction – the product provider (originator), the intermediary (salesman) and the purchaser (customer) – the structure of the process contains a salient feature (high commission) which has the capability to skew the process.

It can be argued that there is nothing wrong with such a structure, which simply reflects an established method of doing business around the world. However, there are fundamental differences in the financial services industry which particularly may affect the relationship between the salesman and the customer. If you buy a car, you can see it, you can try it out and you will discover very quickly whether it performs in the manner advertised and which you expect. You will also be provided, in the case of a new car, with a warranty from the manufacturer. You can thus make your purchase decision with considerable confidence, despite knowing that the reward system in the motor industry means that the salesman will almost certainly receive a commission.

Contrast this with an imaginary financial product. This may be an arena in which you are less than knowledgeable, and the product may be one to which, once committed, you can have no idea about its quality for many years to come, by which time it may be too late to make changes or seek redress.

An ethical salesperson should therefore take you through the structure of, say, a long-term investment instrument in such a manner that you may be reasonably assured that you understand what it is and from whom you are buying the product. The salesperson should explain the factors which determine the rate of return that is offered, and tell you whether that is an actual rate, or an anticipated rate which is dependent upon certain other things happening, over which the product originator may have no control. They should also tell you what they are being paid if you buy the product.

In other words, the salesperson will give you all the facts that you need to make an informed decision as to whether you wish to invest. They will be **open, honest, transparent and fair**.

7.3 An Ethical Corporate Culture

'Culture' can be described but not easily defined. Nor can it be imposed in an organisation by just putting in a programme; it must be recognised by those inside who are employed, and by those outside who come into contact with the business. At its most basic, corporate culture expresses itself in behaviour and the way a business is run. Staff are sensitive to management style. When faced with a business problem, a manager has to balance the legitimate requirements of attaining business objectives and the ethical requirements of honesty and integrity in the way this is achieved. If staff see from their managers' decisions that the prevailing culture is one of trust, integrity and openness, they generally will feel comfortable at work and be proud of the organisation. And this is likely to be reflected in their own dealings with others.

For an ethical culture to be successful, it must have regard to all of those people and organisations who are affected by it. The principal constituents of an organisation and their financial relationships are summarised in the table below.

Stakeholder	Financial Relationship
Shareholder	Dividends and asset value growth
Provider of finance (lender)	Interest and capital repayments
Employee	Wages, salary, pensions, bonus, other financial benefits
Customer	Payments for goods and services (receipts)
Suppliers	Payments for goods and services (invoices)
Community	Taxes and excise duties, licence fees

These are all the people, groups and interests with whom a business has a relationship and who thus will be affected by its fundamental ethical values.

Example

A builder (supplier) offers a customer an apparent incentive: the frequently seen 'discount for cash payment'. But what is his primary motivation? While it may be to give the customer a good deal and so to win the business for himself, this is being achieved through the likely under-reporting of his income and thus under-collection of legitimate taxes, both income and VAT.

So what would you do? Would you insist that you will make payment only against a proper invoice, knowing that you will also have to pay VAT? Or would you be willing to compromise your ethical standards, using the argument that what you are doing 'goes on all the time'.

Would you do that on a business contract at work? Does your company policy allow it? Almost certainly not.

This is a simple example, but in the business context there are numerous other interests to be taken into account when considering who will be affected and in what way. This starts with the smallest participant – you as an individual – and can be followed through to affect all of the stakeholders in the business. Your actions will affect your team, which may be defined as any colleagues with whom you work, up to the whole business itself depending upon its size. The business will have shareholders and, as a result of your actions improving the profitability of the business, a dividend may be paid that otherwise would not have been paid. So your action will have impacted them, apparently positively. Had you asked them whether they supported your activities, however, knowing what was involved, is it likely that they would have agreed?

And what about the impact upon your external stakeholders: other suppliers and customers who become aware of the standards which your firm has adopted? Are they likely to be reassured?

So what may start out as a well-intentioned but inadequately thought-out action may have consequences which extend far beyond your immediate area.

7.4 The Positive Effects of Ethical Approaches on Corporate Sustainability

Regrettably, we are only too familiar with examples of unethical behaviour having a terminal impact on business, with the names of Enron, Tyco, Worldcom and Parmalat springing readily to mind. Equally, the generally low public regard in which the banking industry is held, as a result of what are perceived to be unethical remuneration practices, provides another salutary example.

One reason for the poor regard that people have for business people and their integrity is that business leaders rarely discuss business values and ethics in public or even in private. As a result, there tends to be reluctance among employees to question decisions of management or raise concerns.

The reticence of leaders to speak up about standards in commercial life may be partly due to uncertainty about the business case for insisting on high ethical standards in business. If a link could be established, therefore, between always doing business responsibly and consistently good financial performance, then there would be more reason for directors of companies to speak up about, and insist on, high ethical standards in their organisations. This includes policy and strategy decisions in the boardroom, and integrity throughout their organisations.

And it is feasible to make such a link.

Research[1] shows more business leaders now understand that 'the way they do business' is an important aspect of fulfilling their financial obligations to their stockholders, as well as other stakeholders. They are responding to accusations of poor behavioural standards in various ways.

First, more companies are putting in place corporate responsibility policies or ethics policies, the principal feature of which is a code of ethics/conduct/behaviour to guide their staff. Companies now accept that an ethics policy is one of the essential ingredients of good corporate governance.

Second, modern corporate governance procedures include risk assessments, and until recently these tended to be confined to the financial, legal and safety hazards of the organisation, but growing numbers of companies are recognising reputation and branding issues around lack of integrity as a possible source of future problems. For example, Royal Dutch Shell identifies this among its risk factors in its 2008 Annual Review: *'An erosion of Shell's business reputation would adversely impact our licence to operate, our brand, our ability to secure new resources and our financial performance.'*

But can the time and effort put into designing and implementing such guidance, including a code of conduct/ethics/practice, be shown to make a difference? Does doing business ethically pay?

Recent studies have provided a positive answer to this question. In 2002–03 the Institute of Business Ethics (IBE) undertook research showing that, for large UK companies, having an ethics policy (a code) operating for at least five years correlated with above-average financial performance based on four measures of value. The performance of a control cohort of similar companies without an explicit ethics policy – no code – was used for comparison. This was published by IBE in April 2003 under the title *'Does Business Ethics Pay?'*[2]

---

1 Webley, S. and Werner, A., *'Employee Views of Ethics at Work'*, Institute of Business Ethics, 2009.
2 Webley, S. and More, E., *'Does Business Ethics Pay? Ethics and Financial Performance'*, Institute of Business Ethics, 2003.

The methodology developed for this project was used in a more recent study by researchers at Cranfield University and the IBE using more up-to-date data. They came to a similar conclusion.[3]

So what makes the difference? A pilot study to the Cranfield/IBE report investigated the distinguishing features, if any, of the operations of companies with explicit ethics policies compared with those with a less robust policy.

Employee Retention

One non-financial indicator is the retention of high-quality staff, recognised as vital to a profitable and sustainable organisation. The attraction and retention of high-quality staff would be expected to be reflected in higher productivity and, ultimately, profitability. This is well explained in *'Putting the Service-Profit Chain to Work'*[4] in which the authors describe the links in the service-profit chain. They argue that profit and growth are stimulated by customer loyalty; loyalty is a direct result of customer satisfaction; satisfaction is largely influenced by the value of services provided to customers; value is created by satisfied, loyal and productive employees; and employee satisfaction, in turn, results from high-quality support services and policies that enable employees to deliver results to customers.

Customer Retention

A second non-financial indicator is customer retention; it too is recognised as a significant factor in the long-term viability of a company. A research paper in 2002[5] showed that corporate ethical character makes a difference to the way that customers (and other stakeholders) identify with the company (brand awareness).

Besides maintaining good staff and customers, how providers of finance and insurance rate an organisation is a major factor in determining the cost of each. What ratings agencies have developed, with varying degrees of success, are measures of risk – the lower the risk, the lower the capital cost. One study, using Standard & Poor's and Barclays Bank data, has indicated that companies with an explicit ethics policy generally have a higher rating than those without one. This in turn generated a significantly lower cost of capital.[6]

What is apparent from these research projects, and others in the US, is that the leadership of consistently well managed companies accepts that having a corporate responsibility/ethics policy is an important part of their corporate governance agenda.

---

3   Ugoji, K., Dando, N. and Moir, L., *'Does Business Ethics Pay? Revisited: The Value of Ethics Training'*, Institute of Business Ethics, 2007.
4   *'Putting the Service Profit Chain to Work'*, HBR, July/August 2008.
5   Chun, R., *'An Alternative Approach to Appraising Corporate Social Performance: Stakeholder Emotion'*, Manchester Business School. Submitted to Academy of Management Conference, Denver, Colorado, 2002.
6   Webley, S. and Hamilton, K., *'How Does Business Ethics Pay?'* in Appendix 3 of *'Does Business Ethics Pay? Revisited'*, 2007, op.cit.

7.5 Assessing Dilemmas

Many firms and individuals maintain the highest standards without feeling the need for a plethora of formal policies and procedures documenting conformity with accepted ethical standards. Nevertheless, it cannot be assumed that ethical awareness will be absorbed through a sort of process of osmosis. Accordingly, if we are to achieve the highest standards of ethical behaviour in our industry, and in industry more generally, it is sensible to consider how we can create a sense of ethical awareness.

If we accept that ethics is about both thinking and doing the right thing, then we should seek first of all to instil the type of thinking which causes us, as a matter of habit, to reflect upon what we are considering doing, or what we may be asked to do, before we carry it out.

There will often be situations, particularly at work, when we are faced with a decision where it is not immediately obvious whether what we are being asked to do is actually right.

A simple checklist will help to decide. Is it:

- **Open** – is everyone whom your action or decision affects fully aware of it, or will they be made aware of it?
- **Honest** – does it comply with applicable law or regulation?
- **Transparent** – is it clear to all parties involved what is happening/will happen?
- **Fair** – is the transaction or decision fair to everyone involved in it or affected by it?

A simple and often quoted test is whether you would be happy to appear in the media in connection with, or in justification of, the transaction or decision.

7.6 Codes of Ethics, Codes of Conduct, and Regulation

For any industry in which trust is a central feature, demonstrable standards of practice and the means to enforce them are a key requirement. Hence the proliferation of professional bodies in the fields of health and wealth – areas in which consumers are more sensitive to performance and have higher expectations than in many other fields.

It should be noted that, although the terms 'code of ethics' and 'code of conduct' are often used synonymously, using the term 'ethics' to describe the nature of a code whose purpose is to establish standards of behaviour does, undoubtedly, imply that it involves commitment to and conformity with standards of personal morality, rather than simply complying with rules and guidance relating to professional dealings. Such 'instructions' may be contained more appropriately within a document described as a **code of conduct**. If it is considered that more specific guidance of standards of professional practice would be beneficial, such standards might be set out in an appropriately entitled document, or in **regulatory standards**.

Within financial services we have a structure where, in most countries, detailed and prescriptive regulation is imposed by regulatory bodies (see Section 1). Nevertheless, professional bodies operating in the field of financial services have developed codes of conduct for their members, and the chart below indicates the areas of responsibility that a sample of these cover.

Financial Services Regulation and Professional Integrity

Body	Society	Client	Employer	Professional Association	Profession	Colleagues/Employer	Self	Others
A	✓	✓	✓	✓	✓	✓	✓	✓
B		✓	✓		✓	✓	✓	✓
C		✓		✓	✓		✓	✓
D	✓	✓	✓	✓	✓	✓	✓	✓
E		✓	✓	✓	✓	✓	✓	✓
F	✓	✓		✓	✓	✓	✓	
G	✓	✓		✓	✓		✓	✓
H		✓	✓	✓	✓		✓	✓
I	✓	✓			✓			✓

It is apparent from this chart that there are only two areas, 'responsibility to the client' and 'responsibility to the profession', which all the sampled codes of professional bodies have in common. This falls short of the aim of regulatory standards, which by their very nature must apply to everyone.

Consequently, while regulatory standards may *draw on* professional codes of conduct, they will not simply mirror them. However, the overarching connection between all three of these areas is an explicit requirement for the highest standards of personal and professional ethics.

One of the paradoxical outcomes of the financial crisis is that rule-based compliance is being strengthened, as it is judged that reliance upon principles-based decision-making is deemed to have failed. However, while this may be a natural reaction, the strengthening of regulation, far from being an indication of the failure or weakness of an ethically-based approach, should in fact be seen as clarion call for the strengthening of ethical standards.

These are the principal features of what we can describe as the 'ethics versus compliance' approach:

Ethics	Compliance
Prevention	Detection
Principles-based	Law/rules-based
Values-driven	Fear-driven
Implicit	Explicit
Spirit of the law	Letter of the law
Discretionary	Mandatory

Once again it is back to the choice of doing things because you *ought* to, it is the right thing to do, (ethics) rather than because you *have* to (rules).

7.6.1 UK Regulatory Principles

From the outset of its role as the sole regulator for the UK financial services industry on 1 December 2001, the FSA operated without a formal code of ethics, since the original view was that establishing ethical standards and the policing of ethical behaviour was not an appropriate responsibility for a regulator.

However, as outlined in Section 1.3, there were principles established both for regulated business itself and also for 'approved persons', and both sets of principles were capable of being invoked when considering the behaviour of industry participants that, while not being breaches of actual regulation, were considered to be inappropriate or damaging to the industry.

It is worth noting that the key verb in both sets of principles is the word '**must**', a command verb indicating that the subject has no discretion in what decision they make, because the principle determines the correct course of action.

Events since 2001 caused the UK regulator to revise its belief in the adequacy of the approach that combines regulation with principles, since it is felt that this results in an overly black and white approach, ie, if an action is not specifically prevented by the regulations or principles then it is acceptable to follow that course of action. Such an approach is popular in a number of countries, but is now felt to fall short of what is required in order to produce properly balanced decisions and policies.

7.6.2 CISI Code of Conduct

Learning Objective

8.1.6 Know the CISI's Code of Conduct

For any industry in which trust is a central feature, demonstrable standards of practice and the means to enforce them are a key requirement.

Financial services is one such industry, and the CISI already has in place its own Code of Conduct. Membership of the Chartered Institute for Securities & Investment (CISI) requires members to meet the standards set out within the Institute's Principles. These words are from the introduction:

Professionals within the securities and investment industry owe important duties to their clients, the market, the industry and society at large. Where these duties are set out in law, or in regulation, the professional must always comply with the requirements in an open and transparent manner.

Members of the Chartered Institute for Securities & Investment (CISI) are required to meet the standards set out within the Institute's Principles. These Principles […] impose an obligation on members to act in a way beyond mere compliance and to support the underlying values of the Institute.

They set out clearly the expectations upon members of the industry 'to act in a way beyond mere compliance'. In other words, we must understand the obligation upon us to act with integrity in all aspects of our work and our professional relationships.

Accordingly, it is appropriate to examine the Code of Conduct and to remind ourselves of the stakeholders in each of the individual principles.

	The Principles	Stakeholder
1.	To act honestly and fairly at all times when dealing with clients, customers and counterparties and to be a good steward of their interests, taking into account the nature of the business relationship with each of them, the nature of the service to be provided to them and the individual mandates given by them.	Client
2.	To act with integrity in fulfilling the responsibilities of your appointment and to seek to avoid any acts, omissions or business practices which damage the reputation of your organisation or the financial services industry.	Firm/industry
3.	To observe applicable law, regulations and professional conduct standards when carrying out financial service activities, and to interpret and apply them to the best of your ability according to principles rooted in trust, honesty and integrity.	Regulator
4.	To observe the standards of market integrity, good practice and conduct required or expected of participants in markets when engaging in any form of market dealing.	Market participant
5.	To be alert to and manage fairly and effectively and to the best of your ability any relevant conflict of interest.	Client
6.	To attain and actively manage a level of professional competence appropriate to your responsibilities, to commit to continuing learning to ensure the currency of your knowledge, skills and expertise and to promote the development of others.	Client Colleagues Self
7.	To decline to act in any matter about which you are not competent unless you have access to such advice and assistance as will enable you to carry out the work in a professional manner.	Client
8.	To strive to uphold the highest personal and professional standards.	Industry Self

The Code of Conduct is intended to provide direction to members of the professional bodies and, via the FCA code, other members of the financial services industry, as to what are their behavioural requirements in dealing in all areas and with all stakeholders involved in the activity of financial services.

At the corporate and institutional level this means operating in accordance with the rules of market conduct, dealing fairly (honestly) with other market participants and not seeking to take unfair advantage of either. That does not mean that firms cannot be competitive, but that rules and standards of behaviour are required to enable markets to function smoothly, on top of the actual regulations which provide direction for the technical elements of market operation. At the individual client relationship level, we are reminded of our ethical responsibilities towards our clients, over and above complying with the regulatory framework and our legal responsibilities.

But, as we have been discussing throughout this section, if you are guided by ethical principles, compliance with regulation is made very much easier!

At the conclusion of this section, let us consider the words of Guy Jubb, investment director and head of corporate governance at Standard Life, when speaking at the CISI annual ethics debate in 2009.

It's personal – we as individuals are the City. We must take our responsibility for restoring trust and there can be no abdication of responsibility to third parties; we must conduct our affairs as good stewards; we must sort out right from wrong and behave accordingly […] members must live out being good stewards in the interests of their clients.

End of Chapter Questions

Think of an answer for each question and refer to the appropriate section for confirmation.

1. What is the rationale behind the checks that the FCA undertakes to make sure that a firm is 'fit and proper' prior to authorisation?
   Answer Reference: Section 1.3

2. What are the five groups of controlled functions that require approved person status?
   Answer Reference: Section 1.4

3. In what circumstances might simplified due diligence be appropriate?
   Answer Reference: Section 2.1.3

4. What is EDD and when might it be needed?
   Answer Reference: Section 2.1.3

5. What information should be kept in order to be compliant with the JMLSG guidance?
   Answer Reference: Section 2.1.3

6. What is the corporate offence in relation to bribery, and what defence may be made when charged with it?
   Answer Reference: Section 2.2

7. What types of securities do the insider dealing rules apply to?
   Answer Reference: Section 3

8. What types of behaviour might lead to a charge of market abuse?
   Answer Reference: Section 4

9. What action should a firm take before it allows another firm to process customer data for it?
   Answer Reference: Section 5

10. What is the name of the body that handles dispute resolution and complaints about financial services firms?
    Answer Reference: Sections 6.1 & 6.2

11. If an authorised firm went bust, who could an investor seek compensation from?
    Answer Reference: Section 6.3

Chapter Nine
Taxation, Investment Wrappers and Trusts

1. Introduction	167
2. Taxation	167
3. Individual Savings Accounts (ISAs)	171
4. Pensions	174
5. Trusts	177

This syllabus area will provide approximately 6 of the 50 examination questions

1. Introduction

In this chapter, we look at the main UK taxes that apply to individuals, as well as some of the investment wrappers that are available and their tax attractiveness to investors. We conclude with an overview of trusts and their uses.

2. Taxation

Learning Objective

9.1.1 Know the direct and indirect taxes as they apply to individuals: income tax; capital gains tax; inheritance tax; stamp duty; VAT

9.1.2 Know the main exemptions in respect of the main personal taxes

In this section, we will review the main taxes that affect private individuals, with a focus on the impact of tax on investment income.

The main taxes that affect private investors are income tax, capital gains tax, stamp duty and inheritance tax.

2.1 Income Tax

Individuals are liable to income tax on their earnings and any interest or dividends that arise. Income is classified into three types:

- **Non-savings income** – this category includes earnings from employment and pension income.
- **Savings income** – this includes interest from bank accounts and bonds.
- **Dividend income** – the final category includes dividends payable by companies and investment funds.

Private investors are liable to pay tax on the income generated from their savings and investments. In this context, taxable income includes interest on bank deposits, the dividends payable on shares, income distributions paid by unit trusts and the interest on government stocks and corporate bonds.

Income from savings and investments is added to the investor's other income, such as salary or pension, and income tax is charged on the total amount. In simple terms, the calculation of the tax payable by each individual is done in the following three steps:

Step 1

All of the income from the three categories is added up for the year, first non-savings income (such as wages) and then savings income (interest) and finally dividend income.

Step 2

Deduct the annual personal allowance from the bottom of the 'pile' of income in step 1. All individuals have an **annual personal allowance** on which no tax is due, and the remaining income is grouped into bands and taxed at different rates. The personal allowance applies up to an earnings limit of £100,000, after which it is gradually reduced.

Dividends are treated as the 'top slice' of taxable income, savings as the next slice and other non-savings income as the lowest slice. This means that the personal allowance will always be deducted first from the other (eg, earned) income, and, if there is any remaining, then from savings income, and finally from dividend income.

Step 3

Calculate the tax due on the remaining income after deducting the personal allowance and any other deductions using the published bands and rates.

There are a number of other **deductions** that an individual is allowed to make from gross income before tax is payable; for example, subject to certain limitations, contributions made to a personal or corporate pension scheme; and charitable donations made by individuals on or after 6 April 2000.

Some income is tax-free, including Premium Bond prizes; interest on national savings certificates; income from Individual Savings Accounts (ISAs); gambling and National Lottery wins; compensation for loss of employment of up to £30,000 and statutory redundancy payments; and dividends on ordinary shares of a venture capital trust (VCT).

2.1.1 Savings Interest

Interest income is referred to by HMRC as **non-dividend savings income** and is taxed **after** earned income. Non-dividend savings income applies to UK and overseas savings income from the following sources:

- interest from banks and building societies
- interest from gilts and corporate bonds
- purchased life annuities (income component)
- the taxable amount on deep-discounted securities (eg, zero coupon bonds)
- some distributions from unit trusts.

From 6 April 2016, a new personal savings allowance was introduced to remove tax on up to £1,000 of savings income for basic rate taxpayers and up to £500 for higher rate taxpayers. Additional rate taxpayers will not receive an allowance. As part of this change, from April 2016, banks and building societies stopped automatically taking 20% in income tax from the interest earned on non-ISA savings and so this will remove the need for non-taxpayers to complete a form R85.

How much tax is then due will depend upon what rate the investor pays tax at.

Taxation, Investment Wrappers and Trusts

The taxation of dividends changed significantly as of April 2016, with the first £5,000 of dividend income in each tax year now tax-exempt. Sums above that amount will be taxed at 7.5% for basic rate taxpayers, 32.5% for higher rate taxpayers and 38.1% for additional rate taxpayers.

2.2 Capital Gains Tax (CGT)

Capital gains tax (CGT) is a tax levied on an increase in the capital value of an asset; you normally only pay CGT when the asset is disposed of. For example, if an individual bought shares for £2,000 and later sold them for £17,000, then that individual has made a capital gain of £15,000.

CGT may be payable when an asset is sold or disposed of which includes when you:

- sell, give away, exchange, or transfer – 'dispose of' – all or part of an asset
- receive a capital sum, such as an insurance payout for a damaged asset.

Most types of assets are liable to CGT and include items such as:

- shares
- unit trusts
- certain bonds
- property (except your main home, or principal private residence, see below).

As you can see from the list above, nearly all types of assets are caught by capital gains tax.

There are, however, a number of notable **exemptions**:

- Although property is chargeable to CGT, any gain on the sale of your **main home** is exempt. For CGT purposes, your main home is referred to as your 'principal private residence'.
- Your **car**, and other personal possessions worth up to £6,000 each, such as jewellery or paintings.
- Gains on **gilts** and certain other sterling bonds, called 'qualifying corporate bonds'.
- Gains on assets held in accounts that benefit from **tax exemptions**, such as an ISA, Junior ISA or approved pension.
- **Betting, lottery or pools winnings**.
- **Transfers between spouses**.

In addition, individuals have an annual tax-free allowance which is known as the **annual exempt amount**, which allows them to make a certain amount of gains tax-free each year. Any net gains in excess are chargeable as follows:

- 18% and 28% for individuals (the rate used will depend on the amount of their total taxable income and gains)
- 28% for trustees or personal representatives
- 10% for gains qualifying for entrepreneurs' relief.

169

2.3 Inheritance Tax (IHT)

Inheritance tax (IHT) is usually paid on the estate that someone leaves when they die. It is also sometimes payable on trusts or gifts made during someone's lifetime.

IHT is based on the value of assets that are transferred during the individual's lifetime or that are remaining at death, known as the estate of the deceased. Each individual has a **nil rate band** which is currently set at £325,000; and any transfers in excess of the nil-rate band are then charged at 40%.

Inheritance tax is a complex area but some of the major **exemptions** are:

- assets left to the deceased person's spouse
- assets left to registered charities
- gifts made more than seven years before death can be exempt if certain conditions are met.

Since October 2007, it has also been possible to transfer any unused nil-rate band from a late spouse or civil partner to the second spouse or civil partner when they die. The percentage that is unused on the first death can then be used to reduce the IHT liability on the second death and can increase the inheritance tax threshold of the second partner from £325,000 to as much as £650,000, depending on the circumstances.

The Finance Act 2012 introduced a reduction in the rate of IHT from 40% to 36% where 10% or more of a deceased person's net estate (after deducting IHT exemptions, reliefs and the nil-rate band) is left to charity. The measure applies to deaths on or after 6 April 2012.

2.4 Stamp Duty and Stamp Duty Reserve Tax (SDRT)

Stamp duty is a tax paid on UK share trades when a stock transfer form is used. SDRT is payable when an individual buys shares electronically and no stock transfer form is used. The rate is 0.5% of the purchase price and is paid only by the purchaser.

There is no stamp duty payable on the purchase of most foreign shares, bonds, OEICs, unit trusts or ETFs.

2.5 Value Added Tax (VAT)

VAT is chargeable by firms and individuals whose turnover exceeds a certain amount, when they supply what are known as taxable goods or services. Although this affects all firms except those below the VAT threshold, they are allowed to deduct tax they have paid on purchases, so reducing their liability.

The standard rate of VAT is 20% and is relevant to a number of investment services. For example, fees charged for providing an investment management service to an authorised unit trust (AUT) would be VAT-exempt, while those charged to clients (eg, private individuals) would be VATable. There are also exceptions when no VAT is payable, such as with broker's commission for the execution of a stock market trade.

3. Individual Savings Accounts (ISAs)

Learning Objective

9.2.1 Know the definition of, and tax incentives provided by, ISAs

9.2.2 Know the main types of ISA available: Cash; Stocks & Shares; Junior ISA

9.2.3 Know the following aspects of investing in ISAs: subscriptions; transfers; eligibility

Individual Savings Accounts (ISAs) were set up by the government to encourage individual investment. The particular incentive for investment was that the investments held within an ISA account were free of income tax and capital gains tax.

The ISA itself is often referred to as an investment wrapper because it is essentially an account that holds other savings and investments, such as deposits, shares, OEICs and unit trusts, and allows them to be invested in a tax-efficient manner.

Firms offering investments in ISAs, such as banks, building societies and fund management companies, must be approved by HMRC. The approved entity is known as the 'ISA Manager'. HMRC is also responsible for setting the detailed rules applicable to ISAs.

3.1 ISAs

Over the years, the rules surrounding the types of ISA had become complex and this had made them less than straightforward for investors to understand and caused firms difficulties in administering them.

As a result, the government has simplified the rules. Two main types of ISAs can be opened: a Stocks & Shares ISA and a Cash ISA.

- Stocks & Shares ISAs are available only to residents of the UK over the age of 18.
- Cash ISAs are available to those aged 16 or over.

Investors do not have to hold the two types of account, however many savers may prefer to hold separate accounts for their cash and their stocks and shares investments.

ISAs were introduced in 1999 and have since been the main vehicle for saving and investing tax efficiently. The ISA acts as a wrapper, shielding the return on savings and investments held in it from tax, and ISAs must be run by an HMRC-approved manager. Significant changes were made to ISAs in both the 2014 and 2015 Budgets to introduce greater flexibility and increase their use and attraction as a savings vehicle. As a result, many changes are being introduced and more can be expected.

From April 2016, there are three types of ISA:

1. The most common is the Cash ISA which includes deposits with banks and building societies and some cash-type products. Cash ISAs are the tax-free equivalent of traditional savings accounts.

2. The Stocks & Shares ISA can hold most fixed-interest securities and virtually all unit trusts, investment trusts and open-ended investment companies (OEICs), except cash-like and limited redemption funds. They also include life assurance policies (but not pensions) which, before 2005–06, formed a separate component.
3. From April 2016, a third type of ISA was introduced – the Innovative Finance ISA. This ISA covers peer-to-peer lending, where lenders are matched with borrowers so each enjoys better rates and will mean those lending through peer-to-peer platforms will be able to get their interest tax-free.

For the 2016–17 tax year, the ISA subscription limit is unchanged at £15,240. New subscriptions can be split in any proportion between a Cash ISA, a Stocks & Shares ISA or an Innovative Finance ISA as the saver chooses. However, a saver will only be able to pay into a maximum of one of each type of ISA per year.

Under the rules, savers are able to open one of each type of ISA each year, with the same or different providers.

- In the year when a subscription is made, therefore, an investor can open a Cash ISA with one manager, a separate Stocks & Shares ISA with another manager and a further Innovative Finance ISA with another.
- Any amounts can be subscribed to each ISA so long as the overall subscription limit is not exceeded.
- However, an investor cannot open more than one of each type in any one year. For example, a saver cannot invest half of the annual subscription limit in a Cash ISA with one manager and then later in the year open another one with another manager to hold the balance of the subscription limit; each component must all be with one manager. The same is the case for the Stocks & Shares ISA and the Innovative Finance ISA.

In subsequent years, a saver can open an ISA with a completely different provider so that they can have ISAs with more than one provider.

Investors are also allowed to transfer shares into a Stocks & Shares ISA which they have received from approved profit-sharing schemes, share incentive plans or Save As You Earn (SAYE) share options. They have to transfer such shares at market value within 90 days of receipt. The value of these transfers will reduce the remaining ISA subscription balance available to the investor for that year.

Investors are able to transfer an existing ISA from one manager to another manager providing that the receiving manager is prepared to accept it. Transfers of previous years' subscriptions can be in whole or just in part. Transfers of the same year's subscriptions, however, must be for the full amount.

Investors can also transfer their savings between Stocks & Shares ISAs and Cash ISAs and vice versa.

- Any previous year's savings (eg, amounts paid in before 5 April 2016) can be transferred in whole or in part between Stocks & Shares ISAs and Cash ISAs as the account holder wishes, subject to the agreed terms and conditions of their account.
- Savings made in the current year (ie, amounts subscribed after 6 April 2016) can only be transferred as a whole, and cannot be split.

Taxation, Investment Wrappers and Trusts

Example

An investor opened a new Cash ISA mid-way through the tax year with £5,000 with one ISA manager. Later in the tax year, they wish to make a further subscription to a new Cash ISA offered by another ISA manager as their rates are more attractive. They cannot open more than one Cash ISA each year and so they have to either deposit the money in the existing account or transfer the whole balance to the new ISA manager (assuming that the new manager will accept the transfer) and then make the further subscription.

Money can be withdrawn from an ISA at any time without losing the tax benefits for the remaining funds in the account. Until April 2016, once a withdrawal was made, it was permanent and could not be redeposited. The only way in which further funds could be added to an ISA was if the investor had any of the current year's subscription allowance remaining.

The March 2015 Budget announced changes to the rules on withdrawals to add more flexibility to ISAs. Its introduction was delayed but, from April 2016, individuals are able to withdraw money from their Cash ISA and replace it in the year without it counting towards their annual ISA subscription limit for that year.

3.2 Junior ISAs

The government announced in October 2010 that it intended to create a new tax-free children's savings account to replace the Child Trust Fund. The new accounts, described as Junior ISAs, offer a simple and tax-free way to save for a child's future.

The start date for the new Junior ISA (or JISA as HMRC refers to them) was 1 November 2011 and the key features are as follows:.

- **Eligibility** – all UK resident children (aged under 18) who do not have a CTF are eligible.
- **Types of account** – both Cash and Stocks & Shares JISAs are available. The qualifying investments for each of these are the same as for existing ISAs and children are able to hold up to one Cash and one Stocks & Shares JISA at a time.
- **Annual subscription limit** – each eligible child is able to receive contributions of up to a fixed amount each year (£4,080 in 2015–16) into their JISA. The subscription limit is indexed by CPI.
- **Account opening** – anyone with parental responsibility for an eligible child is able to open a JISA on their behalf. Eligible children over the age of 16 are also able to open a JISA for themselves.
- **Account operation** – until the child reaches 16, accounts will be managed on their behalf by a person who has parental responsibility for that child. At age 16, the child assumes management responsibility for their account. Withdrawals are not permitted until the child reaches 18 except in cases of terminal illness or death.
- **Transfers** – it is possible to transfer accounts between providers, but it is not possible to hold more than one Cash or Stocks & Shares Junior ISA at any time. It had previously not been possible to transfer CTFs into JISAs, but this changed in April 2015.
- **Maturity** – at the age of 18, the JISA will automatically become a normal adult ISA. The funds will then be accessible to the child.

Having a Junior ISA does not affect an individual's entitlement to adult ISAs. It will be possible for JISA account holders to open adult Cash ISAs from the age of 16, and JISA contributions will not impact upon their adult ISA subscription limits.

Example

Someone aged between 16 and 18 can hold a Cash ISA but cannot open a Stocks & Shares ISA. They will be able to pay up to £15,240 into a Cash ISA for the tax year 2015–16. This is in addition to any amounts that they pay into a Junior ISA that they hold. So, in 2015–16, they could pay £4,080 into a JISA and £15,240 into a Cash ISA.

4. Pensions

Learning Objective

9.3.1 Know the benefits provided by pensions

9.3.2 Know the basic characteristics of the following: state pension scheme; occupational pension schemes; personal pensions including self-invested personal pensions (SIPPs)

4.1 Retirement Planning

For many people their pension and their house are their main assets.

Pensions are becoming increasingly important as people live longer, and commentators speak of a 'pensions time bomb', when the pension provided by the state, the individuals and their employers will be inadequate to meet needs in retirement. When the state pension was introduced in the UK, the initial need was funding for the rare event of people living beyond the age of 65. Today this is very common. As an example, it is predicted that by 2040 over 50% of the people in the UK will be over 65.

4.2 Benefits

A pension is an investment fund where contributions are made, usually during the individual's working life, to provide a lump sum on retirement plus an annual pension payable thereafter. Pension contributions are tax-effective, as tax relief is given on contributions.

Some of the main tax incentives of pensions include:

- Tax relief on contributions made by individuals and employers.
- Pension funds are not subject to income tax and CGT and so the pension fund can grow tax-free.
- The ability to take a pension from age 55.
- An option to take a tax-free lump sum at retirement.
- The option to include death benefits as part of the scheme.

These tax advantages were put in place by the government to encourage people to provide for their own old age. Pensions are subject to income tax when they are received.

State pensions are provided out of current National Insurance contributions, with no investment for future needs. This is a problem as dependency ratios (the proportion of working people to retired people) are forecast to fall from 4:1 in 2002 to 3:1 by 2030 and 2.5:1 by 2050.

This means that by 2050 either each worker will have to support almost twice as many retired people, or the support per head will need to fall substantially, or some combination of these changes.

As a result of these cost pressures, major changes are underway to the state pension scheme:

- The age at which the state pension is payable is rising such that the pension age for both men and women will be 65 from 6 April 2018, ie, everyone will draw their pensions at the same age. Those born after 6 October 1954, but before 6 April 1968, however, will not draw their pensions until the age of 66. For those born after 1968, the pension age will increase from 66 to 67 and then to 68. It may subsequently rise even further.
- The state pension currently comes in two parts – a basic state pension and an additional state pension, or state second pension (S2P). This is being replaced by a flat rate pension, although the amount payable will depend on whether the individual has made sufficient national insurance contributions during their working life.

4.3 Occupational Pension Schemes

One of the earliest kinds of scheme supplementing state funding was the occupational pension scheme. Occupational pension schemes are run by companies for their employees. In an occupational pension scheme, the employer makes pension contributions on behalf of its workers.

The advantages of these schemes are:

- Employers must contribute to the fund (some pension schemes do not involve any contributions from the employee – these are called **non-contributory** schemes).
- Running costs are often lower than for personal schemes and the costs are often met by the employer.
- The employer must ensure the fund is well run, and for defined benefit schemes must make up any shortfall in funding.

The occupational pension scheme could take the form of a **defined benefit scheme**, also known as a 'final salary scheme', when the pension received is related to the number of years of service and the individual's final salary. For example, an occupational pension scheme might provide an employee with 1/60th of their final salary for every year of service; the employee could then retire with an annual pension the size of which was related to the number of years' service.

Employers have generally stopped providing defined benefit schemes to new employees because of rising life expectancies and volatile investment returns, and the implications these factors have on the funding requirement for defined benefit schemes.

Instead, occupational pension schemes are now typically provided to new employees on a **defined contribution** basis – when the size of the pension is driven by the contributions paid and the investment performance of the fund. Under this type of scheme, an investment fund is built up and the amount of pension that will be received at retirement will be determined by the value of the fund and the amount of pension it can generate.

The higher cost of providing a defined benefit scheme is part of the reason why many companies have closed their defined benefit schemes to new joiners and make only defined contribution schemes available to staff. A key advantage of defined contribution schemes for employers over defined benefit schemes is that poor performance is not the employer's problem; it is the employee who will end up with a smaller pension.

Occupational pension schemes are structured as **trusts**, with the investment portfolio managed by professional asset managers. The asset managers are appointed by, and report to, the trustees of the scheme. The trustees will typically include representatives from the company (eg, company directors) as well as employee representatives.

4.4 Private Pensions or Personal Pensions

Private pensions or personal pensions are individual pension plans. They are **defined contribution** schemes that might be used by employees of companies that do not run their own scheme or when employees opt out of the company scheme; or they might be used in addition to an existing pension scheme; and also they are used by the self-employed.

Many employers actually organise **group personal pension schemes** for their employees, by arranging the administration of these schemes with an insurance company or an asset management firm. Such employers may also contribute to the personal pension schemes of their employees.

Employees and the self-employed who wish to provide for their pension and do not have access to occupational schemes or employer-arranged personal pensions have to organise their own personal pension schemes. These will often be arranged through an insurance company or an asset manager, where the individual can choose from the variety of investment funds offered.

Individuals also have the facility to run a **self-invested personal pension (SIPP)**, commonly administered by a stockbroker or IFA on their behalf. In a SIPP, it is the individual who decides which investments are included in the scheme, subject to HMRC guidelines.

The schemes are approved by HMRC, which means that they are **tax-exempt**. The contributions are tax-deductible and there is no tax either on investment income or capital gains. Although there is no further tax due, however, the tax credit on any dividends received cannot be reclaimed.

In a private scheme, the key responsibility that lies with the individual is that the individual chooses the investment fund in a scheme administered by an insurance company or asset manager, or the actual investments in a SIPP. It is then up to the individual to monitor the performance of their investments and assess whether it will be sufficient for their retirement needs.

5. Trusts

Learning Objective

9.4.1 Know the features of the main trusts: discretionary; interest in possession; bare

9.4.2 Know the definition of the following terms: trustee; settlor; beneficiary

9.4.3 Know the main reasons for creating trusts

5.1 What is a Trust?

A trust is the legal means by which one person gives property to another person to look after on behalf of yet another individual or a set of individuals.

Starting with the individuals involved, the person who creates the trust is known as the **settlor**. The person they give the property to, to look after on behalf of others, is called the **trustee**, and the individuals for whom it is intended are known as the **beneficiaries**.

5.2 Uses of Trusts

Trusts are widely used in estate and tax planning for high net worth individuals and are encountered throughout retail investment firms from execution-only stockbrokers to private banks.

Some of their main uses include:

- providing funds for a specific purpose, such as the maintenance of young children
- setting aside funds for disabled or incapacitated children in order to protect and provide for their financial maintenance
- to reduce future inheritance tax liabilities by transferring assets into a trust and so out of the settlor's ownership
- separating out rights to income and capital so that, for example, the spouse of a second marriage receives the income from an asset during their life and the capital passes on that person's death to the settlor's children.

Trusts are also the underlying structure for many major investment vehicles, such as pension funds, charities and unit trusts.

5.3 Types of Trusts

There are a number of different types of trust. Some of the main ones that are encountered are:

- **Bare or absolute trusts** – in which a trustee holds assets for one or more persons absolutely.
- **Interest in possession trusts** – in which a beneficiary has a right to the income of the trust during their life and the capital passes to others on their death. These include life interest trusts.
- **Discretionary trusts** – in which the trustees have discretion over to whom the capital and income is paid, within certain criteria.

End of Chapter Questions

Think of an answer for each question and refer to the appropriate section for confirmation.

1. What rates of tax will be paid on a dividend by a higher-rate taxpayer?
   Answer Reference: Section 2.1

2. What assets are liable to CGT?
   Answer Reference: Section 2.2

3. At what rate is CGT payable?
   Answer Reference: Section 2.2

4. How does the eligibility for an ISA differ between a Cash ISA and a Stocks & Shares ISA?
   Answer Reference: Section 3.1

5. What proportion of the annual ISA allowance can be invested in a Cash ISA?
   Answer Reference: Section 3.1

6. What happens to a Junior ISA on maturity?
   Answer Reference: Section 3.2

7. When can a child take over management responsibility for their Junior ISA?
   Answer Reference: Section 3.2

8. What is the key difference between a defined benefit pension scheme and a defined contribution pension scheme?
   Answer Reference: Section 4.3

9. What is the type of trust in which a trustee holds assets for another person absolutely?
   Answer Reference: Section 5.3

Chapter Ten
Other Financial Products

1. Loans	181
2. Property and Mortgages	184
3. Investment Bonds	188
4. Life Assurance	189
5. Protection Insurance	192

This syllabus area will provide approximately 4 of the 50 examination questions

1. Loans

Learning Objective

10.1.1 Know the differences between bank loans, overdrafts and credit card borrowing

10.1.4 Know the difference between secured and unsecured borrowing

Individuals can borrow money from banks and other lenders in three main ways:

- overdrafts
- credit card borrowing
- loans.

1.1 Overdrafts

When an individual draws out more money than they hold in their current account, they become overdrawn. Their account is described as being 'in overdraft'.

If the amount overdrawn is within a limit previously agreed with the bank, the overdraft is said to be **authorised**. If it has not been previously agreed, or exceeds the agreed limit, it is **unauthorised**.

Unauthorised overdrafts are very expensive, usually incurring both a high rate of interest on the borrowed money and a fee. The bank may refuse to honour payments from an unauthorised overdrawn account, commonly referred to as 'bouncing' cheques.

Authorised overdrafts agreed with the bank in advance are charged interest at a lower rate. Some banks allow small overdrafts without charging fees to avoid infuriating a customer who might be overdrawn by a relatively low amount.

Overdrafts are an expensive way of borrowing money, and borrowers should try to restrict their use to temporary periods and avoid unauthorised overdrafts as far as possible.

1.2 Credit Cards

Customers in the UK are very attached to their credit cards from savings institutions like banks and building societies and other cards from retail stores known as store cards. In other countries, including much of Europe, the use is much less widespread.

A wide variety of retail goods such as food, electrical goods, petrol and cinema tickets can be paid for using a credit card. The retailer is paid by the credit card company for the goods sold; the credit card company charges the retailer a percentage fee, but this enables the store to sell goods to customers using their credit cards.

Customers are typically sent a monthly statement by the credit card company. Customers can then choose to pay all the money owed to the credit card company, or just a percentage of the total sum owed. Interest is charged on the balance owed by the customer.

Generally, the interest rate charged on credit cards is relatively high compared to other forms of borrowing, including overdrafts. However, if a credit card customer pays the full balance each month, they are borrowing interest-free. It is also common for credit card companies to offer 0% interest to new customers for balances transferred from other cards and for new purchases for a set period, often six months. However, these offers are often only available if a fee is paid.

1.3 Loans

Loans can be subdivided into two groups:

- secured loans
- unsecured loans.

Unsecured loans are typically used to purchase consumer goods. Another example is a student loan to be repaid after university. The lender will check the creditworthiness of the borrower – assessing whether they can afford to repay the loan and interest over the agreed term of, say, 48 months from their income given their existing outgoings.

The unsecured loan is not linked to the item that is purchased with the loan (in contrast to mortgages, which are covered in Section 2), so if the borrower defaults it can be difficult for the lender to enforce repayment. The usual mechanism for the unsecured lender to enforce repayment is to start legal proceedings to get the money back.

In contrast, if **secured** loans are not repaid, the lender can repossess the specific property which was the security for the loan.

Example

Jenny borrows £500,000 to buy a house.

The loan is secured on the property. Jenny loses her job and is unable to continue to meet the repayments and interest.

Because the loan is secured, the lender is able to take the house to recoup the money. If the lender takes this route, the house will be sold and the lender will take the amount owed and give the rest, if any, to Jenny.

As seen in this example, it is common for loans made to buy property to be secured. Such loans are referred to as **mortgages** and the security provided to the lender means that the rate of interest is likely to be lower than on other forms of borrowing, like overdrafts and unsecured loans.

For more on mortgages, see Section 2.

1.4 Interest Rates

Learning Objective

10.1.2 Know the difference between the quoted interest rate on borrowing and the effective annual rate of borrowing

10.1.3 Be able to calculate the effective annual rate of borrowing, given the quoted interest rate and frequency of payment

The costs of borrowing vary depending on the form of borrowing, how long the money is required for, the security offered and the amount borrowed.

Mortgages, secured on a house, are much cheaper than credit cards and authorised overdrafts. Unauthorised overdrafts will incur even higher rates of interest plus charges.

Borrowers also have to grapple with the different rates quoted by lenders; loan companies traditionally quote flat rates that are lower than the true rate or **effective annual rate**.

Example

The Moneybags Credit Card Company quotes its interest rate at 12% per annum, charged on a quarterly basis.

The effective annual rate can be determined by taking the quoted rate and dividing by four (to represent the quarterly charge). It is this rate that is applied to the amount borrowed on a quarterly basis. 12% divided by 4 = 3%.

Imagine an individual borrows £100 on their Moneybags credit card. Assuming they make no repayments for a year – how much will be owed?

At the end of the first quarter, £100 x 3% = £3 will be added to the balance outstanding, to make it £103.

At the end of the second quarter, interest will be due on both the original borrowing and the interest. In other words there will be interest charged on the first quarter's interest of £3, as well as the £100 original borrowing. £103 x 3% = £3.09 will be added to make the outstanding balance £106.09.

At the end of the third quarter, interest will be charged at 3% on the amount outstanding (including the first and second quarters' interest). £106.09 x 3% = £3.18 will be added to make the outstanding balance £109.27.

At the end of the fourth quarter, interest will be charged at 3% on the amount outstanding (including the first, second and third quarters' interest). £109.27 x 3% = £3.28 will be added to make the outstanding balance £112.55.

In total the interest incurred on the £100 was £12.55 over the year. This is an effective annual rate of 12.55/100 x 100 = 12.55%.

There is a shortcut method to arrive at the effective annual rate seen above. It is simply to take the quoted rate, divide by the appropriate frequency (four for quarterly, two for half-yearly, 12 for monthly) and express the result as a decimal – in other words 3% will be expressed as 0.03, 6% as 0.06 etc. The decimal is then added to 1, and multiplied by itself by the appropriate frequency. The result minus 1 and then multiplied by 100 is the effective annual rate.

From the above example:

- 12% divided by 4 = 3%, expressed as 0.03.
- 1 + 0.03 = 1.03.
- 1.03^4 = 1.03 x 1.03 x 1.03 x 1.03 = 1.1255.
- 1.1255 – 1 = 0.1255 x 100 = 12.55%.

This formula can also be applied to deposits to determine the effective annual rate of a deposit paying interest at regular intervals.

To make comparisons easier, lenders must quote the true cost of borrowing, embracing the effective annual rate and including any fees that are required to be paid by the borrower. This is known as the **annual percentage rate (APR)**. The additional fees that the lender adds to the cost of borrowing might be, for example, loan arrangement fees.

2. Property and Mortgages

Learning Objective

10.2.1 Understand the characteristics of the mortgage market: interest rates; loan to value

10.2.2 Know the definition of and types of mortgage: repayment; interest-only; offset

2.1 Characteristics of the Property Market

In the UK the proportion of families who own, or are buying, their home is higher than in many other countries in the EU. In the past, home ownership has been encouraged by the government, for example by providing tax relief on mortgage interest payments, and encouraging local authority tenants to buy their homes from their local council.

As well as buying their own home, some people have taken out second mortgages to buy holiday homes in places like Cornwall, France and Spain, while others have taken out a 'buy-to-let' mortgage loan with a view to letting a property out to tenants.

Because of the past performance of property prices, property came to be seen as a reasonably safe investment. There is the additional attraction that any capital gains made on a home ('principal private residence', according to the tax authorities) is not subject to capital gains tax (CGT) (see Chapter 9, Section 2.2).

However, the costs of purchasing a property are substantial, embracing solicitors' fees and stamp duty.

Each individual property is also unique, with no two properties the same, and the attractiveness or otherwise is driven heavily by personal preference. As was seen by the last crash in the property market during 2008–09, prices can fall as well as rise.

2.2 Mortgages

A mortgage is simply a secured loan, with the security taking the form of a property.

A mortgage is typically provided to finance the purchase of that property, and for most people their main form of borrowing is the mortgage on their house or flat. Mortgages tend to be taken out over a long term, with most mortgages running for 20 or 25 years.

Whether a mortgage is to buy a house or flat, or to 'buy-to-let', the factors considered by the lender are much the same. The mortgage lender, such as the building society or bank, will consider each application for a loan in terms of the credit risk – the risk of not being repaid the principal sum loaned and the interest due.

Applicants are assessed in terms of:

- income and security of employment
- existing outgoings – utility bills, other household expenses, school fees
- the size of the loan in relation to the value of the property being purchased. This is referred to as the **loan-to-value** ratio.

A second mortgage is sometimes taken out on a single property. If the borrower defaults on their borrowings, the first mortgage ranks ahead of the second one in terms of being repaid out of the proceeds of the property sale.

2.3 Interest Rates

There are four main methods by which the interest may be charged. These are:

- variable rate
- fixed rate
- capped rate
- tracker rate.

In a standard **variable rate mortgage** the borrower pays interest at a rate that varies with prevailing interest rates. The lender's standard variable rates will reflect increases or decreases in the rates set by the Bank of England. Once they have entered into a variable rate mortgage, the borrower will benefit from rates falling and remaining low, but will suffer the additional costs when rates increase.

In a **fixed rate mortgage** the borrower's interest rate is set for an initial period, usually the first three or five years. If interest rates rise, the borrower is protected from the higher rates throughout this period, continuing to pay the lower, fixed rate of interest. However, if rates fall, and perhaps stay low, the fixed rate loan can only be cancelled if a redemption penalty is paid. The penalty is calculated to recoup the loss suffered by the lender as a result of the cancellation of the fixed rate loan. It is common for fixed rate borrowers to be required to remain with the lender and pay interest at the lender's standard variable rate for a couple of years after the fixed rate deal ends – commonly referred to as a 'lock-in' period.

Capped mortgages protect borrowers from rates rising above a particular rate – the 'capped rate'. For example, a mortgage might be taken out at 6%, with the interest rate based on the lender's standard variable rate, but with a cap at 7%. If prevailing rates fall to 5% the borrower pays at that rate, but if rates rise to 8% the rate paid cannot rise above the cap, and is only 7%.

A **tracker mortgage** is one that is linked to another rate such as the Bank of England base rate. The tracker rate will be set at a percentage above the Bank of England base rate, say 1% above, and will then increase or decrease as base rate changes, hence why it is called a tracker.

Lending institutions sometimes also attract borrowers by offering **discounted rate mortgages**. A 6% loan might be discounted to 5% for the first three years. Such deals might attract 'switchers' – borrowers who shop around and remortgage at a better rate; they may also be useful for first-time buyers as they make the transition to home ownership with a relatively low but growing level of income.

2.4 Types of Mortgage

2.4.1 Repayment Mortgages

The most straightforward form of mortgage is a repayment mortgage. This is simply a mortgage in which the borrower will make monthly payments to the lender, with each monthly payment comprising both interest and capital.

Example

Mr Mullergee borrows £100,000 from XYZ Bank to finance the purchase of a flat on a repayment basis over 25 years. Each month he is required to pay £600 to XYZ Bank.

Mr Mullergee will pay in total £180,000 to XYZ Bank (£600 x 12 months x 25 years), a total of £80,000 interest over and above the capital borrowed of £100,000.

Each payment he makes will be allocated partly to interest and partly to capital. In the early years the payments are predominantly interest. Towards the middle of the term the capital begins to reduce significantly, and at the end of the mortgage term the payments are predominantly capital.

The key advantage of a repayment mortgage over other forms of mortgage is that, as long as the borrower meets the repayments each month, they are guaranteed to pay off the loan over the term of the mortgage.

The main risks attached to a repayment mortgage from the borrower's perspective are:

- The cost of servicing the loan could increase, when interest is charged at the lender's standard variable rate of interest. This rate of interest will increase if interest rates go up. Mortgage repayments can rise significantly at the end of a fixed rate deal when they revert to the standard variable rate.
- The borrower runs the risk of having the property repossessed if they fail to meet the repayments – remember, the mortgage loan is secured on the underlying property.

These also apply to other forms of mortgage.

2.4.2 Interest-Only Mortgages

As the name suggests, an interest-only mortgage requires the borrower to make interest payments to the lender throughout the period of the loan. At the same time, the borrower generally puts money aside each month, into some form of investment.

The borrower's aim is for the investment to grow through regular contributions and investment returns (such as dividends, interest and capital growth) so that at the end of the mortgage the accumulated investment is sufficient to pay back the capital borrowed and perhaps offer some additional cash.

Example

Ms Ward borrows £100,000 from XYZ Bank to finance the purchase of a flat on an interest-only basis over 25 years. Each month she is required to pay £420 interest to XYZ Bank. At the same time, Ms Ward pays £180 each month into an investment fund run by an insurance company. At the end of the 25-year period, Ms Ward hopes that the investment in the fund will have grown sufficiently to repay the £100,000 loan from XYZ Bank and offer an additional lump sum.

The main risks attached to an interest-only mortgage from the borrower's perspective are:

- Borrowers with interest-only mortgages still face the risks that repayment mortgage borrowers face – namely that interest rates may increase and their property is at risk if they fail to keep up the payments to the lender.
- There is also an additional risk that the investment might not grow sufficiently to pay the amount owing on the mortgage. In the example above, there is nothing guaranteeing that, at the end of the 25-year term, the investment in the fund will be worth £100,000 – indeed, it might be worth considerably less.

Lenders must ensure that borrowers have robust investment plans in place to repay the mortgage.

2.4.3 Offset Mortgages

An offset mortgage is a simple concept which works on the basis that, for the calculation and charging of interest, any mortgage is offset against, for example, any savings you may hold.

Example

Let's assume you have a mortgage of £100,000 and have a savings account with £8,000 and £2,000 in a current account. For the purpose of calculating interest, the £100,000 is offset by the £10,000 worth of savings, so in effect you only pay interest on £90,000 of your mortgage borrowing.

Obviously you would not receive any interest on your savings.

There are two main benefits to this approach:

- A higher-rate tax payer will not incur tax on any savings interest earned because it has been offset against the mortgage borrowing.
- As interest is being paid on a slightly lower mortgage, it provides some flexibility to manage finances, pay off the mortgage a little quicker and have more control.

3. Investment Bonds

Learning Objective

10.3.1 Know the main characteristics of investment bonds

An investment bond is a **single-premium life assurance policy that is taken out for the purposes of investment**. It is a common form of investment in the UK as it used to receive favourable tax treatment from governments interested in promoting savings and investment.

The benefit of this potential favourable treatment has been made less attractive now that capital gains tax is charged at either 18% or 28%. When comparing investment bonds with other types of investments, such as OEICs or unit trusts, a case-by-case analysis is required, taking into account the investor's risk appetite, cash flow needs and marginal income tax rates at the time of the investment. In the right circumstances, however, investment bonds can still receive favourable tax treatment.

Investment bonds are issued by insurance companies and may be linked to one or more of the insurance company's unit-linked investment funds. They are structured in various ways in order to provide either capital growth or a regular income to investors. There is a wide range of investment bonds available including:

- with-profits investment bonds
- distribution bonds
- guaranteed equity bonds
- unit-linked bonds.

Within these bonds, the investor will have a choice of investment fund with differing levels of risk, geographic coverage and investment style.

They will usually have a choice of two basic charging structures: an initial charge structure and an establishment charge structure. An initial charge involves all of the costs being taken up front, while the other spreads the costs, usually over the first five years. There may also be exit charges for early encashment.

Investment bonds can be a very useful tool for tax planning purposes. Up to 5% of the original investment can be taken from an investment bond each year for 20 years without incurring an immediate tax liability. Also, if the 5% is not taken at the beginning of the investment bond's life, this can be rolled up on a cumulative basis and taken at a later stage, again without an immediate tax liability.

When investment bonds are encashed, the profits made are taxed as income rather than capital gains. As a result, basic rate taxpayers would not be liable to any tax on the proceeds of the bond, providing that the withdrawal does not push them into the higher-rate tax band. Higher-rate taxpayers are currently liable to tax at their higher rate less the basic rate (for example, a 40% taxpayer can deduct the basic rate of 20% to leave a further 20% liability) on policy gains.

The ability to defer any tax liability until encashment makes investment bonds particularly attractive to higher-rate taxpayers who know that they will become basic rate taxpayers at some point in the future. This means that during the lifetime of the bond they can make withdrawals and defer the liability on any tax until the policy is encashed. If at the time of encashment the policyholders have become basic rate taxpayers, then there is a good chance that they will incur no tax liability.

Investment bonds are also issued by life assurance companies based in offshore tax havens such as the Channel Islands. The structure of these bonds is similar to the ones available in the UK but their tax treatment differs. A notable difference is that income tax is charged at the full rates and so a basic rate taxpayer faces a 20% charge and a higher-rate or additional rate taxpayer will pay tax at a full 40% or 45%.

4. Life Assurance

Learning Objective

10.4.1 Understand the basic principles of life assurance

10.4.2 Know the definition of the following types of life policy: term assurance; whole-of-life

A life policy is simply an insurance policy in which the event insured is a death. Such policies involve the payment of premiums in exchange for life cover – a lump sum that is payable upon death.

Instead of paying a fixed sum on death, there are investment-based policies which may pay a sum calculated as a guaranteed amount plus any profits made during the period between the policy being taken out and the death of the insured. The total paid out, therefore, depends on the guaranteed sum, the date of death and the investment performance of the fund.

There are two types of life cover we need to consider, namely whole-of-life assurance and term assurance. A **whole-of-life policy** provides permanent cover, meaning that the sum assured will be paid whenever death occurs, as opposed to if death occurs within the term of a **term assurance policy**.

While looking at these, it is important to know some key terms.

Key Terms	
Proposer	The person who proposes to enter into a contract of insurance with a life insurance company to insure themselves or another person on whose life they have insurable interest.
Life Assured	The person on whose life the contract depends is called the 'life assured'. Although the person who owns the policy and the life assured are frequently the same person, this is not necessarily the case. A policy on the life of one person, but effected and owned by someone else, is called a 'life of another' policy. A policy effected by the life assured is called an 'own life policy'.
Single Life	A single life policy pays out on one individual's death.
Joint Life	When cover is required for two people, this can typically be arranged in one of two ways: through a joint life policy or two single life policies.
	A joint life policy can be arranged so that the benefits would be paid out following the death of either the first, or, if required for a specific reason, the second life assured. The majority of policies are arranged ultimately to protect financial dependants, with the sum assured or benefits being paid on the first death.
	With two separate single life policies, each person is covered separately. If both lives assured were to die at the same time, as the result of a car accident for example, the full benefits would be payable on each of the policies. If one of the lives assured died, benefits would be paid for that policy, with the surviving partner having continuing cover on their life.
Insurable Interest	To buy a life insurance policy on someone else's life, the proposer must have an interest in that person remaining alive, or expect financial loss from that person's death. This is called an 'insurable interest'.

4.1 Whole-of-Life Assurance

There are three types of whole-of-life policy:

- **non-profit** that is for a guaranteed sum only
- **with-profits**, which pays a guaranteed amount plus any profits made during the period between the policy being taken out and death
- **unit-linked policies** in which the return will be directly related to the investment performance of the units in the insurance company's fund.

In **a non-profit policy** the insured sum is chosen at the outset and is fixed. For example, £500,000 payable on death.

With-profits funds are used to build up a sum of money to buy an annuity or pension on retirement, to pay off the capital of a mortgage, or to insure against an event such as death. One advantage of with-profits schemes is that profits are locked in each year. If an investor bought shares or bonds directly, or within a unit trust or investment trust, the value of the investments could fall just as they are needed because of general declines in the stock market. With-profits schemes avoid this risk by 'smoothing' the returns.

A typical scheme might pay out:

- the **sum assured** or **guaranteed sum**, which is usually an amount a little less than the premiums paid over the term
- **annual bonuses**, which are declared each year by the insurance company, and which can vary. If the underlying performance of the investments in the fund is better than expected, this is a good year, and a part of the surplus will be held back to enable the insurance company to award an annual bonus in a bad year. In this way, the returns 'smooth' the peaks and troughs that may be occurring in the underlying stock market
- a **terminal bonus** at the end of the period. This could be substantial, for example 20% of the sum insured, but is not declared until the end of the policy term.

The final kind of policy is a **unit-linked** or **unitised** scheme. Each month, premiums are used to purchase units in an investment fund. Some units are then used to purchase term insurance and the rest remain invested in the investment fund run by the insurance company. When it is held to fund a mortgage, the insurance company will review the policies every five or ten years, making the investor aware of any potential shortfall and perhaps suggesting an increase in the premiums to boost the life cover or the guaranteed sum.

The reason for such policies being taken out is not normally just for the insured sum itself. Usually they are bought as part of a protection planning exercise to provide a lump sum in the event of death to pay off the principal in a mortgage or to provide funds to assist with the payment of any tax that might become payable on death. They can serve two purposes, therefore, both protection and investment.

Purchasing a life assurance policy is the same as entering into any other contract. When a person completes a proposal form and submits it to an insurance company, that constitutes a part of the formal process of entering into a contract. The principle of utmost good faith applies to insurance contracts. This places an obligation on the person seeking insurance to disclose any material facts that may affect how the insurance company may judge the risk of the contract they are entering into. Failure to disclose a material fact gives the insurance company the right to avoid paying out in the event of a claim.

There is a wide range of variations on the basic life policy that are driven by mortality risk, investment and expenses and premium options – all of which impact on the structure of the policy itself.

4.2   Term Assurance

Term assurance is a type of policy that pays out a lump sum in the event of death occurring within a specified period. (Technically, the term 'life assurance' should be used to refer to a whole-of-life policy that will pay out on death, while 'life insurance' should be used in the context of term policies that pay out only if death occurs within a particular period.)

Term assurance has a variety of uses, such as ensuring there are funds available to repay a mortgage in case someone dies or providing a lump sum that can be used to generate income for a surviving partner or to provide funds to pay any tax that might become payable on death.

When taking out life cover, the individual selects the amount that they wish to be paid out if the event happens and the period that they want the cover to run for. If, during the period when the cover is in place, they die, then a lump sum will be paid out that equals the amount of life cover selected. With some policies, if an individual is diagnosed as suffering from a terminal illness which is expected to cause death within 12 months of the diagnosis, then the lump sum is payable at that point.

The amount of the premiums paid for term assurance will depend on:

- the amount insured
- age, sex and family history
- other risk factors, including state of health (for example, whether the individual is a smoker or non-smoker), their occupation and whether they participate in dangerous sports such as hang-gliding
- the term over which cover is required.

When selecting the amount of cover, an individual is able to choose three types of cover, namely level, increasing or decreasing cover.

Level cover, as the name suggests, means that the amount to be paid out if the event happens remains the same throughout the period in which the policy is in force. As a result, the premiums are fixed at the outset and do not change during the period of the policy.

With **increasing cover**, the amount of cover and the premium increase on each anniversary of the taking out of the policy. The amount by which the cover will increase will be determined at the outset and can be an amount that is the same as the change in the CPI, so that the cover maintains its real value after allowing for inflation. The premium paid will also increase, and the rate of increase will be determined at the start of the policy.

As you would expect, with **decreasing cover** the amount that is originally chosen as the sum to be paid out decreases each year. The amount by which it decreases is agreed at the outset and, if it is used to repay a mortgage, it will be based on the expected reduction in the outstanding mortgage that would occur if the client had a repayment mortgage. Although the amount of cover will diminish year by year, the premiums payable will remain the same throughout the policy.

5. Protection Insurance

Learning Objective

10.5.1 Know the main product features of the following: critical illness insurance; income protection; mortgage protection; accident and sickness cover; household cover; medical insurance; long-term care insurance; liability insurance

There are four main areas that might be in need of protection – family and personal, mortgage, long-term care and business. There are a wide range of protection products marketed by insurance companies to meet these needs, and the characteristics of some of the more common types of products are considered below.

5.1 Critical Illness Insurance Cover

Critical illness cover is designed to pay a lump sum in the event that a person suffers from any one of a wide range of critical illnesses. Looking at how many people suffer from a major illness before they reach 65, its use and value can readily be seen. Illness may force an individual to give up work and so could cause financial hardship, to say nothing of how they will pay for specialist medical treatment or afford the additional costs that permanent disability may bring about.

Some of the key features of such policies include:

- The critical illnesses that will be covered will be closely defined.
- Some significant illnesses may be excluded.
- Illness resulting from certain activities, such as war or civil unrest, will not be covered.

Critical illness cover is available to those aged between 18 and 64 years of age and must end before an individual's 70th birthday. It will pay out a lump sum if an individual is diagnosed with a critical illness and will normally be tax-free. The cover will then cease.

There will be conditions attached to the cover that determine whether any payment will be made. A standard condition applying to all illnesses covered is that the insured person must survive for 28 days after the diagnosis of a critical illness to claim the benefit, and the illness must be expected to cause death within 12 months.

Critical illness cover can usually be taken out on a level, decreasing or increasing cover basis and can often be combined with other cover, such as life cover.

5.2 Income Protection Cover

Income protection insurance is designed to pay out an income benefit when a person is unable to work for a prolonged period due to sickness or incapacity. Since this may need to be paid for a significant period of time, the premiums are relatively expensive. Their use and value can be readily appreciated by considering how a family would continue to pay its bills if the main income-earner were to fall ill. Some of the key features of such policies include:

- They run for a set term and an individual must be aged between 18 and 59 when the cover starts and it will stop when they reach 65.
- The circumstances under which a benefit will be payable are clearly defined. The illness or injury that an individual may suffer is referred to as 'incapacity', and the insurance policy will define what constitutes this in relation their occupation.
- They provide a regular income after a certain waiting period but there will be maximum limits on the amount of benefits paid related to a percentage of annual earnings. Payments will differ or cease on return to work.
- The cover pays out a regular monthly benefit if the individual becomes unable to work for longer than a deferred period, which is the time they must wait from when they first become unable to work until benefits start under the cover.
- The benefit starts once the deferred period finishes. The longer the deferred period chosen, the lower the premiums will be; the options available will be periods such as four, eight, 13, 26, 52 and 104 weeks.

Once a claim is made, the insurance company may extend the deferred period or even decline the claim. The claim will not be met if incapacity arises as a result of specific situations including unreasonable failure to follow medical advice, alcohol or solvent abuse, intentional self-inflicted injury and so on.

5.3 Mortgage Payment Protection Cover

Mortgage payment protection is designed to ensure that the payments that are due for a mortgage continue to be paid if the borrower is unable to work because of accident, sickness or unemployment.

They tend to be available from the lending institution, as well as insurance companies, although costs need to be carefully compared. They are designed to cover short-term problems, such as covering the costs if an individual loses their job and until they find alternative work, rather than long-term benefits.

The same basic features as reviewed above under income protection cover will apply, along with the following further considerations:

- The protection provided will be on a level basis, so regular reviews are needed so that the cover reflects the payments due as mortgage interest rates change.
- The amount of benefit payable can be reduced to take account of income from other sources and there may be limits on the maximum amounts that will be paid. As a result, the amount of benefit paid may not cover the mortgage payments.

5.4 Accident and Sickness Cover

Personal accident policies are generally taken out for annual periods and can provide for income or lump sum payments in the event of an accident. Although they are relatively inexpensive, care needs to be taken to look in detail at the exclusions and limits that apply. These may include:

- The amount of cover may be the lower of a set amount or a maximum percentage of the individual's gross monthly salary.
- The waiting period between when an individual becomes unable to work and when benefits start may be 30 or 60 days.

The insurance company will assess eligibility at the time of the claim and may refuse a claim as a result of pre-existing medical conditions even if they have been disclosed.

5.5 Household Cover

House and contents insurance are well established products and are well understood by consumers, so these will only be covered briefly.

Key considerations include:

- Is the cover enough to pay for the complete rebuild of a home?
- To what extent are external features of a house covered, such as walls, gates, drives and pathways?
- What cover is there in case a neighbour sues you for your tree falling on their property or a similar accident?
- What is the extent of cover for personal possessions?
- Is legal cover included?

5.6 Medical Insurance

Private medical insurance is obviously intended to cover the cost of medical and hospital expenses. It may be taken out by individuals, or provided as part of an individual's employment.

Some of the key features of such policies include:

- The costs that will be covered are usually closely defined.
- There will be limits on what will be paid out per claim, or even over a period such as a year.
- Standard care that can be dealt with by a person's local doctor may not be included.

Again, there will be exclusions such as for pre-existing conditions.

5.7 Long-Term Care

The purpose of long-term care cover is to provide the funds that will be needed in later life to meet the cost of care. Simply considering the cost of nursing home care explains the need for such a policy, but its value to an individual will depend on the amount of state funding for care costs that will be available.

Premiums will be expensive, reflecting the cost of care, and the benefit will normally be paid as an income that can be used to cover the expenditure.

5.8 Business Insurance

Business insurance protection can take many forms, and the two main types are liability insurance, such as public liability insurance, and indemnity insurance. Some examples of its use are:

- Providing indemnity cover for claims against the business for faulty work or goods.
- Protecting loans that have been taken out and secured against an individual's assets.
- Providing an income if the owner is unable to work and the business ceases.
- Providing payments in the event of a key member of a business dying, to cover any impact on its profits.
- Providing money in the event of death of a major shareholder or partner so that the remaining shareholders can buy out their share and his estate can distribute the funds to their family.

End of Chapter Questions

Think of an answer for each question and refer to the appropriate section for confirmation.

1. When can a lender repossess the specific property which was purchased with a loan?
   Answer Reference: Section 1.3

2. How can the interest rates on different types of loans or accounts be readily compared?
   Answer Reference: Section 1.4

3. Firm A charges interest annually at 6% pa on loans and Firm B charges interest quarterly at 6% pa. Which is the more expensive?
   Answer Reference: Section 1.4

4. A firm offers fixed rate loans at 6% pa charged quarterly. Ignoring charges, what is the APR on the loan?
   Answer Reference: Section 1.4

5. An individual took out a second mortgage through your firm to finance the purchase of a second home in Spain. It was secured on his property in the UK on which he had an existing mortgage through another company. If he is unable to meet his outgoings and his UK property is repossessed, which mortgage will be repaid first?
   Answer Reference: Section 2.2

6. What are the main differences between the different ways in which interest is calculated on mortgages?
   Answer Reference: Section 2.3

7. What are the principal risks associated with interest-only mortgages?
   Answer Reference: Section 2.4.2

8. How much can be withdrawn from an investment bond each year without triggering an income tax charge?
   Answer Reference: Section 3

9. What is the difference between whole-of-life assurance and term assurance?
   Answer Reference: Section 4

10. What are the key differences between non-profit, with-profits and unit-linked life policies?
    Answer Reference: Section 4.1

11. What are the main factors that will influence the premium for a term assurance policy?
    Answer Reference: Section 4.2

12. What are the main differences between critical illness cover, income protection cover and accident and sickness cover?
    Answer Reference: Section 5

Glossary and Abbreviations

Glossary and Abbreviations

Active Management

A type of investment approach employed to generate returns in excess of the market.

Additional Rate (of Income Tax)

Tax on top band of income, currently 45%.

Alternative Investment Market (AIM)

Established by the London Stock Exchange. It is the junior market for smaller company shares.

Annual Equivalent Rate (AER)

The annualised compound rate of interest applied to a cash deposit or to a loan. Also known as the Annual Effective Rate or Effective Annual Rate.

Annual General Meeting (AGM)

Yearly meeting of shareholders. Mainly used to vote on dividends, appoint directors and approve financial statements.

Approved Persons

Employees in controlled functions, who must be approved by the regulator.

Articles of Association

The legal document which sets out the internal constitution of a company. Included within the Articles will be details of shareholder voting rights and company borrowing powers.

Auction

Sales system used by the Debt Management Office (DMO) when it issues gilts. Successful applicants pay the price they bid.

Authorisation

Required status under FSMA for firms that wish to provide financial services.

Authorised Corporate Director (ACD)

Fund manager for an OEIC.

Authorised Unit Trust (AUT)

Unit trust which is freely marketable. Authorised by the FCA.

Balance of Payments

A summary of all the transactions between a country and the rest of the world. The difference between a country's imports and exports.

Bank of England (BoE)

The UK's central bank. Implements economic policy decided by the Treasury and determines interest rates.

Basic Rate (of Income Tax)

Rate of tax charged on income that is below the higher-rate tax threshold.

Bearer Securities

Those whose ownership is evidenced by the mere possession of a certificate. Ownership can therefore pass from hand to hand without any formalities.

Beneficiaries

The beneficial owners of trust property, or those who inherit under a will.

Bid Price

Price at which dealers buy stock. It is also the price quoted by unit trusts that are dual-priced for sales of units.

Bonds

Interest-bearing securities which entitle holders to annual interest and repayment at maturity. Commonly issued by both companies and governments.

Bonus Issue

A free issue of shares to existing shareholders. No money is paid. The share price falls pro rata. Also known as a *Capitalisation* or *Scrip Issue*.

CAC 40

Index of the prices of 40 major French company shares.

Call Option

Option giving its buyer the right to buy an asset at an agreed price.

Capital Gains Tax (CGT)

Tax payable by individuals on profit made on the disposal of certain assets.

Capitalisation Issue

See *Bonus Issue*.

Central Bank

Central banks typically have responsibility for setting a nation's or a region's short-term interest rate, controlling the money supply, acting as banker and lender of last resort to the banking system and managing the national debt.

Certificated

Ownership (of shares) designated by certificate.

Certificates of Deposit (CDs)

Certificates issued by a bank as evidence that interest-bearing funds have been deposited with it. CDs are traded within the money market.

Clean Price

The quoted price of a gilt. The price quoted for a gilt excludes any interest that has accrued from the last interest payment date and is known as the 'clean' price. Accrued interest is added on afterwards and the price is then known as the 'dirty' price.

Closed-Ended

Organisations such as companies which are a fixed size as determined by their share capital. Commonly used to distinguish investment trusts (closed-ended) from unit trusts and OEICs (open-ended).

Closing

Reversing an original future position by, for example, selling what you have previously bought.

Commercial Paper (CP)

Money market instrument issued by large corporates.

Commission

Charges for acting as agent or broker.

Commodity

Items including sugar, wheat, oil and copper. Derivatives of commodities are traded on exchanges (eg, oil futures on ICE Futures).

Contract

A standard unit of trading in derivatives.

Controlled Functions

Job roles which require the employee to be approved by the FCA. There are groups of controlled functions, including significant influence functions, customer functions and LIBOR functions.

Convertible Bond

A bond that is convertible, at the investor's choice, into the same company's shares.

Coupon

Amount of interest paid on a bond.

Credit Creation

Expansion of loans which increases the money supply.

CREST

Electronic settlement system used to hold stock and settle transactions for UK shares.

Data Protection Act 1998

Legislation regulating the use of client data.

Debt Management Office (DMO)

The agency responsible for issuing gilts on behalf of the Treasury.

Dematerialised (Form)

System where securities are held electronically without certificates.

Glossary and Abbreviations

Derivatives

Options, futures and swaps. Their price is derived from an underlying asset.

Dilution Levy

An additional charge levied on investors buying or selling units in a single-priced fund to offset any potential effect that large purchases or sales can have on the value of the fund.

Dirty Price

The price quoted for a gilt excludes any interest that has accrued from the last interest payment date and is known as the 'clean' price. Accrued interest is added on afterwards and the price is then known as the 'dirty' price.

Diversification

Investment strategy of spreading risk by investing in a range of investments.

Dividend

Distribution of profits by a company.

Dividend Yield

Most recent dividend expressed as a percentage of current share price.

Dow Jones Industrial Average (DJIA)

Major share index in the USA, based on the prices of 30 major company shares.

Dual Pricing

System in which a unit trust manager quotes two prices at which investors can sell and buy.

Economic Cycle

The course an economy conventionally takes as economic growth fluctuates over time. Also known as the business cycle.

Economic Growth

The growth of GDP expressed in real terms, usually over the course of a calendar year. Often used as a barometer of an economy's health.

Effective Annual Rate

The annualised compound rate of interest applied to a cash deposit or loan. Also known as the Annual Equivalent Rate (AER).

Equity

Another name for shares. Can also be used to refer to the amount by which the value of a house exceeds any mortgage or borrowings secured on it.

Eurobond

An interest-bearing security issued internationally.

Euronext

European stock exchange network formed by the merger of the Paris, Brussels, Amsterdam and (later) Lisbon exchanges.

European Securities and Markets Authority (ESMA)

Responsible for drafting, implementing and monitoring EU financial regulation.

Exchange

Marketplace for trading investments.

Exchange Rate

The rate at which one currency can be exchanged for another.

Exchange-Traded Fund (ETF)

Type of collective investment scheme that is open-ended but traded on an investment exchange, rather than directly with the fund's managers.

Ex-Dividend (xd)

The period during which the purchase of shares or bonds (on which a dividend or coupon payment has been declared) does not entitle the new holder to this next dividend or interest payment.

Exercise an Option
Take up the right to buy or sell the underlying asset in an option.

Exercise Price
The price at which the right conferred by an option can be exercised by the holder against the writer.

Financial Conduct Authority (FCA)
One of the bodies that replaced the FSA in 2013 and which is responsible for regulation of conduct in retail, as well as wholesale, financial markets and the infrastructure that supports those markets.

Financial Services and Markets Act 2000 (FSMA)
Legislation which provides the framework for regulating financial services.

Fiscal Policy
The use of government spending, taxation and borrowing policies to either boost or restrain domestic demand in the economy so as to maintain full employment and price stability.

Fit and Proper
FSMA 2000 requires that every firm conducting financial services business must be 'fit and proper'.

Fixed-Interest Security
A tradable negotiable instrument, issued by a borrower for a fixed term, during which a regular and predetermined fixed rate of interest, based upon a nominal value, is paid to the holder until it is redeemed and the principal is repaid.

Fixed-Rate Borrowing
Borrowing when a set interest rate is paid.

Floating Rate Notes (FRNs)
Debt securities issued with a coupon periodically referenced to a benchmark interest rate, such as LIBOR.

Forex
Abbreviation for foreign exchange trading. Also FX.

Forward
A derivatives contract that creates a legally binding obligation between two parties for one to buy and the other to sell a prespecified amount of an asset at a prespecified price on a prespecified future date. As individually negotiated contracts, forwards are not traded on a derivatives exchange.

Forward Exchange Rate
An exchange rate set today, embodied in a forward contract, that will apply to a foreign exchange transaction at some prespecified point in the future.

FTSE 100
Main UK share index of 100 leading shares ('Footsie').

FTSE 250
UK share index based on the 250 shares immediately below the top 100.

FTSE 350
Index combining the FTSE 100 and FTSE 250 indices.

FTSE All Share Index
Index comprising around 98% of UK-listed shares by value.

Full Listing
Those public limited companies (plcs) admitted to the London Stock Exchange's (LSE) official list. Companies seeking a full listing on the LSE must satisfy the UK Listing Authority's (UKLA) stringent listing requirements and continuing obligations once listed.

Fund Manager
Firm that invests money on behalf of clients.

Glossary and Abbreviations

Fund Supermarket

An internet-based service that provides a convenient way of investing in collective investment funds by allowing a variety of funds to be purchased from a number of different management groups in one place.

Future

An agreement to buy or sell an item at a future date, at a price agreed today. Differs from a forward in that it is a standardised amount and therefore the contract can be traded on an exchange.

Gilt-Edged Market Maker (GEMM)

A firm that is a market maker in gilts.

Gilt-Edged Stock (Gilt)

UK government bond.

Gross Domestic Product (GDP)

A measure of a country's output.

Harmonised Index of Consumer Prices (HICP)

Standard measurement of inflation throughout the European Union.

Hedging

A technique employed to reduce the impact of adverse price movements in financial assets held. Often uses derivatives to achieve this aim.

Higher Rate (of Income Tax)

Tax on the band of income above the basic rate and below the additional rate, currently 40%.

Holder

Investor who buys put or call options.

Independent Financial Adviser (IFA)

A financial adviser who is not tied to the products of any one product provider and is duty-bound to give clients best advice and offer them the option of paying for advice. IFAs must establish the financial planning needs of their clients through a personal fact-find, and satisfy these needs with the most appropriate products offered in the marketplace.

Individual Savings Account (ISA)

Savings scheme introduced in 1999 which provided a wrapper in which cash, stocks and shares can benefit from tax concessions.

Inflation

An increase in the general level of prices.

Inheritance Tax (IHT)

Tax on the value of an estate when a person dies.

Initial Public Offering (IPO)

A new issue of ordinary shares, whether made by an offer for sale, an offer for subscription or a placing. Also known as a new issue.

Insider Dealing

Criminal offence by people with unpublished price-sensitive information who deal, advise others to deal or pass the information on.

Integration

Third stage of money laundering.

IntercontinentalExchange (ICE)

ICE operates regulated global futures exchanges and over-the-counter (OTC) markets for agricultural, energy, equity index and currency contracts, as well as credit derivatives. ICE conducts its energy futures markets through ICE Futures Europe, which is based in London, and also owns LIFFE.

In-the-Money

Call option when the exercise price is below current market price (or put option when exercise price is above).

Investment Bank

Business that specialises in raising debt and equity for companies.

Investment Company with Variable Capital (ICVC)

Alternative term for an OEIC.

Investment Trust

A company, not a trust, which invests in a diversified range of investments.

Irredeemable Gilt
A gilt with no redemption date. Investors receive interest in perpetuity.

Layering
Second stage in money laundering.

LIFFE
The UK's principal derivatives exchange for trading financial and soft commodity derivatives products. Owned by Intercontinental Exchange (ICE).

Liquidity
The ease with which an item can be traded on the market. Liquid markets are described as deep.

Liquidity Risk
The risk that shares may be difficult to sell at a reasonable price.

Listing
Companies whose securities are listed on the London Stock Exchange and available to be traded.

Lloyd's of London
The world's largest insurance market.

Loan Stock
A corporate bond issued in the domestic bond market without any underlying collateral, or security.

London InterBank Offered Rate (LIBOR)
A benchmark money market interest rate.

London Metal Exchange (LME)
The market for trading in derivatives of certain metals, such as copper, zinc and aluminium.

London Stock Exchange (LSE)
The main UK market for securities.

Long Position
The position following the purchase of a security or buying a derivative.

Market
All exchanges are markets – electronic or physical meeting places where assets are bought or sold.

Market Capitalisation
Total market value of a company's shares. The share price multiplied by the number of shares in issue.

Market Maker
An LSE member firm which is obliged to offer to buy and sell securities in which it is registered throughout the mandatory quote period. In return for providing this liquidity to the market, it can make its profits through the differences at which it buys and sells.

Maturity
Date when the capital on a bond is repaid.

Memorandum of Association
The legal document that principally defines a company's powers, or objects, and its relationship with the outside world.

Merger
The combining of two or more companies into one new entity.

Markets in Financial Instruments Directive (MiFID)
The directive that introduced European-wide rules and regulations regarding the conduct of business and which enables the passporting of investment services across member states.

Mixed Economy
Economy which works through a combination of market forces and government involvement.

Monetary Policy
The setting of short-term interest rates by a central bank in order to manage domestic demand and achieve price stability in the economy.

Monetary Policy Committee (MPC)
Committee run by the Bank of England which sets interest rates.

Multilateral Trading Facilities (MTFs)
Systems that bring together multiple parties that are interested in buying and selling financial instruments including shares, bonds and derivatives.

Mutual Fund
A type of collective investment scheme found in the US.

Names
Participants at Lloyd's of London who form syndicates to write insurance business. Both individuals and companies can be names.

NASDAQ
National Association of Securities Dealers Automated Quotations. US market specialising in the shares of technology companies.

NASDAQ Composite
NASDAQ stock index.

National Debt
A government's total outstanding borrowing resulting from financing successive budget deficits, mainly through the issue of government-backed securities.

National Savings and Investments (NS&I)
Government agency that provides investment products for the retail market.

Nikkei 225
The main Japanese share index.

Nominal Value
The amount of a bond that will be repaid on maturity. Also known as face or par value.

Nominated Adviser (NOMAD)
Firm which advises AIM companies on their regulatory responsibilities.

Offer Price
Price at which dealers sell stock. It is also the price quoted by unit trusts that are dual-priced for purchases of units.

Open
To initiate a transaction, eg, an opening purchase or sale of a future. Normally reversed by a closing transaction.

Open Economy
Country with no restrictions on trading with other countries.

Open-Ended
Type of investment such as OEICs or unit trusts which can expand without limit.

Open-Ended Investment Company (OEIC)
Collective investment vehicle similar to a unit trust. Alternatively described as an ICVC (Investment Company with Variable Capital).

Open Outcry
Trading system used by some derivatives exchanges. Participants stand on the floor of the exchange and call out transactions they would like to undertake.

Option
A derivative giving the buyer the right, but not the obligation, to buy or sell an asset.

Out-of-the-Money
A call option when the exercise or strike price is above the market price, or a put option when it is below.

Over-the-Counter (OTC) Derivatives

Derivatives that are not traded on a derivatives exchange, owing to their non-standardised contract specifications.

Passive Management

An investment approach that aims to track the performance of a stock market index. Employed in those securities markets that are believed to be price-efficient.

Personal Allowance

Amount of income that each person can earn each year tax-free.

Placement

First stage of money laundering.

Platform

Platforms are online services such as fund supermarkets and wraps that are used by intermediaries to view and administer their investment clients' portfolios.

Pre-Emption Rights

The rights accorded to ordinary shareholders under company law to subscribe for new ordinary shares issued by the company in which they have the shareholding, for cash, before the shares are offered to outside investors.

Preference Share

Shares which pay fixed dividends. Do not have voting rights, but do have priority over ordinary shares in default situations.

Premium

The amount of cash paid by the holder of an option to the writer in exchange for conferring a right.

Premium Bond

National Savings & Investments bonds that pay prizes each month. Winnings are tax-free.

Primary Market

The function of a stock exchange in bringing new securities to the market and raising funds.

Protectionism

The economic policy of restraining trade between countries by imposing methods such as tariffs and quotas on imported goods.

Proxy

Appointee who votes on a shareholder's behalf at company meetings.

Prudential Regulation Authority (PRA)

The UK body that is responsible for prudential regulation of all deposit-taking institutions, insurers and investment banks.

Public Sector Net Cash Requirement (PSNCR)

Borrowing needed to meet the shortfall of government revenue compared to government expenditure.

Put Option

Option where buyer has the right to sell an asset.

Quote-Driven

Dealing system driven by securities firms who quote buying and selling prices.

Real Estate Investment Trust (REIT)

An investment trust that specialises in investing in commercial property.

Redeemable Security

A security issued with a known maturity, or redemption, date.

Redemption

The repayment of principal to the holder of a redeemable security.

Redemption Yield

A measure that incorporates both the income and capital return – assuming the investor holds the bond until its maturity – into one figure.

Glossary and Abbreviations

Registrar

The official of a company who maintains the share register.

Resolution

Proposal on which shareholders vote.

Retail Bank

Organisation that provides banking facilities to individuals and small/medium businesses.

Retail Prices Index (RPI)

Index that measures the movement of prices.

Rights Issue

The issue of new ordinary shares to a company's shareholders in proportion to each shareholder's existing shareholding, usually at a price deeply discounted to that prevailing in the market.

Robo-Advice

The application of technology to the process of providing financial advice but without the involvement of a financial adviser.

Scrip Issue

See *Bonus Issue*.

Secondary Market

Marketplace for trading in existing securities.

Securities

Bonds and equities.

Settlor

The creator of a trust.

Share Capital

The nominal value of a company's equity or ordinary shares. A company's **authorised share capital** is the nominal value of equity the company may issue, while **issued share capital** is that which the company has issued. The term share capital is often extended to include a company's preference shares.

Short Position

The position following the sale of a security not owned, or selling a derivative.

SICAV

Type of European collective investment scheme that is open-ended.

Single Pricing

Refers to the use of the mid-market prices of the underlying assets to produce a single price for units/shares in collective investment schemes.

Special Resolution

Proposal put to shareholders requiring 75% of the votes cast.

Spread

Difference between a buying (bid) and selling (ask or offer) price.

Stamp Duty

Tax at ½% on the purchase of certain assets including certificated securities.

Stamp Duty Land Tax (SDLT)

Tax charged on the purchase of properties and land above a certain value.

Stamp Duty Reserve Tax (SDRT)

Stamp duty levied at ½% on purchase of dematerialised equities.

State-Controlled Economy

Country where all economic activity is controlled by the state.

Stock Exchange Automated Quotations (SEAQ)

LSE screen display system where market makers display the prices at which they are willing to deal. Used mainly for fixed-income stocks and small cap shares.

Stock Exchange Electronic Trading Service (SETS)

LSE's electronic order-driven trading system.

Stock Exchange Electronic Trading Service – quotes and crosses (SETSqx)

A trading platform for securities less liquid than those traded on SETS. It combines a periodic electronic auction book with stand-alone quote-driven market making.

STRIPS

The principal and interest payments of those designated gilts that can be separately traded as zero coupon bonds (ZCBs). STRIPS is the acronym for Separate Trading of Registered Interest and Principal of Securities.

Swap

An over-the-counter (OTC) derivative whereby two parties exchange a series of periodic payments based on a notional principal amount over an agreed term. Swaps can take the form of interest rate swaps, currency swaps and equity swaps.

Swinging Price

When a single-priced investment fund moves its pricing as a result of a large number of buy or sell orders.

Syndicate

Lloyd's names joining together to write insurance.

T+2

The two-day rolling settlement period over which all certificated deals executed on the London Stock Exchange's (LSE) SETS are settled.

Takeover

When one company buys more than 50% of the shares of another.

Third Party Administrator (TPA)

A firm that specialises in undertaking investment administration for other firms.

Treasury

Government department ultimately responsible for the regulation of the financial services industry.

Treasury Bills

Short-term (usually 90-day) borrowings of the UK government. Issued at a discount to the nominal value at which they will mature. Traded in the money market.

Trustees

The legal owners of trust property who owe a duty of skill and care to the trust's beneficiaries.

Two-Way Price

Prices quoted by a market maker at which they are willing to buy (bid) and sell (offer).

Underlying

Asset from which a derivative is derived.

Unit Trust

A system whereby money from investors is pooled together and invested collectively on their behalf into an open-ended trust.

Wrap

A type of fund platform that enables advisers to take a holistic view of the various assets that a client has in a variety of accounts.

Writer

Party selling an option. The writers receive premiums in exchange for taking the risk of being exercised against.

Xetra DAX

German shares index, comprising 30 shares.

Yield

Income from an investment as a percentage of the current price.

Zero Coupon Bond (ZCB)

Bonds issued at a discount to their nominal value that do not pay a coupon but which are redeemed at par on a prespecified future date.

Glossary and Abbreviations

ABS	Asset-Backed Security	**ESMA**	European Securities and Markets Authority
ACD	Authorised Corporate Director	**ETF**	Exchange-Traded Fund
AGM	Annual General Meeting	**EU**	European Union
AIM	Alternative Investment Market	**FCA**	Financial Conduct Authority
AML	Anti-Money Laundering	**FIA Europe**	Futures Industry Association
APR	Annual Percentage Rate	**FOS**	Financial Ombudsman Service
AUT	Authorised Unit Trust	**FPC**	Financial Policy Committee
BBA	British Bankers' Association	**FSAP**	Financial Securities Action Plan
BIS	Bank for International Settlements	**FSCS**	Financial Services Compensation Scheme
BoE	Bank of England	**FRN**	Floating Rate Note
CBOE	Chicago Board Options Exchange	**FSMA**	Financial Services and Markets Act (2000)
CC	Competition Commission	**GDP**	Gross Domestic Product
CCP	Central Counterparty	**HICP**	Harmonised Index of Consumer Prices
CD	Certificate of Deposit	**HMRC**	Her Majesty's Revenue & Customs
CGT	Capital Gains Tax	**ICE**	IntercontinentalExchange
CIS	Collective Investment Scheme	**ICMA**	International Capital Market Association
CMA	Competition and Markets Authority	**ICSD**	International Central Securities Depository
CP	Commercial Paper	**ICVC**	Investment Companies with Variable Capital
CPI	Consumer Prices Index	**IFA**	Independent Financial Adviser
CSD	Central Securities Depository	**IHT**	Inheritance Tax
CTF	Child Trust Fund	**IA**	Investment Association
DJIA	Dow Jones Industrial Average	**IOSCO**	International Organization of Securities Commissions
DMO	Debt Management Office		
DVP	Delivery versus Payment		
ECB	European Central Bank		
EEA	European Economic Area		

IPO	Initial Public Offering	**PIBS**	Permanent Interest-Bearing Shares
ISA	Individual Savings Account	**PLC**	Public Limited Company
ISD	Investment Services Directive	**POCA**	Proceeds of Crime Act
ITC	Investment Trust Company	**PRA**	Prudential Regulation Authority
JISA	Junior ISA	**PSNCR**	Public Sector Net Cash Requirement
JMLSG	Joint Money Laundering Steering Group	**RDR**	Retail Distribution Review
LIBOR	London InterBank Offered Rate	**REIT**	Real Estate Investment Trust
LME	London Metal Exchange	**RIE**	Recognised Investment Exchange
LSE	London Stock Exchange	**RPI**	Retail Prices Index
MAD	Market Abuse Directive	**RUR**	Register Update Request
MiFID	Markets in Financial Instruments Directive	**S2P**	State Second Pension
MLRO	Money Laundering Reporting Officer	**SDLT**	Stamp Duty Land Tax
		SDRT	Stamp Duty Reserve Tax
MPC	Monetary Policy Committee	**SEAQ**	Stock Exchange Automated Quotation system
MTF	Multilateral Trading Facility	**SETS**	Stock Exchange Electronic Trading Service
MTS	An electronic exchange for trading European government bonds	**SFO**	Serious Fraud Office
NAV	Net Asset Value	**SICAV**	*Société d'Investissement à Capital Variable*
NOMAD	Nominated Adviser	**SIPP**	Self-Invested Personal Pension
NSI	National Savings and Investments	**SSAS**	Small Self-Administered Scheme
NURS	Non-UCITS Retail Schemes	**STP**	Straight-Through Processing
NYSE	New York Stock Exchange	**STRIPS**	Separate Trading of Registered Interest and Principal of Securities
OEIC	Open-Ended Investment Company		
OTC	Over-the-Counter	**TISA**	Tax Incentivised Savings Association
PEP	Personal Equity Plan/Politically Exposed Person	**TSE**	Tokyo Stock Exchange

UCITS	Undertakings for Collective Investment in Transferable Securities
UKLA	United Kingdom Listing Authority
UN	United Nations
VAT	Value Added Tax
VCT	Venture Capital Trust
WMA	Wealth Management Association
WTO	World Trade Organisation
xd	Ex-dividend
ZCB	Zero Coupon Bond

Multiple Choice Questions

Multiple Choice Questions

The following questions have been compiled to reflect as closely as possible the standard you will experience in your examination. Please note, however, they are not the CISI examination questions themselves.

Tick one answer for each question. When you have completed all questions, refer to the end of this section for the answers.

1. Which of the following is a wholesale market activity associated with an investment bank?

    A. Execution-only stockbroking
    B. Life assurance
    C. Mergers and acquisitions
    D. Private banking

2. Holding assets in safe-keeping is one of the principal activities of:

    A. A custodian bank
    B. An international bank
    C. An investment bank
    D. A retail bank

3. An economy that is characterised by an absence of barriers to trade and controls over foreign exchange is known as:

    A. A market economy
    B. A mixed economy
    C. A state-controlled economy
    D. An open economy

4. For those on a fixed income, high levels of inflation would normally:

    A. Allow them to save more
    B. Reduce their tax allowances
    C. Allow them to invest for longer periods
    D. Reduce the amount of goods they can buy

5. What is the definition of a country's invisible trade balance?

    A. International transactions related to the purchase and sale of domestic and foreign investment assets
    B. The difference between the value of imported and exported goods
    C. The total value of goods and services that flow in and out of the country
    D. The difference between the value of imported and exported services

6. Which organisation provides compensation in the event that a bank goes bust?

    A. FCA
    B. FOS
    C. FSCS
    D. PRA

7. Which of the following instruments is zero coupon?

    A. Certificates of deposit
    B. Cash ISAs
    C. Bank current accounts
    D. Treasury bills

8. Which type of foreign exchange transaction would normally settle two days later?

    A. Forward
    B. Future
    C. Spot
    D. Swap

9. Energy commodity futures contracts are traded on which market?

    A. LIFFE
    B. Eurex
    C. ICE Futures
    D. LME

10. Which of the following markets would normally trade aluminium and tin derivatives?

    A. LIFFE
    B. ICE
    C. LME
    D. LSE

11. Which stock market index provides the widest view of the US stock market?

    A. Dow Jones Industrial Average
    B. NASDAQ Composite
    C. Nikkei 225
    D. S&P 500

12. The key difference between the primary market and the secondary market is that:

    A. The primary market relates to equities and the secondary market relates to bonds
    B. The primary market covers regulated and protected activities and the secondary market covers unregulated and unprotected activities
    C. The primary market is where new shares are first marketed and the secondary market is where existing shares are subsequently traded
    D. The primary market involves domestic trading and the secondary market involves overseas trading

13. In the event of a company going into liquidation, who would normally have the lowest priority for payment?

    A. Banks
    B. Bondholders
    C. Ordinary shareholders
    D. Preference shareholders

14. What type of corporate action would have taken place if an existing shareholder purchased new shares in the company, thereby increasing the total shares issued?

    A. Bonus issue
    B. Capitalisation issue
    C. Rights issue
    D. Scrip issue

15. The passing of a special resolution at a company meeting requires what MINIMUM percentage of votes in favour?

    A. 50
    B. 75
    C. 90
    D. 100

16. What is the corporate equivalent of Treasury bills known as?

    A. Supranational bonds
    B. Commercial paper
    C. Structured products
    D. Certificates of deposit

17. Which of the following is a mandatory corporate action with options?

    A. Bonus issue
    B. Merger
    C. Rights issue
    D. Takeover

18. Which types of instrument would you expect to see traded on SETS?

    A. Options
    B. Futures
    C. Unit trusts
    D. FTSE 350 shares

19. A UK company has issued a fixed coupon bond into the Japanese market denominated in yen to make it attractive to Japanese investors. What type of bond is this known as?

    A. Asset-backed bond
    B. Eurobond
    C. Foreign bond
    D. Covered bond

20. Which type of bond gives the bondholder the right to require the issuer to repay it early?

    A. Floating rate note
    B. Convertible
    C. Medium-term note
    D. Puttable

21. You have a holding of £10,000 5% Treasury Gilt 2018 which is currently priced at 112 and on which you receive half yearly interest of £250. What is its flat yield?

    A. 5.0%
    B. 4.46%
    C. 2.50%
    D. 2.23%

22. If interest rates increase, what will be the effect on a 5% government bond?

    A. Price will rise
    B. Price will fall
    C. Coupon will rise
    D. Coupon will fall

23. Which of the following statements concerning call and put options is TRUE?

    A. The buyer of a call has the right to sell an asset
    B. The buyer of a put has the right to buy an asset
    C. The seller of a call has the right to sell an asset
    D. The buyer of a call has the right to buy an asset

24. An investor who has entered into a contract which commits him to buying the underlying asset at a future date is described as?

    A. Holder
    B. Long
    C. Short
    D. Writer

25. Which of the following is most likely to be traded as an OTC derivative?

    A. Covered warrant
    B. Future
    C. Option
    D. Swap

26. Which type of collective investment scheme would you expect to trade at a discount or premium to its net asset value?

    A. Unit trust
    B. ETF
    C. Investment trust
    D. OEIC

27. Which of the following types of collective investment scheme has traditionally been dual-priced, but may now also use single pricing?

    A. ETF
    B. REIT
    C. Investment trust
    D. Unit trust

28. A fund that aims to mimic the performance of an index deploys which type of investment style?

    A. Contrarian
    B. Growth
    C. Passive
    D. Momentum

29. An investment fund which can be sold throughout the EU, subject to regulation by its home country regulator, is known as:

    A. An investment trust
    B. An OEIC
    C. A SICAV
    D. A UCITS

30. The standard settlement period for the sale of a unit trust is which of the following?

    A. T+1
    B. T+3
    C. T+4
    D. T+5

31. What MINIMUM percentage of profits, after expenses, must be distributed for a real estate investment trust (REIT) to retain its tax status?

    A. 90
    B. 85
    C. 75
    D. 60

32. What type of investment vehicle would you expect to have the highest minimum investment limit?

    A. ETF
    B. Hedge fund
    C. Investment trust
    D. SICAV

33. From 2013, which UK regulatory body is responsible for the supervision of investment exchanges?

    A. Financial Conduct Authority
    B. Financial Policy Committee
    C. Financial Services Authority
    D. Prudential Regulatory Authority

34. A money launderer is actively switching monies between investment products. The stage of money laundering relevant to these activities is known as:

    A. Investment
    B. Integration
    C. Layering
    D. Placement

35. The type of customer due diligence necessary when an individual is identified as a politically exposed person (PEP) is known as:

    A. Sensitive
    B. Enhanced
    C. Simplified
    D. Non-standard

36. Insider dealing rules apply to which ONE of the following securities?

    A. Commodity derivatives
    B. OEIC shares
    C. Government bonds
    D. Unit trusts

37. What is the MAXIMUM payout that can be awarded by the Financial Ombudsman Service?

    A. £30,000
    B. £50,000
    C. £100,000
    D. £150,000

38. Behaviour likely to give a false or misleading impression of the supply, demand or value of the investments deemed under the legislation to be qualifying, is most likely to constitute which of the following offences?

    A. Front running
    B. Money laundering
    C. Market abuse
    D. Insider dealing

39. Which of the following assets is exempt from capital gains tax?

    A. Buy-to-let properties
    B. Shares
    C. UK government bonds
    D. Unit trusts

40. What income tax will an additional rate taxpayer with an overall income of £250,000 per annum pay on a UK dividend?

    A. 7.5%
    B. 32.5%
    C. 38.1%
    D. 45%

41. What is the minimum age for holding a Stocks & Shares ISA?

    A. 16
    B. 18
    C. 25
    D. There is no minimum age

42. Sue, a higher rate taxpayer aged 43, receives £10,000 in dividend income. How much income tax is due?

    A. £375
    B. £750
    C. £3,250
    D. £1,625

43. At what age can a child withdraw money from their Junior ISA?

    A. 15
    B. 16
    C. 18
    D. 21

44. If an individual investor wishes to be able to manage the investments in a pension themselves, which type of pension would be the most suitable?

    A. SSAS
    B. SIPP
    C. Occupational pension
    D. Stakeholder pension

45. When an investment bond is encashed, the profits are subject to which tax?

    A. Capital gains tax
    B. Corporation tax
    C. Income tax
    D. Inheritance tax

46. The individual charged with looking after the assets of a trust is known as the:

    A. Beneficiary
    B. Executor
    C. Settlor
    D. Trustee

47. You have a loan where interest is charged quarterly at 20% pa. What is the effective annual rate of borrowing?

    A. 21%
    B. 21.18%
    C. 21.35%
    D. 21.55%

48. If you expect interest rates to rise over the next few years, which type of mortgage payment would you expect to be most attractive?

    A. Tracker
    B. Discounted
    C. Fixed
    D. Variable

49. A policy that only pays out if death occurs during the term of the policy is:

    A. An endowment plan
    B. A term assurance
    C. An income replacement plan
    D. A whole-of-life assurance

50. Which of the following types of investment fund is most likely to utilise gearing?

    A. ETF
    B. Investment trust
    C. OEIC
    D. Unit trust

Answers to Multiple Choice Questions

1. **C** **Chapter 1, Section 3.3**

Advice on mergers and acquisitions is a wholesale market activity provided by investment banks.

2. **A** **Chapter 1, Section 3.8**

The primary role of a custodian is the safe-keeping of assets.

3. **D** **Chapter 2, Section 2**

In an open economy there are few barriers to trade or controls over foreign exchange.

4. **D** **Chapter 2, Section 4.2**

High levels of inflation mean that prices rise and so someone on a fixed income would be able to buy fewer goods.

5. **D** **Chapter 2, Section 5.2.3**

The invisible trade balance is the difference between the value of imported and exported services. B is known as the visible trade balance, C is the country's current account, and A is the capital account.

6. **C** **Chapter 3, Section 2.1**

The Financial Services Compensation Scheme (FSCS) provides protection in the event of a deposit-taking institution going bust.

7. **D** **Chapter 3, Section 3**

Treasury bills do not pay interest but instead are issued at a discount to par.

8. **C** **Chapter 3, Section 5**

The 'spot rate' is the rate quoted by a bank for the exchange of one currency for another with immediate effect; however, spot trades are settled two business days after the transaction date.

9. **C** **Chapter 6, Section 5.3**

ICE operates the electronic global futures and OTC marketplace for trading energy commodity contracts. These contracts include crude oil and refined products, natural gas, power and emissions.

10. **C** **Chapter 6, Section 5.3**

A range of metals including aluminium, copper, nickel, tin, zinc and lead are traded on the London Metal Exchange (LME).

11. **D** **Chapter 4, Section 8**

The S&P 500 is generally regarded as providing the widest view of the US market compared to the Dow Jones and the NASDAQ Composite.

Multiple Choice Questions

12.   C   **Chapter 4, Section 7.1**

The primary market is where new shares in a company are marketed for the first time. When these shares are subsequently resold, this is normally done on the secondary market.

13.   C   **Chapter 4, Section 3.1**

If the company closes down, often described as the company being 'wound up', the ordinary shareholders are paid after everybody else.

14.   C   **Chapter 4, Section 6.2**

Under a rights issue, a shareholder is offered the right to subscribe for further 'new' shares at a fixed price per share.

15.   B   **Chapter 4, Section 2.3**

Matters of major importance, such as a proposed change to the company's constitution, require a 'special resolution' and at least 75% to vote in favour.

16.   B   **Chapter 3, Section 3**

Commercial paper is issued by companies and is effectively the corporate equivalent of a Treasury bill.

17.   C   **Chapter 4, Section 6.2**

A rights issue is a mandatory with options type of corporate action.

18.   D   **Chapter 4, Section 9**

SETS is used to trade equity shares.

19.   C   **Chapter 5, Section 4.3**

A foreign bond is one issued by an overseas entity into a domestic market and is denominated in the domestic currency.

20.   D   **Chapter 5, Section 4.1.2**

Puttable bonds give the bondholder the right to require the issuer to redeem early, on a set date or between specific dates.

21.   B   **Chapter 5, Section 5.2**

The flat yield is calculated by taking the annual coupon and dividing by the bond's price, and then multiplying by 100 to obtain a percentage. So the calculation is 5/112 x 100 = 4.46%.

22.   B   **Chapter 5, Section 5.1.3**

Bonds have an inverse relationship with interest rates so if interest rates rise, then bond prices will fall.

23. D Chapter 6, Section 3.3

A call option is when the buyer has the right to buy the asset at the exercise price, if he chooses to. The seller is obliged to deliver if the buyer exercises the option.

24. B Chapter 6, Section 2.3

A contract to buy an underlying asset at a future date is a future and the buyer is referred to as long.

25. D Chapter 6, Section 4.1

A swap is a type of OTC derivative.

26. C Chapter 7, Section 5.4

Investment trusts are structured and listed on a stock market as with any other type of share and able to borrow money to gear up the portfolio. The share price, however, is not necessarily the same as the value of the underlying investments (determined on a per share basis and referred to as the net asset value). The share price could therefore trade at a premium or discount to the net asset value.

27. D Chapter 7, Section 4.1

Unit trusts have traditionally been dual priced, that is to quote separate prices for buying and selling the units. They now have a choice whether to use dual or single pricing.

28. C Chapter 7, Section 1.3

A passive fund aims to generate returns in line with a chosen index or benchmark.

29. D Chapter 7, Section 1.5

The UCITS directives have been issued with the intention of creating a framework for cross-border sales of investment funds throughout the EU. They allow an investment fund to be sold throughout the EU subject to regulation by its home country regulator.

30. C Chapter 7, Section 4.2

Fund groups are required to settle sales within four days of the receipt of all required documentation.

31. A Chapter 7, Section 5.2

At least 90% of profits, after expenses, must be distributed to shareholders for a REIT to retain its tax status.

32. B Chapter 7, Section 8

Hedge funds typically have high minimum investment levels, ranging from £50,000 to over £1 million in some cases.

33. A Chapter 8, Section 1.2.1

The Financial Conduct Authority is responsible for the regulation of all firms in retail and wholesale financial markets, as well as the infrastructure that supports these markets. This includes supervision of investment exchanges.

Multiple Choice Questions

34. C Chapter 8, Section 2.1.1

Layering is the second stage and involves moving the money around in order to make it difficult for the authorities to link the placed funds with the ultimate beneficiary of the money.

35. B Chapter 8, Section 2.1.3

JMLSG guidance requires enhanced due diligence to take account of the greater potential for money laundering in higher risk cases, specifically when the customer is not physically present when being identified, and in respect of PEPs (politically exposed persons) and correspondent banking.

36. C Chapter 8, Section 3

The instruments (securities) covered by the insider dealing legislation in the Criminal Justice Act include government bonds, but does not embrace commodity derivatives, shares in OEICs or unit trusts.

37. D Chapter 8, Section 6.2

The FOS can make an award against what it considers to be fair compensation; however, the sum cannot exceed £150,000.

38. C Chapter 8, Section 4

Market abuse includes behaviour likely to give a false or misleading impression of the supply, demand or value of qualifying investments.

39. C Chapter 9, Section 2.2

UK government bonds (gilts) are exempt from CGT.

40. C Chapter 9, Section 2.1.1

From April 2016, dividends are taxed at 7.5% for basic rate taxpayers, 32.5% for higher rate taxpayers and 38.1% for additional rate taxpayers.

41. B Chapter 9, Section 3.1

Stocks & Shares ISAs are available only to residents of the UK over the age of 18. Cash ISAs are available to UK residents aged 16 and over.

42. D Chapter 9, Section 2.1.1

The first £5,000 of dividend income in each tax year is tax-free, and sums above that will be taxed at 32.5% for higher rate taxpayers. Therefore, the income tax due is (£10,000–£5,000) x 32.5% = £1,625.

43. C Chapter 9, Section 3.2

At the age of 16, a child assumes management responsibility for their Junior ISA, but they cannot withdraw funds until the age of 18, except in the case of terminal illness or death.

44.   B   Chapter 9, Section 4.4

Individuals can manage the investments held within a self-invested personal pension (SIPP) subject to HMRC guidelines.

45.   C   Chapter 10, Section 3

When investment bonds are encashed, the profits made are taxed as income rather than capital gains.

46.   D   Chapter 9, Section 5.1

A settlor creates the trust and the person he gives the property to, to look after for the beneficiaries is the trustee.

47.   D   Chapter 10, Section 1.4

Interest will be charged on the outstanding balance at 5% per quarter so the effective annual rate is [(1.05 x 1.05 x 1.05 x 1.05)] – 1 x 100 = 21.55%.

48.   C   Chapter 10, Section 2.3

A fixed rate mortgage should be the most attractive if interest rates are expected to rise over the next few years.

49.   B   Chapter 10, Section 4.2

Term assurance is designed to pay out only if death occurs within a specified period.

50.   B   Chapter 7, Section 5.3

One of the distinguishing features of an investment trust is its ability to borrow funds for investment, in other words to use gearing.

Syllabus Learning Map

Syllabus Learning Map

Syllabus Unit/ Element		Chapter/ Section
Element 1	**Introduction**	**Chapter 1**
1.1	**The Financial Services Industry** On completion, the candidate should:	
1.1.1	know the role of the following within the financial services industry: • retail banks • building societies • investment banks • pension funds • insurance companies • fund managers • stockbrokers • custodians • platforms • third party administrators (TPAs) • industry trade and professional bodies	3
1.1.2	know the function of and differences between retail and professional business and who the main customers are in each case: • retail clients and professional clients	2
1.1.3	know the role of the following investment distribution channels: • independent financial adviser • restricted advice • execution-only • robo advice	4
Element 2	**The Economic Environment**	**Chapter 2**
2.1	**The Economic Environment** On completion, the candidate should:	
2.1.1	know the factors which determine the level of economic activity: • state-controlled economies • market economies • mixed economies • open economies	2
2.1.2	know the role of central banks: • the Bank of England • the Federal Reserve • the European Central Bank	3
2.1.3	know the functions of the Monetary Policy Committee	3.2.1
2.1.4	know how goods and services are paid for and how credit is created	4.1
2.1.5	understand the impact of inflation/deflation on economic behaviour	4.2
2.1.6	know the meaning of the following measures of inflation: • consumer prices index • retail prices index	5.1

231

Syllabus Unit/ Element		Chapter/ Section
2.1.7	understand the impact of the following economic data: • gross domestic product (GDP) • balance of payments • budget deficit/surplus • level of unemployment • exchange rates	5.2

Element 3	**Financial Assets and Markets**	**Chapter 3**
3.1	**Cash Deposits** On completion, the candidate should:	
3.1.1	know the characteristics of fixed term and instant access deposit accounts	2
3.1.2	be able to calculate the net interest due given the gross interest rate, the deposited sum, the period and tax rate	2
3.1.3	know the advantages and disadvantages of investing in cash	2.1
3.2	**The Money Market** On completion, the candidate should:	
3.2.1	know the difference between a capital market instrument and a money market instrument	3
3.2.2	know the definition and features of the following: • Treasury bill • Commercial paper • Certificate of deposit • Money market funds	3
3.2.3	know the advantages and disadvantages of investing in money market instruments	3
3.3	**Property** On completion, the candidate should:	
3.3.1	know the characteristics of property investment: • commercial/residential property • direct/indirect investment	4
3.3.2	know the potential advantages and disadvantages of investing in property	4
3.4	**Foreign Exchange Market** On completion, the candidate should:	
3.4.1	know the basic structure of the foreign exchange market including: • currency quotes • settlement • spot/forward • short-term currency swaps	5

Syllabus Learning Map

Syllabus Unit/ Element		Chapter/ Section
Element 4	**Equities**	**Chapter 4**
4.1	**Equities** On completion, the candidate should:	
4.1.1	know how a company is formed and the differences between private and public companies	2
4.1.2	know the features and benefits of ordinary and preference shares: • dividend • capital gain • share benefits • right to subscribe for new shares • right to vote	3 & 4
4.1.3	be able to calculate the share dividend yield	4
4.1.4	understand the advantages, disadvantages and risks associated with owning shares: • price risk • liquidity risk • issuer risk	5
4.1.5	know the definition of a corporate action and the difference between mandatory, voluntary and mandatory with options	6
4.1.6	understand the following terms: • bonus/scrip/capitalisation issues • rights issues • dividend payments • takeover/merger (may be tested by the use of a simple calculation)	6
4.1.7	know the purpose and format of annual general meetings	2.3
4.1.8	know the function of a stock exchange: • primary/secondary market • listing	7.1
4.1.9	know the types and uses of the main global stock exchange indices	8
4.1.10	know how shares are traded: • on-exchange/over-the-counter • multilateral trading facilities • order-driven/quote-driven	9
4.1.11	know the method of holding title and related terminology: registered; bearer; immobilised; dematerialised	10
4.1.12	understand the role of the central counterparty in clearing and settlement	11
4.1.13	understand how settlement takes place: • participants • process • settlement cycles	12

Syllabus Unit/ Element		Chapter/ Section
Element 5	**Bonds**	**Chapter 5**
5.1	**Characteristics** On completion, the candidate should:	
5.1.1	understand the characteristics and terminology of bonds: • coupon • redemption • nominal value	2
5.2	**Government Bonds** On completion, the candidate should:	
5.2.1	know the definition and features of government bonds: • types • yields	3
5.3	**Corporate Bonds** On completion, the candidate should:	
5.3.1	know the definitions and features of the following types of bond: • domestic • foreign • eurobond • asset-backed securities including covered bonds • zero coupon • convertible	4
5.4	**Bonds** On completion, the candidate should:	
5.4.1	know the potential advantages and disadvantages of investing in different types of bonds	5.1
5.4.2	be able to calculate the flat yield of a bond	5.2
5.4.3	understand the role of credit rating agencies and the differences between investment and non-investment grades	5.3

Syllabus Unit/ Element		Chapter/ Section
Element 6	**Derivatives**	**Chapter 6**
6.1	**Derivatives Uses** On completion, the candidate should:	
6.1.1	know the uses and application of derivatives	1.1
6.2	**Futures** On completion, the candidate should:	
6.2.1	know the definition and function of a future	2.2
6.3	**Options** On completion, the candidate should:	
6.3.1	know the definition and function of an option	3
6.3.2	understand the following terms: • calls • puts	3

Syllabus Learning Map

Syllabus Unit/ Element		Chapter/ Section
6.4	**Terminology** On completion, the candidate should:	
6.4.1	understand the following terms: • long • short • open • close • holder • writing • premium • covered • naked	2.3 2.3 2.3 2.3 3 3 3 2.3 & 3 2.3 & 3
6.5	**Derivatives/Commodity Markets** On completion, the candidate should:	
6.5.1	know the characteristics of the derivatives and commodity markets	5
6.5.2	know the potential advantages and disadvantages of investing in the derivatives and commodity markets	5.4
6.6	**Swaps** On completion, the candidate should:	
6.6.1	know the definition and function of an interest rate swap	4
6.6.2	know the definition and function of credit default swaps	4

Element 7	**Investment Funds**	**Chapter 7**
7.1	**Introduction** On completion, the candidate should:	
7.1.1	understand the potential advantages and disadvantages of collective investment	1.2
7.1.2	know the difference between active and passive management	1.3
7.1.3	know the purpose and principal features of UCITS/NURS	1.5
7.1.4	know the types of funds and how they are classified	1.4
7.2	**Unit Trusts** On completion, the candidate should:	
7.2.1	know the definition and legal structure of a unit trust	2
7.2.2	know the roles of the manager and the trustee	2
7.3	**Open-Ended Investment Companies (OEICs)** On completion, the candidate should:	
7.3.1	know the definition and legal structure of an OEIC/ICVC/SICAV	3
7.3.2	know the roles of the authorised corporate director and the depository	3
7.4	**Pricing, Dealing and Settling** On completion, the candidate should:	
7.4.1	know how unit trust units and OEIC shares are priced	4.1
7.4.2	know how shares and units are bought and sold	4.2
7.4.3	know how collectives are settled	4.2

Syllabus Unit/ Element		Chapter/ Section
7.5	**Investment Trusts** On completion, the candidate should:	
7.5.1	know the characteristics of an investment trust: • share classes • gearing • real estate investment trusts (REITs)	5
7.5.2	understand the factors that affect the price of an investment trust	5
7.5.3	know the meaning of the discounts and premiums in relation to investment trusts	5
7.5.4	know how investment trust shares are traded	5
7.6	**Exchange-Traded Funds (ETFs)** On completion, the candidate should:	
7.6.1	know the main characteristics of exchange-traded funds • trading • replication methods	6
7.7	**Hedge Funds** On completion, the candidate should:	
7.7.1	know the basic characteristics of hedge funds: • risks • cost and liquidity • investment strategies	8

Element 8	**Financial Services Regulation**	**Chapter 8**
8.1	**Introduction** On completion, the candidate should:	
8.1.1	understand the need for regulation	1.1
8.1.2	know the function and impact of UK, European and US regulators in the financial services industry	1.2
8.1.3	understand the reasons for authorisation of firms and approved persons	1.3
8.1.4	know the groups of activity (controlled functions) requiring approved person status	1.4
8.1.5	know the outcomes arising from the FCA's approach to managing good conduct within firms including Treating Customers Fairly	1.5
8.1.6	know the CISI's Code of Conduct	7.6.2
8.1.7	understand the key principles of professional integrity and ethical behaviour in financial services	7
8.2	**Financial Crime** On completion, the candidate should:	
8.2.1	know what money laundering is, the stages involved and the related criminal offences	2.1
8.2.2	know the purpose and the main provisions of the Proceeds of Crime Act and the Money Laundering Regulations	2.1.2

Syllabus Learning Map

Syllabus Unit/ Element		Chapter/ Section
8.2.3	know the action to be taken by those employed in financial services if money laundering activity is suspected and what constitutes satisfactory evidence of identity	2.1.3
8.2.4	know the purpose of the Bribery Act	2.2
8.2.5	know how firms can be exploited as a vehicle for financial crime: theft of customer data to facilitate identity fraud	2.3
8.3	**Insider Dealing and Market Abuse** On completion, the candidate should:	
8.3.1	know the offences that constitute insider dealing and the instruments covered	3
8.3.2	know the offences that constitute market abuse and the instruments covered	4
8.4	**Data Protection** On completion, the candidate should:	
8.4.1	understand the impact of the Data Protection Act on firms' activities	5
8.5	**Complaints and Compensation** On completion, the candidate should:	
8.5.1	know the requirements for handling customer complaints, including the role of the Financial Ombudsman Service	6
8.5.2	know the circumstances under which the Financial Services Compensation Scheme pays compensation and the compensation payable for investment claims	6.3

Element 9	Taxation, Investment Wrappers and Trusts	Chapter 9
9.1	**Tax** On completion, the candidate should:	
9.1.1	know the direct and indirect taxes as they apply to individuals: • income tax • capital gains tax • inheritance tax • stamp duty • VAT	2
9.1.2	know the main exemptions in respect of the main personal taxes	2
9.2	**Investment Wrappers** On completion, the candidate should:	
9.2.1	know the definition of, and tax incentives provided by, ISAs	3
9.2.2	know the main types of ISA available: • Cash • Stocks & Shares • Junior ISA	3
9.2.3	know the following aspects of investing in ISAs: • subscriptions • transfers • eligibility	3

Syllabus Unit/ Element		Chapter/ Section
9.3	**Pensions** On completion, the candidate should:	
9.3.1	know the benefits provided by pensions	4
9.3.2	know the basic characteristics of the following: • state pension scheme • occupational pension schemes • personal pensions including self-invested personal pensions (SIPPs)	4
9.4	**Trusts** On completion, the candidate should:	
9.4.1	know the features of the main trusts: • discretionary • interest in possession • bare	5
9.4.2	know the definition of the following terms: • trustee • settlor • beneficiary	5
9.4.3	know the main reasons for creating trusts	5

Element 10	Other Financial Products	Chapter 10
10.1	**Loans** On completion, the candidate should:	
10.1.1	know the differences between bank loans, overdrafts and credit card borrowing	1
10.1.2	know the difference between the quoted interest rate on borrowing and the effective annual rate of borrowing	1.4
10.1.3	be able to calculate the effective annual rate of borrowing, given the quoted interest rate and frequency of payment	1.4
10.1.4	know the difference between secured and unsecured borrowing	1
10.2	**Mortgages** On completion, the candidate should:	
10.2.1	understand the characteristics of the mortgage market: • interest rates • loan to value	2
10.2.2	know the definition of and types of mortgage: • repayment • interest-only • offset	2
10.3	**Investment Bonds** On completion, the candidate should:	
10.3.1	know the main characteristics of investment bonds	3
10.4	**Life Assurance** On completion, the candidate should:	
10.4.1	understand the basic principles of life assurance	4

Syllabus Unit/ Element		Chapter/ Section
10.4.2	know the definition of the following types of life policy: • term assurance • whole-of-life	4
10.5	**Protection Insurance** On completion, the candidate should:	
10.5.1	know the main product features of the following: • critical illness insurance • income protection • mortgage protection • accident and sickness cover • household cover • medical insurance • long-term care insurance • business insurance • liability insurance	5

Examination Specification

Each examination paper is constructed from a specification that determines the weightings that will be given to each element. The specification is given below.

It is important to note that the numbers quoted may vary slightly from examination to examination as there is some flexibility to ensure that each examination has a consistent level of difficulty. However, the number of questions tested in each element should not change by more than plus or minus 2.

Element Number	Element	Questions
1	Introduction	2
2	The Economic Environment	3
3	Financial Assets and Markets	5
4	Equities	8
5	Bonds	5
6	Derivatives	4
7	Investment Funds	7
8	Financial Services Regulation	6
9	Taxation, Investment Wrappers and Trusts	6
10	Other Financial Products	4
Total		50

CISI Associate (ACSI) Membership can work for you...

Studying for a CISI qualification is hard work and we're sure you're putting in plenty of hours, but don't lose sight of your goal!

This is just the first step in your career; there is much more to achieve!

The securities and investments industry attracts ambitious and driven individuals. You're probably one yourself and that's great, but on the other hand you're almost certainly surrounded by lots of other people with similar ambitions.

So how can you stay one step ahead during these uncertain times?

Entry Criteria:
Pass in either:
- Investment Operations Certificate (IOC), IFQ, ICWIM, Capital Markets in, eg, Securities, Derivatives, Advanced Certificates; or
- one CISI Diploma/Masters in Wealth Management paper

Joining Fee: £25 or free if applying via prefilled application form   **Annual Subscription (pro rata):** £125

Using your new CISI qualification* to become an Associate (ACSI) member of the Chartered Institute for Securities & Investment could well be the next important career move you make this year, and help you maintain your competence.

Join our global network of over 40,000 financial services professionals and start enjoying both the professional and personal benefits that CISI membership offers. Once you become a member you can use the prestigious ACSI designation after your name and even work towards becoming personally chartered.

* ie, Investment Operations Certificate (IOC), IFQ, ICWIM, Capital Markets

Benefits in Summary...
- Use of the CISI CPD Scheme
- Unlimited free CPD seminars, webcasts, podcasts and online training tools
- Highly recognised designatory letters
- Unlimited free attendance at CISI Professional Forums
- CISI publications including *S&I Review* and *Change – The Regulatory Update*
- 20% discount on all CISI conferences and training courses
- Invitation to CISI Annual Lecture
- Select Benefits – our exclusive personal benefits portfolio

The ACSI designation will provide you with access to a range of member benefits, including Professional Refresher where there are currently over 60 modules available on subjects including Behavioural Finance, Cybercrime and Conduct Risk. CISI TV is also available to members, allowing you to catch up on the latest CISI events, whilst earning valuable CPD hours.

Plus many other networking opportunities which could be invaluable for your career.

Revision Express Interactive

You've bought the workbook... now test your knowledge before your exam.

Revision Express Interactive is an engaging online study tool to be used in conjunction with CISI workbooks. It contains exercises and revision questions.

Key Features of Revision Express Interactive:
- Examination-focused – the content of Revision Express Interactive covers the key points of the syllabus
- Questions throughout to reaffirm understanding of the subject
- Special end-of-module practice exam to reflect as closely as possible the standard you will experience in your exam (please note, however, they are not the CISI exam questions themselves)
- Interactive exercises throughout
- Extensive glossary of terms
- Useful associated website links
- Allows you to study whenever you like

IMPORTANT: The questions contained in Revision Express Interactive elearning products are designed as aids to revision, and should not be seen in any way as mock exams.

Price per elearning module: £35
Price when purchased with the CISI workbook: £100 (normal price: £110)

To purchase Revision Express Interactive:

call our Customer Support Centre on:
+44 20 7645 0777

or visit CISI Online Bookshop at:
cisi.org/bookshop

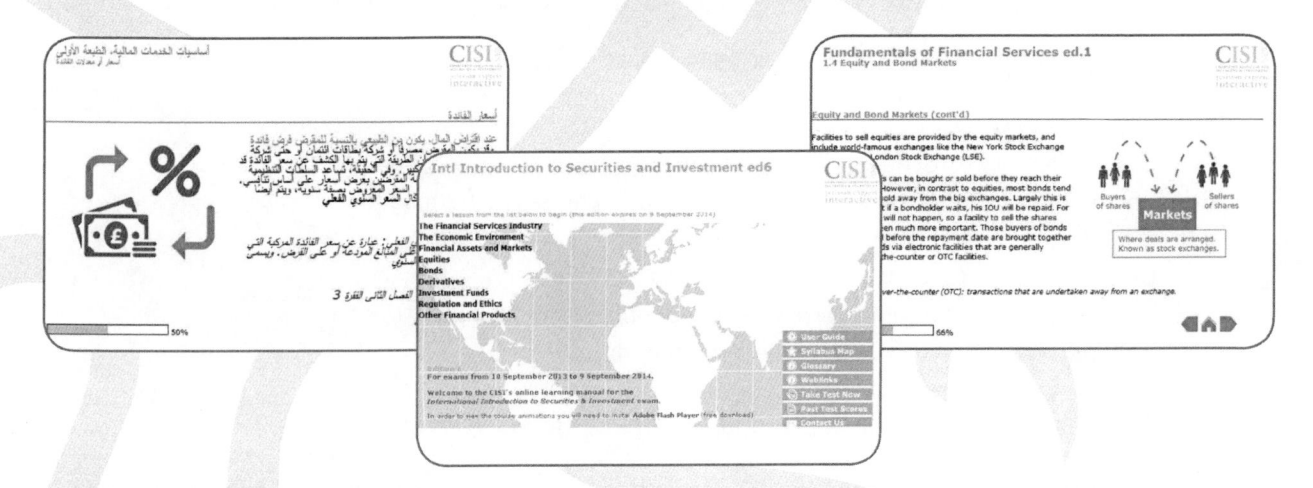

For more information on our elearning products, contact our Customer Support Centre on +44 20 7645 0777, or visit our website at cisi.org/study

Professional Refresher

Self-testing elearning modules to refresh your knowledge, meet regulatory and firm requirements, and earn CPD hours.

Professional Refresher is a training solution to help you remain up-to-date with industry developments, maintain regulatory compliance and demonstrate continuing learning.

This popular online learning tool allows self-administered refresher testing on a variety of topics, including the latest regulatory changes.

There are currently over 70 modules available which address UK and international issues. Modules are reviewed by practitioners frequently and new topics are added to the suite on a regular basis.

Benefits to firms:
- Learning and tests can form part of business T&C programme
- Learning and tests kept up-to-date and accurate by the CISI
- Relevant and useful – devised by industry practitioners
- Access to individual results available as part of management overview facility, 'Super User'
- Records of staff training can be produced for internal use and external audits
- Cost-effective – no additional charge for CISI members
- Available to non-members

Benefits to individuals:
- Comprehensive selection of topics across industry sectors
- Modules are frequently reviewed and updated by industry experts
- New topics introduced regularly
- Free for members
- Successfully passed modules are recorded in your CPD log as Active Learning
- Counts as structured learning for RDR purposes
- On completion of a module, a certificate can be printed out for your own records

The full suite of Professional Refresher modules is free to CISI members or £250 for non-members. Modules are also available individually. To view a full list of Professional Refresher modules visit:

cisi.org/refresher

If you or your firm would like to find out more contact our Client Relationship Management team:

+ 44 20 7645 0670
crm@cisi.org

For more information on our elearning products, contact our Customer Support Centre on +44 20 7645 0777, or visit our website at cisi.org/study

Professional Refresher

Free to CISI members

Top 5

SCORM COMPLIANT

Integrity & Ethics
High Level View
Ethical Behaviour
An Ethical Approach
Compliance vs Ethics

Anti-Money Laundering
Introduction to Money Laundering
UK Legislation and Regulation
Money Laundering Regulations 2007
Proceeds of Crime Act 2002
Terrorist Financing
Suspicious Activity Reporting
MLRO
Sanctions

Financial Crime
What Is Financial Crime?
Insider Dealing and Market Abuse
Legislation, Offences and Rules
Money Laundering Legislation
Regulations, Financial Sanctions and Reporting Requirements
Money Laundering and the Role of the MLRO

Information Security and Data Protection
Information Security: The Key Issues
Latest Cybercrime Developments
Lessons From High-Profile Cases
Key Identity Issues: Know Your Customer
Implementing the Data Protection Act 1998
The Next Decade: Predictions For The Future

UK Bribery Act
Background to the Act
The Offences
What the Offences Cover
When Has an Offence Been Committed?
The Defences Against Charges of Bribery
The Penalties

Latest modules

Crowdfunding
Who Uses Crowdfunding?
The Funding Process
The Risks and Protections

Financial Planning
Related Activities
The Financial Plan
Cash Flow Planning and Modelling
Behavioural Finance and Financial Planning
The Regulatory Framework
The Future Landscape

Offshore Fund Administration (Crown Dependencies)
Legal and Regulatory Framework
Fund Structures
Administration
Fund Distribution

Retirement Planning
Pensions and Provisions
Money In and Money Out

Senior Managers and Certification Regime
Definitions, Obligations & Certification
Conduct Rules
Scope of the Rules
Future Developments

Operations

Best Execution
What Is Best Execution?
Achieving Best Execution
Order Execution Policies
Client Consent & Information
Monitoring
Best Execution for Specific Firms

Approved Persons Regime
The Basis of the Regime
Fitness and Propriety
The Controlled Functions
Principles for Approved Persons
Code of Practice

Corporate Actions
Corporate Structure and Finance
Life Cycle of an Event
Mandatory & Voluntary Events

Wealth

Client Assets and Client Money
Protection & Ring-Fencing
Due Diligence of Custodians
Reconciliations
Records and Accounts
CASS Oversight

Investment Principles and Risk
Diversification
Factfind and Risk Profiling
Investment Management
Modern Portfolio Theory
Direct and Indirect Investments
Socially Responsible Investment
Investment Trusts

Banking Standards
Strengthening Individual Accountability
Reforming Corporate Governance
Securing Better Outcomes for Consumers
Enhancing Financial Stability

Suitability of Client Investments
Assessing Suitability & Risk Profiling
Establishing Risk Appetite
Suitable Q&As
Suitable Investment Selections
Guidance, Reports and Record Keeping

International

Foreign Account Tax Compliance Act (FATCA)
Foreign Financial Institutions
Due Diligence Requirements
Reporting
Compliance

MiFID II
The Organisations Covered
The Products Subject to MiFID
The Origins of MiFID II
The Products Covered by MiFID II
Implementation

UCITS
The Original UCITS Directive
UCITS III
UCITS IV
Non-UCITS Funds
Future Developments

cisi.org/refresher

Feedback to the CISI

Have you found this workbook to be a valuable aid to your studies? We would like your views, so please email us at learningresources@cisi.org with any thoughts, ideas or comments.

Accredited Training Partners

Support for examination students studying for the Chartered Institute for Securities & Investment (CISI) Qualifications is provided by several Accredited Training Partners (ATPs), including Fitch Learning and BPP. The CISI's ATPs offer a range of face-to-face training courses, distance learning programmes, their own learning resources and study packs which have been accredited by the CISI. The CISI works in close collaboration with its ATPs to ensure they are kept informed of changes to CISI examinations so they can build them into their own courses and study packs.

CISI Workbook Specialists Wanted

Workbook Authors

Experienced freelance authors with finance experience, and who have published work in their area of specialism, are sought. Responsibilities include:
- Updating workbooks in line with new syllabuses and any industry developments
- Ensuring that the syllabus is fully covered

Workbook Reviewers

Individuals with a high-level knowledge of the subject area are sought. Responsibilities include:
- Highlighting any inconsistencies against the syllabus
- Assessing the author's interpretation of the workbook

Workbook Technical Reviewers

Technical reviewers provide a detailed review of the workbook and bring the review comments to the panel. Responsibilities include:
- Cross-checking the workbook against the syllabus
- Ensuring sufficient coverage of each learning objective

Workbook Proofreaders

Proofreaders are needed to proof workbooks both grammatically and also in terms of the format and layout. Responsibilities include:
- Checking for spelling and grammar mistakes
- Checking for formatting inconsistencies

If you are interested in becoming a CISI external specialist call:
+44 20 7645 0609

or email:
externalspecialists@cisi.org

For bookings, orders, membership and general enquiries please contact our Customer Support Centre on +44 20 7645 0777, or visit our website at cisi.org